International Real Estate Valuation, Investment and Development

International Real Estate Valuation, Investment and Development

A SELECT BIBLIOGRAPHY

Valerie J. Nurcombe

BIBLIOGRAPHIES AND INDEXES
IN ECONOMICS AND ECONOMIC HISTORY,
NUMBER 7

GREENWOOD PRESS
NEW YORK WESTPORT, CONNECTICUT

Published in the United States and Canada by
Greenwood Press, Westport, Connecticut

English Language edition, except the United States and Canada, published by E. & F.N. Spon Ltd.

First published 1987

Library of Congress Cataloging in Publication Data

Nurcombe, Valerie J.
International real estate valuation, investment, and development:
(Bibliographies and indexes in economics and economic history, ISSN 0749-1786; no. 7)
Includes index.
1. Real estate business – Bibliography. 2. Real property – Valuation – Bibliography. 3. Real estate investment – Bibliography. 4. Real estate development – Bibliography. I. Title. II. Series.
Z7164.L3N87 1987 [HD1375] 016.33333 87-14906
ISBN 0-313-26082-6 (lib. bdg. : alk. paper)

Library of Congress Catalog Card Number: 87-14906

ISBN: 0-313-26082-6

Printed in Great Britain

Contents

Introduction

A few years ago David Clurman in his preface to Wiley's series on 'Real Estate for Professional Practitioners', commented that, 'Perhaps no field of business endeavour is more in need of a series of professional books than real estate.' He went on to point out that property is involved in many aspects of professional and business life: valuation, property investment and development impinge on business, accountancy, law, urban affairs and finance to name but a few. This introduction outlines the way in which these have been covered.

It is difficult to trace much of the relevant literature in the absence of a bibliography. Ten years ago there were few texts in Britain, rather more in the USA, but nothing like the numbers available on other subjects. The last five to ten years have seen a positive explosion in the literature worldwide.

A bibliography on valuations must define its terms. There are many definitions of the term value - some taking whole books, it would be unwise to attempt another. In defining the coverage of this bibliography the introduction gives an indication of the terminology used. Property, landed property, or real estate, are variously used to describe property in land and buildings; personal property is not covered.

Millington (1) suggests that value is generally used with the meaning 'market value' hence there is a need to consider in detail the real estate or property market but not necessarily to cover the legal and other aspects of buying and selling property. The Royal Institution of Chartered Surveyor's Guidance notes on the valuation of assets, quoted by Enever (2), define 'open market value'

'The best price at which an interest in a property might reasonably be expected to be sold by private treaty at the date of valuation, assuming:

(a) a willing seller;

(b) a reasonable period within which to negotiate the sale, taking into account the nature of the property and the state of the market;

(c) values will remain static throughout the period;

(d) the property will be freely exposed to the market;

(e) no account is to be taken of an additional bid by a special purchaser.'

This indicates some of the component parts of a valuation. The interaction of so many factors to create a value suggests a bibliography which relates equally to all those factors. Thus valuation is 'The art, or science, of estimating the value for a specific purpose of a particular interest in property at a particular moment in time, taking into account all the features of the property and also considering all the underlying economic factors of the market, including the range of alternative investments.'

There are many alternatives - hence the few selected references to investment and development. Development of the land enhances its investment value and is therefore also crucial to the problem of valuation.

Alternative sources of information exist for some of the factors influencing the valuation: international political and economic situation; national political and economic situation; national finance and markets of all types, their depression, recession or revival; government policies; local economies; geographical environment - latitude, topography, aspect, climate, communications; fashion and local demand. Individual features of a property and its age, its state of repair, services etc., the timing of sales according to property market fluctuations, development decisions, the demand or inflation conditions at the time, are discussed in the literature. The only items included in this bibliography are those which discuss such features in relation to real estate and valuation. Information relating to some factors is usually gathered from sources other than the written word. Local conditions cannot be covered adequately in any international bibliography, although some information about the local markets is included as an indicator to sources.

Valuations are made for a variety of purposes. The purpose will affect that valuation and therefore different types of valuation are reflected in the literature. The skilled professional valuer discerns exactly what information must be used in a particular situation and which is a mix suited to that instance. No two valuations are ever the same and therefore no bibliography can ever completely cover the valuer's needs.

No bibliography will ever be comprehensive, although some claim to be and a few aim to be. This volume started out to be comprehensive in the field of valuations but, when all the peripheral topics which relate to the valuation of a property were brought into consideration, it became evident that something would have to be either curtailed or omitted.

Exclusions have been governed by the bibliographical control of related topics. Thus planning and certain aspects of finance, including mortgage, which are better covered than real estate aspects, have been omitted generally. Real estate finance is covered selectively, estate management and investment in property are covered selectively also in so far as they relate to value and valuing. Tax is covered by Haikalis' bibliography (3) for the USA, items included in this bibliography are either theoretical, lengthy, or discussions of the impact, or importance of tax in relation to property valuation. Bibliographies relating to many of these aspects already exist - not all are particularly lengthy. They should be identified using sources such as H W Wilson's Bibliographic Index or series of bibliographies such as those from the Greater London Council, Research Library and the Departments of the Environment and Transport in Great Britain, or similar series in the United States, such as those from the Department of Housing and Urban Development or Vance bibliographies in Monticello, Illinois, which include real estate and valuation in their Public Administration series.

Millington, in explaining the problems engendered by this wide range of topics involved in valuations, points out that

> 'Many hours of study are required to understand fully the effect of statutes and government action on property values. ... (The valuer) has to be able to isolate the important factors affecting property value. ... To understand people (and the way they react to various situations is to a large extent to understand values.'(4)

The content of this volume will at least indicate to those concerned with understanding the many factors involved how wide a range of information is already available.

The statutes referred to by Millington are also numerous, too numerous to isolate and list since they range from the Town and Country Planning Acts,

Housing Acts, Landlord and Tenant Acts to the Agricultural Holdings Act and Factories Acts in the UK alone.

Law of property is essential to the valuer. But legal bibliography has advanced somewhat further than property bibliography and the reader, or user, is referred to the numerous law bibliographies, Index to legal periodicals and legal databases such as Lexis. It was suggested to me that a subject approach to legal cases would be useful to the valuer but it presented too many problems for inclusion. To be useful such a list must be comprehensive and in trying to relate to a number of countries it could occupy a whole volume in itself. Cases are written up in the many weekly and monthly journals. Few are indexed as well as in the British services in Estates Gazette, RICS Abstracts and Reviews and the Rating and Valuation Reporter.

Statistical publications are numerous in most countries and easily traced at the national level although sometimes less easily located at the local level. For example, councils in England and Wales make returns of the housing land availability and some have issued returns of industrial and commercial land avilability. These have not been separately listed. Most are reviewed and therefore republished annually. Their volume would distort the bibliography. They are best located through the ACOMPLINE (London Residuary Body) and SIGLE (British Library) databases or the print sources mentioned in this Introduction. Nor is it possible to include every village or town plan and its appraisal where land and property valuation represents only a small part of that report.

In the organisation of this bibliography the type of property takes precedence. This brings together references on the market in a type of property with the appropriate valuation techniques and any other factors which would affect the valuation of that type of property. Where the volume is great the geographical sub-divisions separate the purely local from studies of more general applicability.

All section headings should be interpreted in the light of the main topic of the bibliography - valuations. General references to planning and land use, for example, are not included, only those specifically relevant to valuations and property development. Many section headings could in fact be expanded into a full bibliography - further information should be sought in the sources mentioned in this introduction.

Two specific types of journal and book exist in the property and valuation field: the popular and the academic. While the former have not been totally excluded because they may cover topics which are otherwise poorly documented (especially market and local studies), their inclusion has been severely restricted where they appear to be insubstantial, unduly chatty or heavily geared to the non-professional market. An example might be a guide to investment in housing for the first-time buyer. The quantity of these is great and would detract from the overall use of the bibliography. But many property market surveys are included because they are authoritative and valuable contributions to the overall picture. Readers are also referred to Douglas Scarrett's useful listing (5). Its bias is towards Great Britain but similar research programs will be found in all major international property companies.

However it would be invidious to exclude totally the popular journal titles as they contain some useful items. Some give interesting highlights and angles for the professional, creating a heightened awareness of the viewpoint of the customer. Not all users will be familiar with Ulrich's International Periodicals Directory (6) and therefore the main journals relating to the property industry are listed in an Appendix.

Journals also change during their 'life'. Not only does frequency and name sometimes change but so also do the character of the articles and the content. Two examples might be the Canadian Appraiser, formerly AIM, creating a newer, livelier image for 1983/4; and the Royal Institution of Chartered Surveyor's Chartered Surveyor, monthly until 1982 when it became Chartered Surveyor Weekly with shorter, more newsy articles and more advertising a change which not only makes it more difficult to index but which also affects the value of those articles to the user of this bibliography. Some articles in these new formats date more quickly than those published formerly while others tend to 'scratch the surface' rather than see topics in depth. Such changes are typical of many publications, even long-running text books will alter edition by edition. This should be remembered when using the articles listed here, articles which have been grouped together to review the property market of an area are not referred to individually, unless substantial, but the towns covered are indexed (where they are significant). Reprints of articles occur in different journals and these are noted.

Currency is important in certain aspects of valuations work; theory may remain the same but markets are continually changing. Therefore only a few items which were published prior to 1975-6 have been included and these relate to theory. Although some of the local property market studies of the seventies may appear to be insufficiently current, they represent the background to the eighties and to the continuing scene. Any earlier than that they would be of only historical significance. The cut-off point of December 1984 has been rigidly enforced. Future volumes may up-date this one. Some earlier references may be obtained by consulting other bibliographies(7); these are mainly American. A few, shorter, British bibliographies have appeared in the series already cited.

In many cases there are not adequate databases or indexing and abstracting journals to assist the reader in updating such a bibliography. A number of journal publishers have been contacted during the compilation of the bibliography and many know of no journal in which their title is indexed. Many are available only in their country of origin. This applies to titles covering the local market in particular. The databases Public Affairs Information Service (PAIS), Economic Abstracts and ABI/Inform cover real estate in America and internationally, while in print RICS Abstracts and Reviews and RICS Weekly Briefing with the Departments of the Environment and Transport Library Bulletin cover British and international material, and the database ACOMPLINE also provides useful British information.

This bibliography is aimed toward a broad audience. Some users may need to move beyond the outline coverage of the investment aspects. As well as the databases already mentioned, Management Contents, Business Periodicals Index and SCIMP (Selective Coooperative Indexing of Management Periodicals, in print or database format) will assist with this, as will the printed volumes of Anbar Abstracts and the Institute of Cost & Management Accountant's new abstracting journal among others.

Some sources of information are mentioned in texts such as Darlow's (items 31, 32) or Enever's (item 40). The only guide to sources was published by Gale in 1963 (8) and is now somewhat dated. As many relate to statistics, which are listed here with the property type to which they relate, a section on their sources has been included. Useful developments may be announced in the press, such as the new databank being coordinated by Roger Tym and Partners, independant urban land economists, in conjunction with six London firms of agents to provide raw information from property owning funds and portfolios in excess of £7 billion. All should have five year's record of annual valuations, with individual properties sorted by use and location and being confidential with owners not being identifiable. The firms cooperating currently produce indexes of property information and market surveys (9).

The pamphlet from which this bibliography originated was presented in author order with subject indexing; it was suggested that subject order would be preferable and this approach has been adopted. Despite discussions with members of the profession the usual subject breakdown within the field has had to be adapted to relate to literary requirements. Some topics appear to have very little coverage as separate entities although all appear in the various texts and general works. The list of contents should be seen as reflecting this since it cannot reflect an outline of the principles and practice of valuations. To enable this bibliography to be useful in all English-speaking countries that the index includes many place-name entries and certain sections have been sub-divided geographically.

Although multiple entries have not usually been made there are inevitably some instances where subject arrangement suggests that an item ought to be listed twice. This is kept to a minimum with reliance being placed on indexing to correlate such items. Subject organisation inevitably presents the compiler with a decision as to location and unwarranted duplication of entries increases costs unacceptably.

Terminology in an international bibliography may be confusing. On different sides of the Atlantic techniques may vary either in the way they are applied or in nomenclature. Generally the British terminology is used for the categories and the indexing except where a distinct topic, such as Real Estate Investment Trusts(REITs), relates mainly to a particular country.

All references are presented in standard bibliographical format, indicating where they belong to series (if known). References are adequate to identify items uniquely. This bibliography is not prepared purely for librarians but for those working in the property industry and, as such, while attention has been paid to standard cataloguing practice, entries are presented in a clear and readable format for the professional valuer.

Most academic articles should include references although not all do so. These are only noted where they are significant or substantial. Although the general bibliographies (See reference 7) have been isolated from the subject groupings others have been included with the subject section where they will be most useful. Index entries are provided.

It has not been possible to inspect all items listed - some were not readily available in Britain. Lists of others were requested but not received. A decision was made that, in this instance, the volume of references mattered more than abstracts of their content. Titles are usually indicative and notes on content have been made occasionally where expansion was thought necessary to enhance the value of particular entries. Abstracts are a luxury for which adequate indexing and subject arrangement can attempt to provide some substitute.

This bibliography has been a long time in inception. Work has been done to update and expand the original thin pamphlet compiled while I worked at Leicester Polytechnic Library. The encouragement of members of the staff at the School of Land and Building Studies led to its expansion. Its usefulness was shown as numerous students arrived in my office to request copies. Its sale at a modest price generated unexpected external demand (and a reprint). Thanks are due to all those former colleagues for their help then and since, in particular to Douglas Scarrett and to David Chiddick in the School of Land and Building Studies, to Marilyn Hill, Mary Prior, Marjorie Williams and Alan Bland in the Kimberlin Library for their encouragement, and to Andrew Baum for his constructive criticism.

Special thanks are also due to my husband for assistance and patience when work has had to be done at odd hours of the day or weekends due to the demands of a newly established freelance business.

Introduction

References

(1) Millington, A. F. An introduction to property valuation. 2nd ed. London, Estates Gazette, 1982.

(2) Enever, N. The valuation of property investment. 3rd ed. London, Estates Gazette, 1984. p38.

(3) Haikalis, P & Freeman, J K eds. Real estate: a bibliography of monographic literature. Prepared under the auspices of the California State University, Real Estate Education Endowment, Office of the Chancellor, The California State University, Long Beach, California. Westport, Conn. & London: Greenwood Press, 1983. (Has a lengthy section on popular books. Mainly American)

(4) Millington. op. cit. p159.

(5) Scarrett, Douglas Practice based market research and property indices. Leicester: Leicester Polytechnic, 1983. Second edition 1985.

(6) Ulrich's international periodicals directory. New York, Bowker, biennial. Lists periodicals in borad subject groupings, with a name index.

(7) American Institute of Real Estate Appraisers. Appraisal Journal bibliography 1932-1969. Chicago: American Institute of Real Estate Appraisers, 1969.

- Reader's guide to the Appraisal Journal 1970-1980. Chicago: American Institute of Real Estate Appraisers, 1981.

- Real estate appraisal bibliography. Chicago: American Institute of Real Estate Appraisers, 1973.

Bain, H O California real estate bookshelf Revised edition. Berkeley, California: Center for Real Estate and Urban Economics, University of California, 1970-5. (Research report 32)

Denne, R C The determinants of value: an annotated bibliography. Assessors Journal vol.11 1976 pp153-195.

Society of Real Estate Appraisers. An annotated bibliography of the professional journal of the international Society of Real Estate Appraisers. Part 2 1961-1970. Chicago: Society of Real Estate Appraisers, 1971.

(8) Babb, Janice B and Dordick, B F. Real estate information sources. Detroit, Gale, 1963. (Gale Management Information Guide series no.1)

(9) £7bn data bank starts next summer Chartered Surveyor Weekly vol.9 no.11 13 December 1984 p761.

General

1 Abson, G. Appraisal review - an overview for the non-appraiser. *Canadian Appraiser*, 28(4) November 1984 pp14-17.

2 Albritton, H. D. *Controversies in real property valuation: a commentary*. Chicago, American Institute of Real Estate Appraisers, 1982.

3 American Appraisal Company. *Boeckh building valuation manual*. 2nd ed. Milwaukee, Wi., Boeckh Publications, a division of American Appraisal Associates, 1979. (First edition 1967).

4 American Institute of Real Estate Appraisers. *Appraisal of real estate*. 8th ed. Chicago, American Institute of Real Estate Appraisers 1984. (Previous editions 1935, 1951, 1960, 1964, 1967, 1973, 1978).

5 American Institute of Real Estate Appraisers. *Appraising in a changing economy: collected writings of James E. Gibbons*. Chicago, American Institute of Real Estate Appraisers, 1982.

6 American Institute of Real Estate Appraisers. Evaluation. *Appraisal Journal*, 51(4) October 1983 pp546-568

7 American Institute of Real Estate Appraisers. *Guidelines for appraisal office policies and procedures*. Chicago, American Institute of Real Estate Appraisers, 1980.

8 American Institute of Real Estate Appraisers. *Readings in market value*. Chicago, American Institute of Real Estate Appraisers, 1981. (Originally published in *Appraisal Journal*).

9 American Institute of Real Estate Appraisers. *Readings in real property valuation principles*. Vol.1. Cambridge, Mass., Ballinger, 1977.

10 American Institute of Real Estate Appraisers. *Real estate valuing, counseling, forecasting: selected writings of John Robert White*. Chicago, American Institute of Real Estate Appraisers, 1984.

11 American Society of Appraisers, College of Fellows. *Principles of appraisal*. Washington, D.C., American Society of Appraisers, 1978.

12 Appraisal Institute of Canada. Code of ethics, standards of professional conduct and standards of professional practice for members of the Appraisal Institute of Canada. *AIM*, 24(3) August 1980 insert 6pp with covering letter pp22-24, 32. (Draft version)

13 Appraisal Institute of Canada. Code of ethics, standards of professional conduct and standards of professional practice for members of the Appraisal Institute of Canada. *AIM*, 27(1) February 1983 insert 12pp (Regulation no.1,final version. Revised January 1984 and inserted with *AIM* 28(1) February 1984).

14 Averill, L. H. *Estate valuation handbook*. London, Wiley, 1983.

15 Babcock, H. A. *Appraisal principles and procedures*. Washington, DC, American Society of Appraisers, 1980.

16 Bailey, A. The learned babble. Estates Gazette, 268(6158) 29 October 1983 pp464-466, 469.

17 Bailey, A. Sixty glorious years. Estates Gazette, 272(6208) 27 October 1984 pp387, 389. (Anniversary of ISVA)

18 Barash, Samuel T. Standard real estate appraising manual. Englewood Cliffs, N.J., Prentice Hall, 1979.

19 Barrett, G. V. and Blair, John P. Foundations of real estate analysis. New York, Macmillan, 1981.

20 Barrett, G. V. and Blair, John P. How to conduct and analyze real estate market and feasibility studies. New York, Van Nostrand Reinhold, 1982. (The background to development and valuation)

21 Baum, Andrew. Statutory valuations. London, Routledge & Kegan Paul, 1983.

22 Baum, Andrew. The valuation profession in the 1990s. Estates Gazette, 271(6196) 4 August 1984 pp427-431.

23 Berry, H. Problem definition between the appraiser and client. Appraisal Journal, 52 April 1984 pp237-241.

24 Betts, Richard M. and Ely, S. J. Basic real estate appraisal. London & New York, Wiley, 1982.

25 Bradman, N. Valuations today and in the future. Estates Gazette, 248(5905) 21 October 1978 pp209-213.

26 Bryce, B. N. and Kinnard, W. N. Appraising real property. Lexington, Mass., Lexington for the Society of Real Estate Appraisers, 1984.

27 Cartlidge, D. P. Practical cost planning: a guide for surveyors and architects. London, Hutchinson, 1982.

28 Clatanoff, Robert M. Government assessment manuals: a checklist. Chicago, International Asssociation of Assessing Officers, 1982. (Bibliography series)

29 Cote, J. S. Modern real estate analysis:some practical considerations. Real Estate Appraiser and Analyst, 50 Spring 1984 pp53-58.

30 Crean, M. J. Principles of real estate analysis. New York, Van Nostrand, 1979.

31 Darlow, Clive. Valuation and development appraisal. London, Estates Gazette, 1982.

32 Darlow, Clive. Valuation and investment appraisal. London, Estates Gazette, 1983.

33 Davies, K, Johnson, T., and Britton, W. Modern methods of valuation. 7th ed. London, Estates Gazette, 1980.

34 Directory of associations. Buildings, 77 May 1983 p102. (Related to real estate)

35 Dorchester, John D. The quest for international valuation standards. Appraisal Journal, 52 January 1984 pp142-145.

36 Edgerton, William H. and Hlibok, A. J. Real estate valuation cost file. New York, Van Nostrand Reinhold, 1980.

37 Eikmeyer, C. J. The appraiser and his ethics. AIM, 21(2) April 1977 pp8-9.

38 Elliott, D. The appraisal process - in process. AIM, 22(1) February 1979 pp29-32.

39 Enever, Nigel. Education for valuers. Estates Gazette, 241(5824) 26 March 1977 pp899-903.

40 Enever, Nigel. The valuation of property investments. 3rd ed. London, Estates Gazette, 1984. (Earlier editions 1981, 1977).

41 Epley, D. R. and Boykin, James H. Basic income property appraisal. Reading, Mass., Addison-Wesley, 1982.

42 Erdman, E. Developments in the property profession in the last fifty years. Valuer(ISVA), 51(5) June 1982 pp74-76; 51(6) July 1982 pp104-108.

43 Establishment of a real estate appraisal standards board. Real Estate Appraiser and Analyst, 46 September-October 1980 pp37-38.

44 Estate Agents and Valuers Directory, 1977-1978. London, Kelly's Directories, 1977. (Not regularly updated)

45 Exton, E. Ethics ... they may live to haunt or help you. AIM, 21(2) April 1977 pp24-27.

46 Frey, John H. Real estate appraisal, January, 1974-November, 1980. Springfield, Va., National Technical Information Service, 1980. (Citations from the Management Contents database)

47 Germaine, Max. Professionalism and the valuer. Valuation, 27(1) November 1981 pp112-115.

48 Goulet, P. G. Principles of real estate, a value approach. Encino, Ca., Glencoe Publishing Co., 1979.

49 Hickmott, G. J. R. ed. Insurance valuations for buildings, machinery and plant in the United Kingdom. London, John Foord & Co., 1983.

50 Hillier, Parker, May and Rowden. Valuations: a guide for property owning organisations. London, Hillier, Parker May and Rowden, 1976.

51 Hines, M. A. Real estate appraisal. New York, Macmillan, 1981. (First published by Harcourt Brace, 1978).

52 Hoyes, Tom. The practice of valuation, in University of Reading, College of Estate Management, Centre for Advanced Land Use Studies. Property valuation handbook. Reading, Centre for Advanced Land Use Studies, 1981. (Pamphlet A2)

53 Incorporated Society of Valuers and Auctioneers. Code of measuring practice: a guide for surveyors and valuers. London, Royal Institution of Chartered Surveyors, 1979. (With Royal Institution of Chartered Surveyors)

54 International Association of Assessing Officers. Improving real property assessment: a reference manual. Chicago, International Association of Assessing Officers, 1978.

55 International Association of Assessing Officers. Property assessment valuation. Chicago, International Association of Assessing Officers, 1977.

56 International Association of Assessing Officers. Standard on assessment appeal. Chicago, International Asssociation of Assessing Officers, 1981.

57 International Association of Assessing Officers. Standard on assessment maps and parcel identifiers. Chicago, International Association of Assessing Officers, 1976.

58 International Association of Assessing Officers. Standard on assessment ratio studies. Chicago, International Asssociation of Assessing Officers, 1980.

59 International Association of Assessing Officers. Standard on mass appraisal of real property. Chicago, International Asssociation of Assessing Officers, 1984.

60 International Association of Assessing Officers. Standard on public relations. Chicago, International Asssociation of Assessing Officers, 1977.

61 International Association of Assessing Officers. Standard on property use codes. Chicago, International Asssociation of Assessing Officers, 1980.

62 International Association of Assessing Officers. Standard on the application of the three approaches to value in a mass appraisal. Chicago, International Asssociation of Assessing Officers, 1983.

63 Jonker, A. J. Property valuation in South Africa. Capetown, Wetton and Johannesberg, Juta, 1984. (Refers heavily to US and British practice).

64 Kahn, Sanders A. and Case, F. E. Real estate appraisal and investment. 2nd ed. New York, Ronald Press, 1977. (First ed. 1963)).
65 Kamerschen, David R. and Sirmans, C. F. Methods of awarding appraisal contracts: an economic analysis. Appraisal Journal, 51(4) October 1983 pp569-583.
66 Kinnard, W. N., Messner, Stephen D. and Boyce, B. N. Special applications of appraisal analysis. Rev. ed. Chicago, Society of Real Estate Appraisers, 1979.
67 Klaasen, R. L. Practising real estate appraisal. Winnipeg, Pennex Publications, distributed by Appraisal Institute of Canada, 1977.
68 Kokus, John. Ethics for the real estate appraiser. Appraisal Journal, 51(4) October 1983 pp540-545.
69 Lumby, S. Investment appraisal. New York and London, Van Nostrand, 1984.
70 McGough, R. M. The valuer's problems in a changing economy. New Zealand Valuer, 23(11) September 1978 pp545-555.
71 McKenzie, Dennis J. and Betts, Richard M. The essentials of real estate economics. 2nd ed. London & New York, Wiley, 1980.
72 Mackmin, D. H. Current valuation practice? Valuer(ISVA), 49(3) April 1980 pp74-77.
73 Macpherson, J. O. Professionalism in the modern valuing sense. New Zealand Valuer, 24(3) September 1979 pp130-133.
74 McVeigh, J. P. Land valuation law. 7th ed. Wellington, Butterworth, 1979. (New Zealand practice)
75 Mander, M. M. The professional standards of valuers. New Zealand Valuer, 25(11) September 1984 pp636-638.
76 Match the indemnity to the risk. Chartered Surveyor Weekly, 3(11) 23 June 1983 p675.
77 Messina, John P. Real estate appraisers and the problems of malpractice. Chicago, Society of Real Estate Appraisers, 1977.
78 Messner, Stephen D. and others. Analyzing real estate opportunities: market and feasibility studies. Chicago, Realtors National Marketing Institute, 1977.
79 Miles, W. Porcher. Error and risk in property value estimates. Appraisal Journal, 48(4) October 1980 pp540-549.
80 Miller, B. S. Real estate appraiser's kit. Englewood Cliffs, N.J., Institute for Business Planning, 1981.
81 Millington, Alan F. An introduction to property valuation. 2nd ed. London, Estates Gazette, 1982. (1st ed. 1975)
82 Millington, Alan F. Valuers - thinking men or creatures of habit. in Chiddick, David and Millington, Alan F. Land management: new directions. London, Spon, 1984. pp129-135.
83 Morley, S. and Darlow, Clive. Investment appraisal. London, Estates Gazette, 1983.
84 Motha, P. Approaches to land valuation. Valuer(Commonwealth Institute of Valuers) 25(6) April 1979 pp444-449.
85 Murray, J. F. N. Principles and practice of valuation. 5th ed. Sydney, Australian Institute of Valuers, 1973.
86 Myers, J. Revaluing the valuer. Management Today, February 1977 pp111+ .
87 National Association of Review Appraisers. Reviewer's guide. St. Paul, Minn., Todd Publishing, 1980. (PO Box 246, St. Paul, Minn.55102)
88 National real estate investor directory. National Real Estate Investor, annual in June.
89 Nielsen, D. A. Certification of appraisers: issues, dilemmas, and prospects. AIM, 26(4) November 1982 pp7-11.
90 Opelka, F. Gregory. FHLB board appraisal standards compromise valua-

tion judgements. Savings and Loan News, 99 July 1978 pp90-91.

91 Pearce, D. N. Idris. International valuation standards. AIM, 27(4) November 1983 pp16-22.

92 Pearce, D. N. Idris. Problems in establishing standards. Chartered Surveyor, 113(1) 1980 pp16-17.

93 Pearce, D. N. Idris. Standard measurements of real property values. Journal of Valuation, 1(4) Summer 1983 pp351-362.

94 Pearce, D. N. Idris. Valuers past, present and future. Chartered Surveyor Weekly, 3(9) 9 June 1983 pp562-563.

95 Pearce, I. Taking advice from the professional valuer. Banker's Magazine, 223(1628) November 1979 pp14-16.

96 Pennell, C. E. Role of the professional appraiser in the 1980s. Appraisal Journal, 49 April 1981 pp205-213.

97 Powell, J. G. The valuer's view ... for what it's worth. Estates Times, 24 June 1983 pp12-13.

98 Rams, Edwin M. A new real estate appraisal process. AIM, 20(4) October 1976 pp30-33,35.

99 Rams, Edwin M. Ram's real estate appraising handbook. Englewood Cliffs, N.J., Prentice Hall, 1976.

100 Ratcliffe, J. An introduction to urban land administration. London, Estates Gazette, 1978.

101 Readings in real property valuation principles. Vol.1. Cambridge, Mass., Ballinger, 1977.

102 Rees, W. H. Valuation: principles into practice: a handbook for advanced students and practitioners. 2nd ed. London, Estates Gazette, 1984. (1st ed. 1980)

103 Reynolds, A. J. Theoretical vs. practical appraising (1982) Appraisal Journal, 50(1) January 1982 pp20-24.

104 Reynolds, Judith. Working with the real estate appraiser. Journal of Property Management, 46(5) September/October 1982 pp6+ .

105 Richmond, D. Introduction to valuation. London, Macmillan, 1975.

106 Roberts, T. L. Apprizing: 1648. Appraisal Journal, 52 July 1984 pp457-461.

107 Rose, D. Ideologies of property. Sociological Review, 24(4) n.s. 1976 pp699-730.

108 Rost, R. O. and Collins, H. G. Land valuation and compensation in Australia. 2nd ed. Sydney, Australian Institute of Valuers, 1978. (1st ed. 1971: covers all types of land, buildings and techniques)

109 Rothwell, G. Responsibilities of a valuer to an intending mortgagee. New Zealand Valuer, 25(2) June 1982 pp81-87. (Reprinted from Valuer(Australia) 1981).

110 Row, Judge K. Professionalism - the professional approach. The Valuer(Australia), 28(4) October 1984 pp315-320.

111 Royal Institution of Chartered Surveyors. Code of measuring practice. see Incorporated Society of Valuers and Auctioneers.

112 Royal Institution of Chartered Surveyors. Manual of valuation standards. London, Royal Institution of Chartered Surveyors, 1980 with updates.

113 Royal Institution of Chartered Surveyors. Yearbook. London, Royal Institution of Chartered Surveyors, annual.

114 Royal Institution of Chartered Surveyors, General Practice Division. Valuation standards and reports , conference. 27 November 1980. London, Royal Institution of Chartered Surveyors, 1980.

115 Royal Institution of Chartered Surveyors, Valuation and Rating Committee. The future of the valuation surveyor: report.... Chartered Surveyor, 110(5) 1977 pp131-136.

116 Ruggles, R. K. and Walsh, J. J. Supply, demand and the nature of

value. Appraisal Journal, 51(2) April 1983 pp190-201.
117 The science of valuation - at a time of change. Valuer(ISVA), 48(8) October 1979 pp257-266.
118 Scott, R. Likely demand for valuations in the 1980s. Chartered Surveyor, 113(1) 1980 pp22-23.
119 Searles, Sidney Z. Real estate valuation and condemnation 1979. New York, Practicing Law Institute, 1979. (Real estate law and practice course handbook series 169).
120 Seymour, C. F. Outlook for real estate appraising in the 80s. Appraisal Journal, 48(2) April 1980 pp165-171.
121 Shenkel, W. M. Modern real estate appraisal. New York, McGraw-Hill, 1978.
122 Smith, Halbert C. Real estate appraisal. Columbus, Ohio, Grid, 1976.
123 Society of Real Estate Appraisers. A guide to appraising for federal agencies. Rev. ed. Society of Real Estate Appraisers, 1980.
124 Speedy, S. L. An economic approach to value. New Zealand Valuer, 24(9) March 1981 pp735-737; 24(10) June 1981 pp807-809; 24(11) September 1981 pp896-901; 24(12) December 1981 pp941-948. (May be reprints of the Australian articles)
125 Speedy, S. L. Economic approach to value. Valuer(Australia), 26(3) 1980 pp199-203; 26(4) 1980 pp345-349.
126 Speedy, S. L. Theoretical models of urban land value theory. New Zealand Valuer, 23(7) September 1977 pp359-361.
127 Stabler, M. J. Economics for valuers: two lectures. Reading, University of Reading, College of Estate Management for Incorporated Society of Valuers and Auctioneers, 1977.
128 Standards of professional practice and conduct. Real Estate Appraiser and Analyst, 46 January 1980 pp18-25.
129 Stellmacher, H. B. Real estate appraisal: the world's newest profession. Appraisal Journal, 47(1) January 1979 pp99-125.
130 Thomas, J. R. Valuations for loan purposes, in University of Reading, College of Estate Management, Centre for Advanced Land Use Studies. Property valuation handbook. Reading, Centre for Advanced Land Use Studies, 1981. (Pamphlet B3)
131 Todd, E. C. E. The credibility of appraisers. AIM, 25(3) August 1981 pp12-16.
132 Turner, D. M. An approach to land values. London, Geographical Publications, 1977.
133 Tynan, P. A. C. The appraiser ... as viewed by the client. AIM, 20(2) April 1976 pp24-26, 38-39.
134 Unger, M. A. Elements of real estate appraisal. New York, Wiley, 1982.
135 University of Reading, College of Estate Management, Centre for Advanced Land Use Studies. Property valuation handbook. Reading, Centre for AdvancedLand Use Studies, 1979 onwards. (Issued as separate pamphlets for ring binder - see separate entries, Hoyes, T.; Wiggins, K. P.; Jolly, B. A.; Jonas, C. W.; Thomas, J. R.; Anstey, J.; Smith, K. R. and Bowie, N. W.)
136 Ventolo, W. L., Williams, M. R. and Boykin, James H. Fundamentals of real estate appraisal. 3rd ed. Chicago, Real Estate Education Company, 1983. (Previous editions 1975, 1980).
137 Warren, J. M. Real estate appraisal review. AIM, 22(4) November 1978 pp19-23.
138 Webb, J. R. Micro-real estate: the quintessential dictums: a brief introduction to selected topics in appraisal theory, real estate related economics, real estate finance, and investments. Houston, Texas, Coker Books, 1979.
139 Webb, J. R. Real estate research: past, present and future. Appraisal

Journal, 52 January 1984 pp135-142.
140 Wendt, Paul F. _Real estate appraisal: review and outlook_. Athens, Georgia, University of Georgia Press, 1976.
141 Westbrook, R. _Valuer's casebook of approved valuations: volume one_. London, Estates Gazette, 1968. (Lands Tribunal valuations 1963-7 with case reports and commentary)
142 Westbrook, R. _Valuer's casebook of approved valuations: volume two_. London, Estates Gazette, 1973. (Lands Tribunal valuations 1967-72 with case reports and commentary)
143 White, P. H. Taking a view of valuations. _Estates Gazette_, 242(5834) 4 June 1977 pp799-806.
144 Wiggins, K. P. Principles of valuation, _in_ University of Reading, College of Estate Management, Centre for Advanced Land Use Studies. _Property valuation handbook_. Reading, Centre for Advanced Land Use Studies, 1981. (Pamphlet A1)
145 Wofford, Larry E. and M. L. Goetz. Law, economics, and real estate valuation. _Real Estate Appraiser and Analyst_, 50 Spring 1984 pp69-73.
146 Wood, Ernest. _An introduction to some current ideas in valuation and appraisal_. Liverpool, Liverpool Polytechnic, Faculty of Construction, 1976.
147 Wood, Ernest. _Property and building appraisal in uncertainty_. Liverpool, Liverpool Polytechnic, Faculty of Construction, 1977. (Occasional Paper no. 1)
148 Woolery, A. ed. _The art of valuation_. Lexington, Mass., Lexington Books, 1978: Aldershot, Hants., Heath, 1979. (Transcript of two panel conversations held in Cambridge, Mass., in 1977).

The profession and its practice in various countries

149 Asabere, Paul K. Determinants of land values in an African city: the case of Acra, Ghana. _Land Economics_, 57 August 1981 pp385-397.
150 Button, W. S. The role of the real estate appraiser in Canadian Government. _AIM_, 22(3) August 1978 pp36-37.
151 Byrom, R. J. _The Building Society valuer_. London, Estates Gazette, 1979.
152 Christian, A. C. Thailand - development of landed property valuation: the first steps. _Valuer_(Australia), 28(2) April 1984 pp102-104.
153 Connolly, Robert J. Professional liability of a valuer. _Valuer_(Australia), 27 April 1982 pp170-173.
154 Dalton, A. H. _Review of government valuation services_. London, Inland Revenue, 1983. (Dalton Committee)
155 Dass, R. Professional valuation standards - the Malaysian experience. _The Surveyor_ (Journal of the Institution of Surveyors, Malaysia), 18(2) Second quarter 1983 pp31-34.
156 Dass, R. Valuation and property management in developing countries - its growth and problems. _The Surveyor_ (Journal of the Institution of Surveyors, Malaysia). 11(1&2) January-June 1975 pp33-41.
157 Desimone, Robert C. The real estate business and appraising in Saudi Arabia. _Valuation_, 25(2) March 1979 pp2-7.
158 Geok, N. T. The role of valuers in the public sector. _New Zealand Valuer_, 24(1) March 1979 pp22-25.
159 Great Britain. Inland Revenue. _Report of the Committee reviewing the provision of valuation services in central government_. London, Inland Revenue, 1984. (Review and summary in _Rating and Valuation Reporter_, 24(4) 1984 pp76-77.

160 Great Britain. Scottish Office. Valuation and rating in Scotland: proposals for reform. London, H.M.S.O. 1983. (Cmnd 9018)

161 Greater London Council. Valuation and Estates Department. Valuation and estates: department position statement. London, Greater London Council, 1983. (TSC27)

162 Greater London Council. Valuation and Estates Department. Valuation and estates department in-depth review. London, Greater London Council, 1984. (PPR151: includes review of the department and evidence to the Dalton Committee)

163 Herron, Kerry C. Outback Australia. Valuer(Australia), 27 January 1985 pp104-109.

164 Kahn, Sanders A. Some contrasts between U. S. and U. K. valuation and investing. Real Estate Review. 9(3) Fall 1979 pp25-26.

165 Lewsley, C. Jurisdiction of lands tribunal and local valuation courts. Rating and Valuation Reporter, 20(2) February 1980 pp29-31.

166 Londono, Hernan. The appraising practice in Colombia, S.A. Valuation, 26(1) November 1980 pp74-77.

167 Luscombe, Wendy. American appraisal techniques. Estates Gazette. 237(5766) 7 February 1976 pp401-403.

168 Mackmin, D. H. Valuation in the U.K. market. Appraisal Journal, 47(3) July 1979 pp427-437.

169 Mander, M.R. The appraisal system and education in New Zealand. New Zealand Valuer, 24(8) December 1980 pp627-639.

170 Ohkochi, K. The growth of Japanese real estate appraisal. Appraisal Journal, 50 October 1982 pp499-504.

171 Othick, F. Cost-effective Government valuation services? Local Government Review, 146 4 December 1982 p1071.

172 Pearce, H. No change for Government valuation. Estates Gazette, 270(6183) 5 May 1984 p376. (Following Dalton Committee)

173 Public sector to pay for government valuations. Chartered Surveyor Weekly, 2(7) 17 February 1983 p357. (UK procedure)

174 Purdon, John. ASA in perspective 1952-1977 - special historical issue. Valuation, 25(1) July 1978 pp55-135. (Including history of ASA)

175 Thomas, H. O. History of Pan Pacific Congresses of real estate appraisers, valuers and counselors. Valuer(Australia), 27 January 1982 pp136-139, 144.

Techniques

The many general texts and articles discussing methodology are grouped together in this section. Where a topic has a considerable quantity of literature the references are grouped together in the following section on Technical topics. These do not reflect the organisation of valuations literature but have been selected on literary warrant.

176 Albert, J. D., Banton, H. S. and Pearson, T. D. Valuation of real estate under conditions of bilateral monopoly. *Appraisal Journal*, 50(4) 1982 p532+.

177 Albritton, H. D. A critique of the prevailing definition of market value. *Appraisal Journal*, 48(2) April 1980 pp199-205.

178 Albritton, H. D. Market value: highest price or most probable price? *Appraisal Journal*, 47 July 1979 pp452-453.

179 Albritton, H. D. Valuation of special-use property types. *Appraisal Journal*, 48 July 1980 pp367-371.

180 Aldritch, Peter C. Location is the essence of value in deciding the price of real estate. *Pension and Investments*, 7(4) 12 February 1979 pp27-28.

181 Allan, K. M. Valuations for company prospectus and revaluation purposes. *New Zealand Valuer*, 25(10) June 1984 pp587-588.

182 Ames, R. Appraising the intangibles: is it good will or expertise? *Real Estate Appraiser*, 43 May 1977 pp23-25.

183 Anderson, J. E. Ridge regression: a new regression technique useful to appraiser and assessors. *Real Estate Appraiser and Analyst*, 45 November 1979 pp48-51.

184 Archer, W. R. Towards a model of real estate project demand under uncertainty: an exploratory example of market simulation. *American Real Estate and Urban Economics Association Journal*, 4 Winter 1976 pp19-47.

185 Armfield, Peter D. Casualty loss valuation. *Appraisal Journal*, 50(4) 1982 p505+.

186 Armfield, Peter D. Unusual appraisal assignments: problems and solutions. *Real Estate Appraiser and Analyst*, 48 Spring 1982 pp21-26.

187 Bailey, J. B. Today's real estate transactions require advanced valuation methods. *Appraisal Journal*, 49 April 1981 pp279-283.

188 Bailey, J. B. and others. Market study + financial analysis = feasibility report. *Appraisal Journal*, 45 October 1977 pp550-577.

189 Barrett, G. V. Appraisal should be market study: techniques of analysis. *Appraisal Journal*, 47(4) October 1979 pp538-555.

190 Barrett, G. V. and Blair, John P. Appraisal: pressures and practices.

Real Estate Appraiser and Analyst, 46 January 1980 pp39-42.
191 Baum, Andrew. The all-risks yield: exposing the implicit. Journal of Valuation, 2(3) 1984 pp229-239.
192 Baum, Andrew. Extrapolating comparable evidence. Estates Gazette, 263 3 July 1983 p23.
193 Baum, Andrew. The valuation of reversionary freeholds. Journal of Valuation, 3(1) 1984 pp53-73.
194 Baumgarten, J. Market value when there is no market. Appraisal Journal, 46(1) January 1978 pp79-89.
195 Baxter, C. Impact of government policies and programs on land values. Real Estate Appraiser and Analyst, 45 May 1979 pp42-45.
196 Beard, B. J. Market analysis: a tool for determining market value and rents. Journal of Property Management, 45(5) September/October 1980 pp287-291.
197 Bell, Harold F. Economic future and the property industry. Valuer (Australia) 27 October 1982 pp353-357.
198 Benage, William F. Which offer is worth more? New Zealand Valuer, 25(1) March 1982 pp26-28. (Reprint from Real Estate Appraiser and Analyst, 1981)
199 Bernasconi, John R. Inventories and catalogues for auctioneers. London, Estates Gazette, 1976.
200 Berney, H. M. The understanding and valuation of goodwill. London, Henry Berney Rowland & Partners, 1981.
201 Berney, H. M. Goodwill. Estates Gazette, 258(6039) 20 June 1981 pp1147-1150; 258(6040) 27 June 1981 pp1255-1258.
202 Berry, H. Problem definition between the appraiser and client. Appraisal Journal, 52(2) April 1984 pp237-241.
203 Bickford, H. M. Feasibility approach to varied investment properties. Valuer(Australia), 28(2) April 1984 pp113-115.
204 Bishop, Jeff. The appraisal of buildings - a case study and critique of approaches. Bristol, University of Bristol, School of Advanced Urban Studies, 1979. (Occasional paper no.5)
205 Bishop, R. C. Option value: an exposition and extension. Land Economics, 58(1) 1982 n.p.
206 Blair, John P. Estimating price expectations. Real Estate Appraiser and Analyst, 46 September-October 1980 pp45-49.
207 Blandon, P. and Ward, C. W. R. Questions of investment valuation: a reply. Estates Gazette, 242(5826) 9 April 1977 pp101-103. (Reply to "The valuation of investment properties: two faces of Janus" See no. 562)
208 Blazar, S. M. Valuing real estate: the puzzle of meaningful disclosure. Real Estate Review, 7 Winter 1978 pp72-77.
209 Bohling, J. E. Market analysis: a much needed tool for better loan appraisals. Appraisal Journal, 45 January 1977 pp25-34.
210 Bomar, T. R. Appraiser and the secondary market. Real Estate Appraiser, 42 November 1976 pp42-44.
211 Bowcock, Philip. The valuation of varying incomes: 2 and 3. Journal of Valuation, 1(4) 1983 pp366-376. (For Part 1 see Harker)
212 Bowes, H. R. Handling variable rate mortgages in appraisal problems. Appraisal Journal, 45(1) January 1977 pp122-128.
213 Bowles, Joseph H. Application of exploratory data to the valuation process. Valuation, 27(1) November 1981 pp116-125.
214 Boykin, James H. Real property appraisal in the American colonial area. Appraisal Journal, 44(3) July 1976 pp361-374.
215 BPF suggests alternative to annual valuations. Estates Gazette, 238 (5782) 29 May 1976 pp633-635.
216 Briggs, L. John. The rental valuation of markets: a tender problem.

Journal of Valuation, 1(3) 1983 pp239-245.

217 Brown, Gordon T. Real estate cycles after the valuation perspective. *Appraisal Journal*, 52(4) October 1984 pp539-549.

218 Brown, J. R. A management audit for real estate appraisers. *Appraisal Journal*, 51(3) July 1983 p436-444.

219 Brown, Ralph J. and Johnson, D. A. Inflation, valuation and the discount rate. *Appraisal Journal*, 48(4) October 1980 pp549-555.

220 Bryce, M. L. and McIlwain, A. E. Building efficiency - cost and value. *AIM*, 27(4) November 1983 pp33-39.

221 Building Maintenance Cost Information Service. *Standard form of property occupancy cost analysis*. London, Building Maintenance Cost Information Service, 1984.

222 Burford, R. H. Higher math: an objective or a tool? *Real Estate Appraiser and Analyst*, 44 July 1978 p40.

223 Cairns, W. H. Effect of inflation on capitalisation rates. *Valuer* (Australia), 27 April 1983 pp498-502.

224 A call for new valuation methods. *Estates Gazette*, 238(5780) 15 May 1976 pp481-484.

225 Carn, N. G. Is highest and best use a justification for zoning? *Appraisal Journal*, 52(2) April 1984 pp177-182.

226 Carpenter, M. D. and Shannon, D. S. The effect of inflation on value. *Real Estate Appraiser and Analyst*, 47(1) 1981 pp51-55.

227 Carpenter, M. D. and Shannon, D. S. The effect of inflation on value. *New Zealand Valuer*, 25(3) September 1982 pp169-173. (Reprinted from *Real Estate Appraiser and Analyst*, 1981)

228 Case, F. E. Value of a thing is the price it will bring. *American Real Estate and Urban Economics Association Journal*, 7 1979 pp265-268.

229 Castenholz, W. B. A. *A solution to the appreciation problem*. New York, Arno Press, 1978.

230 Cavanagh, D. Title III, Uniform Act, 1970: its effect on eminent domain appraisal. *Real Estate Appraiser and Analyst*, 46 September-October 1980 pp23-27.

231 Christensen, B. Taking the guesstimating out of adjustments. *Appraisal Journal*, 48(2) April 1980 pp255-260.

232 Christiansen, W. K. S. Urban property investment: a range of options. *New Zealand Valuer*, 25(2) June 1982 pp88-94.

233 Chudleigh, W. H. Application of correlation matrix analysis to real estate appraisal. *Appraisal Journal*, 47(4) October 1979 pp523-531.

234 Clapp, J. M. Elasticity of substitution for land: the effects of measurement errors. *Journal of Urban Economics*, 8 September 1980 pp255-263.

235 Clapp, J. M. Substitution of urban land for other inputs. *Journal of Urban Economics*, 6 January 1979 pp122-134.

236 Clark, R. E. RICS Research into valuation methods, *in* Chiddick, David and Millington, Alan F. *Land management: new directions*. London, Spon, 1984. pp289-292.

237 Clatanoff, Robert M. *Metrication in assessment*. Chicago, International Association of Assessing Officers, 1980 (Research & Information series)

238 Coin, B. J. Valuing real estate subject to tax-free financing. *Appraisal Journal*, 48 April 1980 pp261-266.

239 Colam, M. A more modern method. *Estates Gazette*, 251(5951) 15 September 1979 pp1054-1055.

240 Collingwood, J. C. Alternative use value, *in* Royal Institution of Chartered Surveyors. *Balance sheet valuations - the background: GPD*

seminar 1979. London, Royal Institution of Chartered Surveyors, 1979.

241 Colwell, Peter F. Statistically oriented definiton of market value. Appraisal Journal, 47(1) January 1979 pp53-58.

242 Colwell, Peter F. and Cannaday, R. E. Property residual form of mortgage-equity analysis. Real Estate Appraiser and Analyst, 46 July -August 1980 pp30-34.

243 Colwell, Peter F. and Sirmans, C. F. Area, time. centrality and the value of urban land. Land Economics, 54 November 1978 pp514-519.

244 Confusion of areas: measurement. Estates Gazette, 268(6164) 10 December 1983 pp1127-1128.

245 Contractor's basis vindicated by Rating and Valuation Association report. Chartered Surveyor Weekly, 2(7) 17 February 1983 p357.

246 Cooper, J. M. A statistical based approach to valuation: the educational requirements. Valuer(Australia), 28(2) April 1984 pp91-101.

247 Cooper, Kenneth J. A new sales system for public valuers. New Zealand Valuer, 24(9) March 1981 pp713-721.

248 Copley, R. E. and Clemons, M. K. Choosing the right depreciation method: the impact of marginal tax brackets. Appraisal Journal, 51(3) July 1983 pp355-362.

249 Corgel, J. B. and others. Measuring energy efficiency for selection and adjustment of comparable sales. Appraisal Journal, 50(1) January 1982 pp71-78.

250 Cothern, F. H. Interim use revisited. Appraisal Journal, 48 October 1980 pp556-561.

251 Council of State Governments. Period reappraisal of real property: the Utah approach. Washington, D. C., The Council, 1976.

252 Craig, R. H. Market value for assessment purposes fact or fiction? AIM, 22(2) April 1978 pp7-8.

253 Crawford, K. and Harris, D. Prime property yields - well publicised but discredited indicators of value. Property Management, 2(4) 1984 pp341-348.

254 Crissey, John C. A brief review of statistics for the Ad Valorem Appraiser. Valuation, 29(1) December 1983 pp32-39.

255 Croot, T. J. Interest on outlay: the phantom factor in a hypothetical value. New Zealand Valuer, 24(1) March 1979 pp26-32.

256 Crosby, Neil. The analysis and valuation of freehold investment property. Valuer(ISVA), 53(8) October 1984 pp234-235.

257 Crosby, Neil. Investment valuation technique - the shape of things to come? Valuer(ISVA), 53(7) August/September 1984 pp196-197.

258 Danek, C. E. Creative or favorable financing and its effects on value. Real Estate Appraiser and Analyst, 49(2) 1983 pp31-32.

259 D'Ardenne, Roy H. Valuation subject to existing financing. Appraisal Journal, 47(4) October 1980 pp512-520.

260 Darlow, Clive. Property investment - indexing valuations. Estates Gazette, 263(6094) 24 July 1982 pp327-329.

261 Darlow, Clive and Morley, S. New views on development appraisal. Estates Gazette, 262 26 June 1982 pp1263,1265-1266.

262 Davey, N. Is the season of goodwill over? Chartered Surveyor Weekly, 6(4) 26 January 1984 p236.

263 Davey, N. Profit sharing: can it ever be fair? Chartered Surveyor Weekly, 5(9) 1 December 1983 p577.

264 Davies, D. R. Underlying zoning - 'a remarkable fiction'. Valuer (Australia), 26 October 1980 pp333-336.

265 Davies, L. John D. Wood case: a cautionary tale. Management Today, September 1977 pp161-162.

266 Davis, J. M. Using gross rent multipliers and statistical inference along with the three appraisal approaches. *Valuation*, 25(2) March 1979 pp16-33.

267 Davis, W. D. Impact of public announcement on value. *Appraisal Journal*, 44(4) October 1976 pp533-546.

268 Denne, Robert C. *Determinants of value : an annotated bibliography*. International Association of Assessing Officers, 1976.(Bibliography series)

269 Desmond, Glenn M. Valuing the loss of business goodwill. *Appraisal Journal*, 45 April 1977 pp193-202.

270 Dolman, J. P. Incremental elements of market value due to historical significance. *Appraisal Journal*, 48 July 1980 pp338-353.

271 Du Bois, Ayers J. Theoretical vs practical appraising (1933). *Appraisal Journal*, 50(1) January 1982 pp13-19.

272 Dunham, H. W. Real estate appraising from the viewpoint of the small investor. *Real Estate Appraiser and Analyst*, 45 March 1979 pp31-36.

273 Eldred, G. W. and Zerbst, R. H. Consumer research and the real estate appraiser. *Appraisal Journal*, 44(4) October 1976 pp510-522.

274 Else-Mitchell, Justin R. Uniformity of statutory valuations - feasible ideal? *Valuer*(Australia), 27 July 1982 pp231-233, 252.

275 Entreken, H. C. Are we really seeking market value? *Appraisal Journal*, 48(3) July 1980 pp428-431.

276 Equiquated yield valuations. *Estates Gazette*, 254(5987) 7 June 1980 pp888.

277 Erickson, E. H. Appraising older properties. *Real Estate Appraiser*, 44 May 1978 pp11-12.

278 Evaluation. *Appraisal Journal*, 51(4) October 1983 pp546-568.

279 Evaluation of selected criticisms of traditional real estate appraisal. *Real Estate Appraiser and Analyst*, 46 September-October 1980 pp38-40.

280 Everhart, M. E. *Everhart on easements*. St. Paul, Todd Publishing Co., 1980 & 1981.

281 Farrell, M. D. Review of the appraisal process. *Real Estate Appraiser*, 43 November 1977 pp21-23.

282 Farrell, M. D. Valuation of income-producing properties for loan underwriting purposes. *Appraisal Journal*, 48 October 1980 pp576-578. (Discussion 49 April 1981 pp284-289)

283 Federation Internationale des Geometres. *Assessing property values in capital markets: valuation seminar, Edinburgh, 9 July 1980*. unpublished paper. (Royal Institution of Chartered Surveyors Library)

284 Ferguson, J. T. and Dunham, F. Evaluating distressed properties by after-tax equity yields. *Real Estate Appraiser and Analyst*, 47 Winter 1981 pp16-18.

285 Fineman, S. J. Peeking into the future - the appraiser's crystal ball. *Appraisal Journal*, 49 April 1981 pp301-305.

286 Fisher, W. and others. Method for building a property values index for use in local public policy decisions. *American Real Estate and Urban Economics Association Journal*, 4 Fall 1976 pp77-89.

287 Freeman, A. Myrick. The sign and size of option value. *Land Economics*, 60(1) February 1984 pp1-13.

288 Friedman, J. P. and Lindeman, B. Cash equivalent analysis. *Appraisal Journal*, 47(1) January 1979 pp35-43.

289 Gibbons, A. A. *Valuation and the inner city areas*. London, Royal Institution of Chartered Surveyors, 1977. (Paper given at a study day, 20 May 1977, 'Future of our inner city areas')

290 Gibbons, James E. Equity yield. *Appraisal Journal*, 48(1) January

1980 pp31-55.
291 Gibbons, James E. Equity yield. Valuer(Australia) 27 July 1983 pp615-627.
292 Gibbons, James E. Influence of inflation on real estate valuation and investment analysis. Appraisal Journal, 48 October 1980 pp485-502.
293 Gibbons, James E. Point of view: influence of inflation on real estate valuation and investment analysis. Appraisal Journal, 48(4) October 1980 pp485-502.
294 Gleeson, M. E. Effects of an urban growth management system on land values. Land Economics, 55 August 1979 pp350-365.
295 Gloudemans, Robert J. Use-value assessment in the United States. Chicago, International Association of Assessing Officers, 1979. (Research and Information Series)
296 Goebel, P. R. Discrimination and the appraisal process: some empirical results. Real Estate Appraiser and Analayst, 47 Summer 1981 pp63-67.
297 Goggans, T. P. and Keller, A. Current use valuation: opportunities and restrictions for estate planning. Trusts and Estates, 119 November 1980 pp41-46.
298 Goodwill: the main development ingredient. Estates Gazette, 27 April 1984 p9.
299 Goolsby, W. C. How inflation-induced changes in interest rates affect property values. Appraisal Journal, 51(2) 1983 pp234-239.
300 Gordon, W. S. Incurable functional obsolescence due to lack of an item: is it possible? Real Estate Appraiser and Analyst, 48 Summer 1982 pp32-36.
301 Graaskamp, J. A. The appraisal of 25 N Pickney: a demonstration case for contemporary appraisal methods. Madison, Wisc., Landmark Research Institute, 1978.
302 Grear, A. Aspects of valuation, valuing goodwill. Valuer(ISVA), 52(6) pp170-171, 180.
303 Greaves, M. J. Is the property profession of the dual rate principle out-dated? Valuer(Australia), 26 January 1980 pp18-24.
304 Greer, Willis R. and Buono, Thomas J. Going concern valuations. Appraisal Journal, 49(4) October 1981 pp587-595.
305 Gross, Martin M. Shared development of historic sites. Appraisal Journal, 52(4) October 1984 pp519-527.
306 Gullickson, A. E. and Hewitt, R. Adjusting to reality. Real Estate Appraiser and Analyst, 47 Summer 1981 pp22-27.
307 Hall, P. O. Alternative approaches to performance measurement. Estates Gazette, 259(6052) 19 September 1981 pp935-938.
308 Hall, P. O. Development: appraisal techniques. Estates Gazette, 263(6096) 7 August 1982 pp499-502.
309 Hall, P. and Hargitay, Stephen. Property portfolio performance - a selected approach, in Chiddick, David and Millington, Alan F. Land management: new directions. London, Spon, 1984. pp27-43.
310 Halpin, M. C. Merchandising income properties. Journal of Property Management, 41(6) November/December 1976 pp293-298.
311 Handley, W. B. and Livingston, E. J. Hypothesis testing in appraisal. Real Estate Appraiser and Analyst, 48 Winter 1982 pp19-22.
312 The hardcore/marginal method of valuation and comparisons - 2. Rating and Valuation Reporter, 15(32-35) August 1975 pp326-328.
313 Hardly for students: valuations methods and techniques. Estates Gazette, 248(5907) 4 November 1978 pp404-405.
314 Harju, Melvin W. and Clauretie, Terrence M. New directions in eminent domain: the emerging issue of enhancement. Appraisal Journal, 52(2) April 1984 pp214-229.

315 Harker, N. The valuation of varying incomes: 1. Journal of Valuation, 1(4) 1983 pp363-365. (For parts 2 & 3 see Bowcock)

316 Harps, W. S. Valuation reforms - current concepts under question. Valuer(Australia), 27 January 1982 pp3-9, 15.

317 Harris, D. G. Inflation-indexed price supports and land values. American Journal of Agricultural Economics, 59 August 1977 pp489-495.

318 Harris, Don L., McCormick, Philip A. and Davis, W. D. The valuation of partial interests in real estate. Valuation, 29(1) December 1983 pp62-73.

319 Harris, J. Evaluating participation financing for income properties. Appraisal Journal, 52(2) April 1984 pp198-213.

320 Harris, R. Lee. How to measure market demand. Journal of Property Management, 42(4) July/August 1977 pp178-180.

321 Harrison, H. S. Harrison on Eminent Domain: a guide for appraisers and others. Chicago, Society of Real Estate Appraisers, 1980.

323 Harrison, H. S. What is an amenity? Real Estate Today, 10 February 1977 pp16-19.

324 Harrison, H. S. and Kaye, Barbara J. A new appraisal dilemma: what is actual cash value? Appraisal Journal, 52(3) July 1984 pp348-355.

325 Hartley, H. B. Section 2032A regs detail special use valuation methods, how to make the election. Journal of Taxation 53 December 1980 pp364-367.

326 Haymes, Alan. Full-value assessments can work. Real Estate Review, 11 Summer 1981 pp99-102.

327 Haymes, Alan. When to gamble on a time-of-the-essence clause. Real Estate Review, 7 Spring 1977 pp19-20.

328 Hellewell, E. G. Valuation of variable future incomes on the dual-rate basis. Chartered Land Surveyor/Chartered Minerals Surveyor, 2(2) 1980 pp45-51.

329 Henderson, R. A usability index. Estates Gazette, 257(6020) 7 February 1981 pp453-456.

330 Herney, A. The mysterious case of land values and derelict land. Municipal Review, (49)586 1978 pp158-160.

331 Herps, A. C. B. Land value - its origin, nature and effect. Valuer (Australia), 26 April 1980 pp106-108.

332 Herps, M. D. Uniformity of statutory valuations - practical considerations. Valuer(Australia), 27 July 1982 pp244-246.

333 Hilton, R. W. and Swiering, R. J. Perception of initial uncertainty as a determinant of information value. Journal of Accounting Research, 19(1) 1981 pp109-119.

334 Hirsch, W. Z. Efficiency of restrictive land use instruments. Land Economics, 53 May 1977 pp145-156.

335 Hoag, J. W. Towards indices of real estate value and return. Journal of Finance, 35(2) 1980 pp569-580.

336 Hoagland, G. Are the mechanics of the adjustment process correct? Real Estate Appraiser and Analyst, 48 Spring 1982 pp59-62.

337 Hodges, M. B. Mass appraisal of investment class properties. Valuation, 27(1) November 1981 pp44-65.

338 Holmes, R. L. Inflation, real estate yields and current market aspirations. Real Estate Appraiser, 42 July 1976 pp25-29.

339 How it pays to get the first byte of the apple. Property Confidential, 347 July 1984 pp16-20.

340 Howcroft, P. A. Rational expectations approach to concepts of value. Appraisal Journal, 48(3) July 1980 pp402-413.

341 Howcroft, P. A. A review of appraisal practices and methods of analysis. Appraisal Journal, 46(3) July 1978 p420+.

342 Howes, C. K. Value maps: aspects of land and property values. Nor-

wich, Geo Books, 1980. (Bibliography pp138-145)

343 Hunter, J. C. IVEM revisited: inner city appraising. Real Estate Appraiser, 43 September 1977 pp15-25.

344 Hyde, J. V. New markets for right-of-way appraisers. Appraisal Journal, 46 October 1978 pp523-528.

345 Inflation, money markets and the appraisal process. Real Estate Appraiser and Analyst, 45 September 1979 p49.

346 Interim report of the Institute's Working Party on the Sandilands proosals. Public Finance and Accountancy, 3(9) September 1976 pp275-279. (Chartered Institute of Public Finance and Accountancy)

347 Jacob, Bernard E. Introduction: how to evaluate a new development. International Property Investment Journal, 1(1) 1982 pi+ .

348 Jaffe, Austin J. Is there a new internal rate of return literature. American Real Estate and Urban Economics Association Journal, 5 1977 pp482-502.

349 Jaffe, Austin J. and Sirmans, C. F. Relationship between growth factors, operating expense ratio, and valuation. Real Estate Appraiser, 44 July 1978 pp30-34.

350 Jaffe, Austin J. and Sirmans, C. F. Some myths about real estate. Real Estate Review, 8 Spring 1978 pp39-42.

351 Jahns, J. Fourth method of valuation: the weed tree test. Real Estate Review, 9 Summer 1979 pp85-87.

352 Janata, J. F. Effect of the trend towards requiring assessment of realty at market value. Journal of Taxation, 48 January 1978 pp36-39.

353 Janssen, C. T. L. and McKenzie, D. W. Correction factors for conversion of monthly cash flows to annual equivalents. Canadian Appraiser, 28(2) May 1984 pp22-25.

354 Jason, T. T. C. The effect of financing terms on property values. New Zealand Valuer, 24(12) December 1981 pp953-956.

355 Jason, T. T. C. Valuation mathematics. New Zealand Valuer, 25(1) March 1982 pp29-30.

356 Jenkinson, R. H. Investment, profitability and the valuation ratio. London, Bank of England, 1981. (Discussion paper no.17)

357 Jones, I. G. Equivalent yield analysis. Journal of Valuation, 1(3) 1983 pp246-252.

358 Kahn, Sanders A. Appraising in a volatile market. Real Estate Review. 9 Winter 1980 pp27-28.

359 Kahn, Sanders A. Challenging appraisal concepts. Real Estate Appraiser and Analyst, 49 Spring 1983 pp5-10.

360 Kahn, Sanders A. Infernal rate of return and regressive analysis. Real Estate Review, 9 1979 pp2-22.

361 Kahn, Sanders A. Real estate value: its genesis and demise. Real Estate Appraiser and Analyst, 45 January 1979 pp13-20.

362 Kamanitz, B. How to prepare an assessment case based on comparison valuation. Journal of Property Management, 42(1) January/February 1977 pp37-40.

363 Kanner, G. Buy cheap, sell dear - a look at the re-use appraisal. Appraisal Journal, 47 July 1979 pp461-465.

364 Kapplin, S. D. Economic forecasting for real estate appraisal. Real Estate Appraiser and Analyst, 44 March 1978 pp47-55.

365 Kapplin, S. D. Financial theory and valuation of real estate under conditions of risk. Real Estate Appraiser, 42 September 1976 pp28-37.

366 Kau, James B. and Sirmans, C. F. Changes in urban land values: 1836-1970. Journal of Urban Economics, 15 January 1984 pp18-25.

367 Kernebone, R. A. Capital value: valuation under the New South Wales

Crown Lands legislation. Valuer(Australia), 26 July 1980 pp209-216, 221; October 1980 pp287-294; January 1981 pp370-376, 384.
368 Kirby, T. R. Functional obsolescence: the nemesis of the demonstration report writer. Real Estate Appraiser and Analyst, 47 Summer 1981 pp19-21.
369 Kleinfeld, I. and Healy, J. J. Case study: MRA in different neighbourhoods. Real Estate Appraiser, 42 July 1976 pp30-35.
370 Klink, J. J. and O'Malley, P. J. Net realisable value controversy. Real Estate Review, 10 Summer 1980 pp68-72.
371 Korpacz, Peter F. and Marchitelli, Richard. Market value: a contemporary perspective. Appraisal Journal, 52(4) October 1984 pp485-493.
372 Kummer, D. R. and Schwartz, A. L. Valuing real property purchase options. Real Estate Appraiser and Analyst, 46 January 1980 pp13-17.
373 Lambert, D. W. The three approaches to value - market, market and market. AIM, 20(1) January 1976 pp31-33.
374 Land, Howard G. and Maxted, William M. Valuations...or calculations? Estates Gazette, 259(6049) 29 August 1981 pp682-684.
375 Leach, W. A. Hardcore method of valuation. Estates Gazette, 246(5881) 6 May 1978 pp475-476.
376 Leach, W. A. Marriage value. Estates Gazette, 250(5928) 7 April 1979 pp44-45.
377 Leach, W. A. Pointe Gourde principle. Journal of Planning and Environment Law, February 1977 pp85-92.
378 Leach, W. A. 'Pointe Gourde', rule 3 and section 6. Journal of Valuation, 1(4) 1983 pp386-391.
379 Leaper, R. J. Trends in the market place and the valuer's role. Valuer(Australia), 26 October 1981 pp647-649.
380 Lehari, R. A. The best way to value a real estate company. CA Magazine, 116 July 1983 pp38-42.
381 Lindeman, B. Profit and puff in real estate valuation. Real Estate Review, 6 Summer 1976 pp83-88.
382 Lipman, M. R. Problem property marketing analysis. Appraisal Journal, 46 April 1978 pp287-291.
383 Liteplo, D. N. Mortgage calculations and the appraiser. AIM, 27(4) November 1983 pp27-32.
384 Lloyd, C. A rethink on property values. Property Journal, 89(4) 1982 p9+.
385 Lombardelli, H. P. Big Ben - the appraiser's timepiece. Appraisal Journal, 47 July 1979 pp396-405.
386 Lovell, D. D. Condominium and subdivision discounting. Appraisal Journal, 51 October 1983 pp524-539.
387 Lusht, Kenneth M. Data, the appraisal process and the market value definition. Appraisal Journal, 49(4) October 1981 pp534-546.
388 Lusht, Kenneth M. Inflation and real estate investment value. Real Estate Appraiser and Analyst, 45 November 1979 pp23-29.
389 Lusht, Kenneth M. Most probable selling price. Appraisal Journal, 51(3) July 1983 pp346-354.
390 McClellan, W. M. and Toland, A. D. Capitalization with a variable rate mortgage. Appraisal Journal, 45 July 1977 pp396-404.
391 McClellan, W. M. Inflation/monetary policy/real estate market. Appraisal Journal, 46(4) October 1978 pp547-550.
392 McDonald, J. F. and Bowman, H. W. Land value functions: a reevaluation. Journal of Urban Economics, 6 January 1979 pp25-41.
393 McGough, R. M. Current cost accounting and the valuer. Valuer(Australia), 27 January 1982 pp88-93, 97. (Also in New Zealand Valuer, 25(1) March 1982 pp11-17.

394 McInnes, David R. Resources boom and related property market. Valuer (Australia), 27 April 1982 pp174-180, 186.
395 McIntosh, A. and Sykes, S. Towards a standard property income valuation model - rationalisation or stagnation? Journal of Valuation, 1(2) 1983 pp117-135.
396 Mackmin, D. H. The appraisal process. Estates Gazette, 244(5852) 8 October 1977 pp123-125.
397 Mackmin, D. H. Appraisal v. valuation: some US differences. Journal of Valuation, 1(1) 1983 pp17-23.
398 Mackmin, D. H. A matter of amortisation. Estates Gazette, 245(5867) 28 January 1978 pp289-292.
399 MacLeod, Peter. The mystery of indemnity. New Zealand Valuer, 25(6) June 1983 pp326-336.
400 McMahon, S. J. Fixed assets: a guide to plant and machinery valuation terminology. Valuer(Australia), 27 October 1982 pp381-382, 387.
401 Maes, M. A. Appraised value vs. contract price. Real Estate Today, 10 February 1977 pp10-14.
402 Maes, M. A. The emergence of cash equivalency in valuation. Real Estate Review, 12 Fall 1982 pp87-90.
403 Markandya, Anil. Rents, prices, and expectations in the land market. Berkeley, Cal., University of California, Institute of Business and Economic Research, June 1982.
404 Markusen, J. R. Elements of real asset pricing: a theoretical analysis with special reference to urban land prices. Land Economics, 55 May 1979 pp153-166.
405 Marling, J. H. Real estate valuation in a distressed market. Mortgage Banker, 37 October 1976 pp10+ .
406 Marriage value: a further look. Estates Gazette, 271(6204) 29 September 1984 p1276.
407 Marshall, Phillip. Equated yield analysis: a valuation method of the future? Estates Gazette, 239(5793) 14 August 1976 pp493-497.
408 Marshall, Phillip. Techniques for applied valuation examinations. Estates Gazette, 241(5822) 12 March 1977 pp751-755.
409 Marshall, Richard D. Appraising property values in a world of change. Real Estate Appraiser, 44 May 1978 pp4-7.
410 Marshall, Richard D. Inflation-depreciation-replacement value: windfall or wipeout? Real Estate Appraiser and Analyst, 46 July-August 1980 pp23-29.
411 Marshall, Richard D. Market value: what does it mean in real estate today? Real Estate Appraiser, 44 January 1978 pp31-34.
412 Martin, Eugene J. Building loss appraisal. Valuation, 23(1) March/April 1976 pp112-121.
413 Martin, R. S. Estimating the effect of existing financing on market value using an after tax approach. Real Estate Appraiser and Analyst, 48 Summer 1982 pp67-75.
414 Mason, R. C. The appraiser and the mortgage lender. Canadian Appraiser, 28(4) November 1984 pp18-23.
415 Mason, R. C. Do not demean the mean. Appraisal Journal, 45(1) January 1977 pp65-69.
416 Mason, R. C. Present worth in present dollars. Appraisal Journal, 51(3) July 1983 pp415-421.
417 Mason, R. C. Valuing the effects of a variable rate mortgage. Appraisal Journal, 47(2) April 1979 pp243-247.
418 Mellor, R. M. Valuation and viability criteria of proposed projects. Valuer(Australia), 26 January 1980 pp12-17.
419 Melville, I. Surveys - perils, pitfalls and procedures. Chartered Surveyor Weekly, 3(9) 9 June 1983 p554.

420 Migliorini, Edesio M. A study of valuation methods in practice with reference to future developments. Valuer(Australia) 25 October 1979 pp661-670; 26 January 1980 pp47-49.
421 Milan, R. D. Suggested conceptual foundations for the valuation of partial interests. Appraisal Journal, 45(2) April 1977 pp173-178.
422 Miles, W. Porcher. Error and risk in property value estimates. Appraisal Journal, 48 October 1980 pp540-548.
423 Miller, N. G. Market value and market price:economists and appraisers. Valuation, 25(2) March 1979 pp34-41.
424 Moore, D. Property valuations - disclosure considerations. Valuer (ISVA), 51(9) Novemebr 1982 pp202-203.
425 Moreton, Peter. Common standards of valuation for mortgages. Building Societies Gazette, 115(1399) 1983 pp1178-1180.
426 Moreton, Peter. Valuation for mortgage purposes. Journal of Valuation, 2(2) 1984 pp125-136.
427 Moreton, Peter. Valuing for mortgage purposes in the United Kingdom. Appraisal Review Journal, 7(2) Fall 1984 pp69-79. (Also published in International Real Estate Journal, 8(1) pp66-72.
428 Moreton, Peter. What price? - building society valuations. Valuer (ISVA), 52(9) November 1983 pp276-277.
429 Morley, S. J. E. Methods of valuation. Architect and Surveyor, 52(1) Spring 1977 pp11-12.
430 Morton, T. Factor analysis, multicollinearity, and regression appraisal models. Appraisal Journal, 45 October 1977 pp578-588.
431 Moselle, G. Building cost manual 1982: square foot costs for residential, commercial, industrial, agricultural, and military structures. Carlsbad, Cal., Craftsman Book Co., 1981.
432 Motha, P. Investment valuation. New Zealand Valuer, 24(8) December 1980 pp646-653.
433 Mulquiney, Allan and Allen, Simon. The use of equated yield techniques: a case study. Journal of Valuation, 1(3) 1983 pp229-238.
434 Mumme, Frank. The Morris Report - effects of recommendations for compensation for injurious affection and reinstatement. Valuer(Australia) 27 October 1983 pp712-714, 720.
435 Murdoch, J. R. Holding the balance. Estates Gazette, 268(6258) 29 October 1983 pp469-470, 474, 476.
436 Murrells, P. How a disclaimer deters a borrower's claims. Chartered Surveyor Weekly, 9(3) 18 October 1984 pp196-197.
437 Myers, J. Investment: the services of professional valuers. New Law Journal, 126(5767) 9 September 1976 p923.
438 Nabarro, R. High cost and low value in urban land. Built Environment, 4(3) 1978 pp229-236.
439 Neal, R. How to handle a storm disaster. Journal of Property Management, 41(6) November/December 1976 pp42-46.
440 Needham, M. A simpler route to property valuation. Estates Times, 752 29 June 1984 p9.
441 Net and equated yields. Estates Gazette, 244(5856) 5 November 1977 pp484-485.
442 A new measure for property. Investors Chronicle, 70(888) 16 November 1984 pp8-9. (Hillier Parker May and Rowden's Average yields, quarterly from 1984)
443 New standards for sale, purchase and mortgage of land and buildings. Chartered Surveyor, 112(11) June 1980 pp506-508.
444 Newell, G. J. Application of ridge regression to real estate appraisal Appraisal Journal, 50 January 1982 pp116-119.
445 Newell, G. J. Introduction to ridge regression in mass appraisal work.

Valuer(Australia), 26 October 1980 pp318-319.

446 Nicholls, A. D. New legislative proposals - the valuation provisions. Rating and Valuation, March 1980 pp67-69.

447 Nicholls, A. D. Valuation commentary. Rating and Valuation, August/ September 1983 pp229-231. (Dates when evidence of transactions can be taken into account in making valuations) (Regular column in each issue, not all are indexed)

448 North, Ralph M. Building replacement cost estimating for non-professional estimators. Valuation, 28(1) November 1982 pp128-138.

449 Nutley, W. G. Investment valuation. Chartered Surveyor Urban Quarterly, 3(4) Summer 1976 pp1-3.

450 O'Keefe, J. A. B. The title factor in valuation. New Zealand Valuer, 23(1) November 1976 pp19-22.

451 Oliver, J. W. Appraisal for mortgage purposes. AIM, 25(4) November 1981 pp22-23.

452 Opelka, F. Gregory. Appraisal amendment meant to reinforce appraiser rights. Savings and Loan News, 101 May 1980 p120-121.

453 Opelka, F. Gregory. Appraisal practices don't discriminate, FHLBB study shows. Savings and Loan News, 101 September 1980 p110-111.

454 Opelka, F. Gregory. Are appraisal disclosures next? Savings and Loan News., 97 July 1976 pp82-83.

455 Opelka, F. Gregory. Building guidelines are explicit in policy statements. Savings and Loan News, 100(3) March 1979 p107.

456 Opelka, F. Gregory. Government records reinforce appraisal policy statements. Savings and Loan News, 100(1) January 1979 p87.

457 Opelka, F. Gregory. Inflation jump may trouble appraisal process in 1980. Savings and Loan News, 101 April 1980 p110-111.

458 Opelka, F. Gregory. Lenders don't use low appraisals to discriminate. Savings and Loan News, 101 October 1980 p142-143.

459 Opelka, F. Gregory. Question recurs: how to file data on comparable sale? Savings and Loan News, 100 September 1979 p117.

460 Opelka, F. Gregory. Valuation process proves vexing for inner-city property. Savings & Loan News, 97 August 1976 pp90-91.

461 Ottensman, J. R. Urban sprawl, land values and the density of development. Land Economics, 53 November 1977 pp389-400.

462 Owens, R. W. Measuring a property's periodic performance. Real Estate Review, 12 Winter 1983 pp56-59.

463 Palmon, D. and Seidler, L. J. Current value reporting of real estate companies and a possible example of market inefficiency. Accountant's Review, 53 July 1978 pp776-790.

464 Pannell, P. W. The artistic valuer. Estates Gazette, 250(5929) 14 April 1979 pp129-133.

465 Paschall, Robert H. An exploration of the upper limit of value. Valuation, 24(1) December 1977 pp2-13.

466 Patrick, M. J. Property indices and the interpretation of property investment performance, in Chiddick, David and Millington, Alan F. Land management: new directions. London, Spon, 1984. pp44-49.

467 Patrick, M. J. What use is property performance analysis? Journal of Valuation, 2(2) 1984 pp137-141.

468 Payne, R. R. Multiple valuation dates. Real Estate Appraiser and Analyst, 45 January 1979 pp39-41.

469 Pearce, D. N. Idris. Standard measurements of real property values. Journal of Valuation, 1(4) 1983 pp351-362.

470 Pines, D. and Weiss, Y. Land improvements projects and land values. Journal of Urban Economics, 11 March 1982 pp199-204.

471 Pollack, B. Market data revisited. Real Estate Appraiser and Analyst, 46 July-August 1980 pp35-36. (Discussion 47 Fall 1981 pp68-69)

472 Pollack, B. Ultraconservative valuations can kill co-op conversions. *Real Estate Review*, 10 Winter 1981 pp46-48.

473 Qualification on valuation. *Accountant*, 176 28 April 1977 p480.

474 Quinlivan, J. M. and Johnson, V. R. Nonconforming-use properties: the concept of positive economic obsolescence. *Appraisal Journal*, 49 January 1981 pp45-51.

475 Rabianski, J. Alternative approach to economic base analysis. *Real Estate Appraiser*, 43 September 1977 pp49-54.

476 Rahman, Talhar Abdul. Political uncertainties and land value. *Valuer* (Australia), 27 January 1982 pp16-17,23.

477 Raison, Barrymore, Australian Heritage Commission listings - effect on historic property rights and values, particularly in the Australian Capital Territory. *Valuer*(Australia), 27 April 1982 pp161-165.

478 Rams, Edwin M. The concept of valuation in the property valuation process. *Valuation*, 27(1) November 1981 pp80-83.

479 Ratcliff, R. Appraisal is market analysis. *Appraisal Journal*, 43 October 1975 p485+.

480 Ratcliffe, J. Appraisal and financial partnership. *Estates Gazette*, 250(5936) 2 June 1979 pp841-845.

481 Ratcliffe, J. Valuation - demands and techniques, *in* Royal Institution of Chartered Surveyors. *Annual conference*. Birmingham, 1980. London, Royal Institution of Chartered Surveyors, 1980.

482 Ratcliffe, J. and Trott, A. Valuations: demands and techniques. *Estates Gazette*, 255(5995) 2 August 1980 pp435-439; 255(5996) 9 August 1980 pp529-233.

483 Rating and Valuation Association. *Contractor's basis of valuation: report of a research group*. London, Rating and Valuation Association, 1982.

484 Rayner, Michael. The valuation of 'no-market' property assets. *Journal of Valuation*, 1(2) 1983 pp136-141.

485 Real estate and inflation revisited. *Real Estate Appraiser and Analyst*, 46 September-October 1981 pp34-41.

486 Redford, D. W. Apply property analysis to maximise income. *Journal of Property Management*, 42(3) May/June 1977 pp148-151.

487 Reese, L. Mass appraisals: raffle or racket? *Real Estate Appraiser*, 44 May 1978 pp16-20.

488 Resolving conflicting valuation rules. *CPA Journal*, 51 November 1981 pp75-76.

489 Reynolds, A. Current valuation techniques: a review. *Appraisal Journal* 52(2) April 1984 pp183-197.

490 Reynolds, A. Current valuation techniques: a review. *Valuer*(Australia), 28(3) July 1984 pp198-204.

491 Rhodes, F. G. Inflation discounting: how appraisers can deal with inflation. *Appraisal Journal*, 49(2) 1981 pp234-247.

492 Richardson, D. H. and Thalheimer, R. Alternative methods of variable selection: an application to real estate assessment. *American Real Estate and Urban Economics Association Journal*, 7 Fall 1979 pp393-409.

493 Rickard, J. Mortgage calculations: all you need is a pencil and ruler. *Accountancy*, 94(1083) November 1983 pp125-126,128,130.

494 Ring, A. A. *Valuation of real estate*. 2nd ed. Englewood Cliffs, Prentice-Hall, 1970.

495 Roberts, T. A. The assessment of indemnity value for insurance purposes. *New Zealand Valuer*, 25(3) September 1982 pp131-143.

496 Roberts, T. L. Valuation of project enhancement in eminent domain. *Appraisal Journal*, 50 April 1982 pp220-227.

497 Roddewig, Richard J. and Schlaes, Jared. Preservation easements reconsidered: an alternative approach to value. Appraisal Journal, 52(3) July 1984 pp325-347.
498 Rooklidge, C. H. New indicators and old theories. Real Estate Appraiser and Analyst, 48 Fall 1982 pp25-31.
499 Rose, J. J. Markets and mathematics. Valuer(ISVA), 148(4) May 1979 pp126-128.
500 Rosser, J. B. Theory and policy implications of spatial discontinuities in land values. Land Economics, 54 November 1978 pp430-431.
501 Rothwell, G. Responsibilities of a valuer to an intending mortgagee. Valuer(Australia), 26 October 1981 pp835-643.
502 Roulac, Stephen E. Balancing right brain creativity and left brain discipline to value complex real property interests. Real Estate Appraiser and Analyst, 48 Summer 1982 pp49-53; 48 Fall 1982 pp50-56.
503 Roulac, Stephen E. Valuation decisions in a turbulent economy: challenge to tradition, opportunity for distinction. Appraisal Journal, 50(4) October 1982 pp564-580.
504 Roy, J. O. Price to sell. Real Estate Today, 9 July 1976 pp30-33.
505 Royal Institution of Chartered Surveyors, General Practice Division. Valuation for goodwill. Chartered Surveyor Weekly, 5(4) 27 October 1983 pp238-239.
506 Royal Institution of Chartered Surveyors, Valuation and Rating Committee. Advisory note to members on the effect on valuations of the presence of HACC in buildings. London, Royal Institution of Chartered Surveyors, 1984.
507 Royal Town Planning Institute. Land values and planning in the inner areas: consultation document. London, Royal Town Planning Institute, 1979.
508 Ruggles, R. K. and Walsh, James J. Supply, demand and the nature of value. Appraisal Journal, 5(2) April 1983 pp190-201.
509 Rynders, L. J. Photography for appraisers. Real Estate Appraiser and Analyst, 46 March 1980 pp17-26.
510 Sams, G. S. Severance and the land taken. Journal of Valuation, 1(1) 1983 pp9-16.
511 Sanderson, I. J. V. Future of pioneer properties. Valuer(Australia), 27 October 1982 pp376-380.
512 Sanderson, I. J. V. Pioneer properties - a case for the crystal ball? Valuer(Australia), 27 January 1982 pp34-37, 55.
513 Schaefer, R. C. DCR: an appraisal gate crasher. Appraisal Journal, 50(2) April 1982 pp195-203.
514 Schlaes, Jared. The market in market value. Appraisal Journal, 52(4) October 1984 pp494-518.
515 Schlaes, Jared and Young, Michael S. Evaluating major investment properties. Appraisal Journal, 46(1) January 1978 pp101-111.
516 Schultz, J. C. What is market value? Real Estate Appraiser, 43 November 1977 pp17-19.
517 Seltzer, Mac C. On 'depth of lot' factors, for land value. Valuation, 23(1) March/April 1976 pp20-23.
518 Sheard, M. Mixed base value - a different recipe. Estates Gazette, 272(6211) 17 November 1984 p744.
519 Shenfield, A. Mirage of social land value: lessons from the British experience. Appraisal Journal, 44 October 1976 pp523-531.
520 Shenkel, W. M. Appraiser's role in making investment decisions. Real Estate Appraiser and Analyst, 44 September 1978 pp4-15.
521 Shenkel, W. M. Value in use, value in exchange and investment value. Real Estate Appraiser and Analyst, 46(3) 1980 pp27-38.

522 Shimmon, R. Real estate - the American way. Valuer(ISVA), 52(1) 1983 pp4-5, 13. (Valuation methods)
523 Shonk, J. N. Mass appraisal techniques. Valuer(Australia) 27 October 1982 pp358-359, 361.
524 Shonk, J. N. Notes on precedence in the NSW valuation appeals system. Valuer(Australia), 26 April 1980 pp137-139.
525 Sirmans, C. F. Minimum tax, recapture and choice of depreciation methods. American Real Estate and Urban Economics Association Journal, 8 Fall 1980 pp255-267.
526 Sirmans, C. F. and Newsome, B. After-tax mortgage equity valuation. Appraisal Journal, 52(2) April 1984 pp250-269.
527 Sirmans, C. F. and Newsome, B. Mortgage-equity valuation and alternative financing. Appraisal Journal, 51(2) April 1983 pp240-254.
528 Sirmans, C. F. and Webb, J. R. Mortgage-equity analysis again?! Appraisal Journal, 47(1) January 1979 pp44-52.
529 Smith, Halbert C. Value concepts as a source of disparity among appraisals. Appraisal Journal, 45(2) April 1977 pp203-209.
530 Snyder, E. A. Appraising fractional interests: a short reprise. Real Estate Appraiser, 42 September 1976 pp20-21.
531 Souve, William F. Instant photography in real estate appraisal. Real Estate Appraiser and Analyst, 46(3) May/June 1980 pp23-26.
532 Speaight, Anthony and Stone, Gregory. The law of defective premises. London, Pitman, 1982.
533 Special use valuation of real estate. CPA Journal, 50 October 1980 p70+ .
534 Special valuation for real property updated. CPA Journal, 53 August 1983 pp66-67.
535 Speedy, S. L. Economic approach to value. Valuer(Australia), 26 July 1980 pp199 203; October 1980 pp345-349; January 1981 pp387-390,393.
536 Spies, P. F. The great re-investment debate - myth and fact. Appraisal Journal, 51(3) July 1983 pp401-407.
537 Stehm, R. J. Equity dividend/equity yield conversion. Real Estate Appraiser, 44 March 1978 pp23-25.
538 Sykes, S. Property valuation, investment and risk, in Chiddick, David and Millington, Alan F. Land management: new directions. London, Spon, 1984. pp50-58.
539 Thomas, H. O. Valuation of buildings erected for a specific use. Valuer(Australia), 27 July 1983 pp630-635.
540 Treadwell, D. M. Value in use in perspective. Appraisal Journal, 46(2) April 1978 p223+.
541 Troisi, F. X. Is it one, two, or three approaches to value? Real Estate Review, 10 Fall 1980 pp20-22.
542 Trott, A. RICS research project into property valuation methods: interim report. London, Polytechnic of the South Bank, Department of Estate Management, 1980.
543 Trott, A. RICS research project into property valuation methods: draft glossary of valuation terms. London, Polytechnic of theSouth Bank, Department of Estate Management, 1980.
544 Tucker, G. E. Value of the reversion. Appraisal Journal, 51 July 1983 pp449-451.
545 Tyndall, D. G. The value of a participation clause in a loan contract. Financial Analysts Journal, 35(1) January/February 1979 pp68-72.
546 Valuing for exchange deals or buy-ins. Estates Gazette, 272(6214) 8 December 1984 pp1179-1180.
547 Van Manen, F. J. Economic recession creates economic obsolescence. Real Estate Appraiser and Analyst, 49(1) 1983 pp51-54.
548 Van Manen, F. J. Market sales and market forces. Real Estate Appr-

aiser and Analyst, 47 Summer 1981 pp60-62.

549 Van Manen, F. J. Real estate value as it relates to business value. Appraisal Journal, 46 October 1978 pp592-597.

550 Voisey, C. J. Terminology: equated yeild and equivalent yield. Estates Gazette, 268(6159) 5 November 1983 p544.

551 Ward, C. W. R. Valuing property investment: the implicit question. Investment Analyst, 68 April 1983 pp25-28.

552 Weaver, William C. Measuring the market. Real Estate Today, 9 July 1976 pp7-8.

553 Weaver, William C. The use of telephone data collection in valuation and evaluation assignments. Real Estate Appraiser and Analyst, 48 Fall 1982 pp71-73.

554 Webb, J. R. Negative cash flows: a current appraisal problem. Appraisal Journal, 49(1) January 1981 pp92-101.

555 Webster, J. J. The four valuations. Valuer(Australia), 28(4) October 1984 pp282-284.

556 Wendt, Paul F. Estimating interest and recapture rates - miracle of mirage? Appraisal Journal, 46 July 1978 pp397-408.

557 Westwood, R. M. Valuation of properties subject to National Estate classifications. Valuer(Australia) 27 July 1983 pp628-629, 651.

558 White, John R. Real estate appraisals: how they pay off for investors. Trusts and Estates, 115 August 1976 pp516-519. (Same article in Appraisal Journal, 45 January 1977 pp49-55).

559 White, John R. Valuing megastructures. Real Estate Review, 13(2) Summer 1983 pp15-19.

560 White, John R. and Spies P. F. Towards universally acceptable semantics. Appraisal Journal, 46(1) January 1978 pp67-78.

561 White, P. H. Questions of investment valuation. Estates Gazette, 241(5821) 5 March 1977 pp660-675.

562 White, P. H. The value of investment properties - two faces of Janus. Reading, University of Reading, College of Estate Management, Centre for Advanced Land Use Studies, 1977.(Occasional Paper no. 9)

563 Wiegratz, W. F. Special valuation of real estate: opportunities and pitfalls, Trusts and Estates, 118 November 1979 pp39-45.

564 Wilde, R. L. Mortgage valuation or structural survey? Chartered Surveyor Weekly, 3(11) 23 June 1983 pp676-677.

565 Wiley, Robert J. Testing the sensitivity of break-even points. Real Estate Review, 8 1979 pp95-97.

566 Wilkinson, C. J. Valuer as a contributor to government policy formation. Valuer(Australia), 27 January 1982 pp10-15.

567 Wilkinson, H. W. Mortgage valuer's liability to purchasers. New Law Journal, 131(6028) 19 November 1981 pp1181-1182.

568 Williams, S. R. Problems with percentage adjustments. Real Estate Appraiser and Analyst, 48 Winter 1982 pp48-55.

569 Wilson, P. J. Valuation of high rise buildings: is it useful? Valuer (Australia) 27 October 1982 pp338-349.

570 Woodley, C. Litigation details. Valuer(Australia), 27 October 1982 pp367-368, 371.

571 Woodmore, Frank. The reason why property values rise or fall. Real Estate and Stock Journal, 44(1) January-February 1980 pp13,27,29.

572 Woodward, L. N. Appraisal: a limited form of feasibility analysis. Real Estate Appraiser and Analyst, 48 Summer 1982 pp5-11.

573 Woodward, L. N. Use of remote-sensing photography and maps in appraising. Appraisal Journal, 45(1) January 1977 pp85-94.

574 World Valuation Congress. Estates Gazette, 17 March 1984 p1048. Also Estates Times, 16 March 1984 p15. (First congress, Cambridge 3-6 June, 1984)

575 Worthington, John. Compensation for resumption and acquisition: the Pointe Gourde principle. Valuer(Australia), 27 October 1983 pp737-743.

576 Worthington, John. Family of equated yield - equivalent yield valuation models - an explanation of their form and definition. Valuer (Australia), 28(2) April 1984 pp131-133.

577 Written appraisal concept. Real Estate Appraiser, 43 January 1977 pp10-17.

578 Yasumoto, H. Reconciliation. Appraisal Journal, 44(4) October 1976 pp612-614.

579 Young, Malcolm D. Principles of insurance valuation of buildings. Valuer(Australia), 26 July 1980 pp246-248.

580 Young, Michael S. Inflation, valuation and the Petersburg paradox. Appraisal Journal, 48(1) January 1980 pp85-94.

581 Young, R. P. Reinstatement insurance valuations. New Zealand Valuer, 25(3) September 1982 pp127-130.

582 Zachary, P. L. Appraisal implications of a convertible mortgage. Appraisal Journal, 50(2) April 1982 pp182-186.

583 Zerbst, R. H. and Eldred, G. W. Specification of net operating income. Real Estate Appraiser and Analyst, 45 November 1979 pp39-43.

584 Zerbst, R. H. and Kohlhepp, D. B. Use of equity rates in appraisal theory. Real Estate Appraiser, 43 May 1977 pp26-31.

585 Zoraster, D. Corporate takeover as an appraisal indicator. Appraisal Journal, 48(2) April 1980 pp249-254.

Technical topics

The topics in this chapter have been selected on the basis of literary warrant. They are presented in alphabetical order. Attempts to produce a satisfactory and logical subject grouping were abandoned as there were inadequate references for many of the topics identified.

Accounting

586 Accounting for real estate acquisition, development and construction costs. CPA Journal, 51 July 1981 pp70-72.
587 Amenta, M. J. Accounting for real estate acquisition, development, and construction costs. Real Estate Review, 11 Winter 1982 pp100-102.
588 Association comments on ED18 - Current cost accounting. Certified Accountant, 69(3) June 1977 pp171-174.
589 Banks, F. J. Property values and CCA - problems for the auditor. Accountant, 182 24 January 1980 pp95-96.
590 Blitz, E. and Spiegel, R. J. Rehabilitation: the accountant and the appraiser. Real Estate Appraiser and Analyst, 50 Spring 1984 pp26-31.
591 Cooper, Kenneth J. The contribution of the valuer to current cost accounting in New Zealand. New Zealand Valuer, 24(4) December 1979 pp248-261.
592 Cullis, J. Inflation accounting and the valuer. Valuer(ISVA), 46(1) January/February 1977 pp17-16.
593 Davison, I. H. Property valuations for current cost accounting: an auditor's view. Estates Gazette, 11 March 1978 p826.
594 Gemmell, J. H. F. The RICS accounts regulations. London, Oyez, 1979.
595 Hill, G. P. Current cost accounting. Farm Management, 3(7) Winter 1977/78 pp341-348.
596 Institution of Chartered Accountants of England and Wales. Property valuation and accounts. London, Institution of Chartered Accountants of England and Wales, 1980.
597 Kwong, L. Y. Valuation of land and buildings in current cost accounting. New Zealand Valuer, 23(9) March 1978 pp461-464.
598 The net realizable value controversy. CPA Journal, 54 June 1984 pp7-8.
599 New rules for more uniform real estate accounting. Practical Accountant, 14 May 1981 pp28-29.
600 Norton, C. L. and Porter, G. A. Accountant's views on income producing real estate valuation. Real Estate Appraiser and Analyst, 48

Fall 1982 pp5-7.
601 Ratcliffe, T. A. Accounting for real estate leases. CPA Journal, 49 May 1979 pp64-65.
602 Robertson, T. J. L. Apples, pears and bananas. Accountancy, 94 November 1983 pp62-64.
603 Robertson, T. J. L. Property valuations for CCA one year on. Accountant, 184(5547) 18 June 1981 pp660-661.
604 Royal Institution of Chartered Surveyors, General Practice Division. Valuations for current cost accounting. Conference.3 December 1980. London, Royal Institution of Chartered Surveyors, 1980.
605 Royal Institution of Chartered Surveyors, General Practice Division. Valuation for current cost accounting. Conference. 28 April 1981. London, Surveyors Technical Services, 1981.
606 Royal Institution of Chartered Surveyors, General Practice Division. Valuation of land and buildings for financial statements.6 lectures at the Royal Institution of Chartered Surveyors, 22 October - 26 November 1980.
607 Royal Institution of Chartered Surveyors, General Practice Division. The valuers role in current cost accounting. London 27.6.79. London, Royal Institution of Chartered Surveyors, 1979.
608 Shafto, R. J. A guide to the RICS accounts regulations. London, Institution of Chartered Accountants of England and Wales, 1980. (Accountants Digest no 87)
609 Shue, G. H. Valuations for takeover purposes - a 1982 case study. Accountancy, 93 June 1982 pp56-58. (Discussion 93 September 1982 p22)
610 SSAP 19 - accounting for investment properties. Accountancy, 92 December 1981 pp115-117.
611 Statement of financial accounting standards no.26 - profit recognition on sales-type leases of real estate. Journal of Accountancy, 147 June 1979 pp108-109.
612 Thomas, H. O. Current cost accounting as affecting valuers. Valuer (ISVA), 26(3) 1980 pp178-183.
613 Thomas, H. O. Current cost accounting as affecting values. Valuer (Australia), 26 July 1980 pp178-183.
614 Thompson, A. P. Understanding CCA: ED18 accounts redrafted. Accountant, 176(5344) 16 June 1977 pp685-687.
615 Valuations. Accountant, 182(5476) 24 January 1980 pp91-110.
616 Venmore-Rowland, O. Valuer's approach to SSAP 16. Accountant, 183 17 July 1980 pp97-99.
617 Westwick, C. Property valuation and accounts. London, Institution of Chartered Accountants in England and Wales, 1980.

Approaches and methods

Cost approach and depreciation

618 Accounting for depreciation. Chartered Surveyor, 111(6) January 1979 pp205-214. (Papers given at a one-day seminar 17 November 1978)
619 Baum, Andrew. Depreciation: some alternative approaches. Valuer(ISVA) 51(8) October 1982 pp168-169.
620 Bose, M. Property companies parry SSAP 12 on depreciation. Accountancy, 89 December 1978 pp15-16.
621 Bowie, N. Learning to take account of depreciation. Estates Times, 751 22 June 1984 pp13-14.
622 Bowie, N. The depreciation of buildings. Journal of Valuation, 2(1) 1984 pp5-13.

623 Copley, R. E. and Clemons, M. K. Choosing the right depreciation method: the impact of marginal tax brackets. Appraisal Journal, 51 July 1983 pp355-362.
624 Corgel, J. B. and Goebel, P. R. Choosing depreciable lives: weighing gains vs. risks. Real Estate Review, 9 Summer 1979 pp80-84.
625 Cutsinger, Shannon. The cost approach may produce the lowest valuation estimate. Real Estate Appraiser, 44(1) January-February 1978 pp35-37.
626 Depreciation. Estates Gazette, 269(6178) 31 March 1984 pp1249-1250.
627 Derbes, M. J. Is the cost approach obsolete? Appraisal Journal, 50(4) 1982 p581+.
628 Englebrecht, T. D. Depreciation recapture under the Tax reform act. Real Estate Review, 7 Summer 1977 pp18-20.
629 Entreken, H. C. and Kapplin, S. D. Proper place and purpose of the cost approach. Real Estate Appraiser, 43 January 1977 pp5-9.
630 Fraser, R. R. Depreciation and the value of real estate. Valuer(Australia), 25(4) October 1978 pp276-278.
631 Gilliland, C. E. Component depreciation - the appraiser's role. Appraisal Journal, 48 January 1980 pp78-83.
632 Hargreaves, R. V. Some computer applications to the replacement cost method of valuation. Wellington, New Zealand Institute of Valuers, 1983. (New Technology Committee publication no. 2)
633 Hargreaves, R. V. Further computer applications to the valuation process. Wellington, New Zealand Institute of Valuers, 1983. (New Technology Committee publication no. 3)
634 Hartman, Donald J. Industrial real estate: cost-approach with caution. Appraisal Journal, 45(3) July 1977 pp444-449.
635 Hartman, Donald J. and Shapiro, M. B. Depreciation: incurable functional obsolescence and sequence of deductions. Appraisal Journal, 51(3) July 1983 pp408-414.
636 Higgins, J. W. Maximising depreciation through component depreciation. Real Estate Appraiser, 42 January 1977 pp52-54.
637 Higgins, J. W. and Scribner, D. Simple formula for switching declining balance to straight-line when depreciating real property. Real Estate Appraiser, 42 July 1976 pp36-37.
638 Kanner, G. Reproduction-less-depreciation: real world economics in the Courts. Appraisal Journal, 46(4) October 1978 pp612-614.
639 Krasker, W. S. Building depreciation: which method pays off? Harvard Business Review, November/December 1982 60(6) pp68-70.
640 Noke, Christopher. Property depreciation: now let's be realistic. Accountancy, 90 December 1979 pp50-52.
641 Noke, Christopher. The reality of property depreciation. Accountancy, 90(1035) November 1979 pp129-130.
642 North, L. Propitious use of the cost approach cuts variables. Estates Times, 752 29 June 1984 p10.
643 Patchin, P. J. How depreciation methods conform to actual market experience. Appraisal Journal, 48(4) October 1980 pp503-511.
644 Powell, J. G. Depreciation under current cost accounting. Estates Gazette, 242(5827) 16 April 1977 pp189-195.
645 Rayner, Michael. Valuation of property assets for which no market exists. Estates Gazette, 238(5781) 22 May 1976 pp549-553.
646 Schneider, W. J. Straight line and accelerated depreciation: an analytical approach. Industrial Development, 153 May-June 1984 pp30-34.
647 Sherwood, K. Depreciation, residual values and revaluations. Accountancy, 94(1074) 1983 pp138-140.
648 Speedy, S. L. Recent problems in capital recovery (depreciation).

Valuer(Australia), 27 January 1983 pp440-442, 446.
649 Stapleton, Tim. Capital allowances - the neglected factor. Estates Gazette, 266(6113) 7 May 1983 pp499-501.
650 Thayer, R. E. Rethinking the cost approach to valuation. Appraisal Journal, 51(2) April 1983 pp278-289.
651 Tidwell, V. H. Component depreciation can be a cure for excess depreciation. Taxes, 55 February 1977 pp116-126.
652 Williford, J. S. There's a right way to compute depreciation. Buildings, 72 October 1978 pp95-97.

Comparative approach

653 Craig, R. H. Direct comparison approach to value in appraisal for expropriation adjustment for financing yes or no? AIM, 25(2) May 1981 pp26-31.
654 Hanford, Lloyd D. Capitalization process revisited. Appraisal Journal, 44(3) July 1976 pp393-404.
655 Hardy, C. J. L. Decapitalisation - an essential process. AIM, 27(2 May 1983 pp13-15.)
656 Harper, Brian. Improvements to the direct comparison method, in Chiddick, David and Millington, Alan F. Land management: new directions. London, Spon, 1984. pp118-128.
657 Harrison, H. S. Direct sales comparison approach of market data approach. Real Estate Appraiser and Analyst, 44(5) September/October 1978 pp61-62.
658 Hauser, N. W. Simple comparison control. Appraisal Journal, 45(2) April 1977 pp210-222.
659 Kahn, Sanders A. Comparative-sales approach. Real Estate Review, 7 Winter 1978 pp17-18.
660 Kamanitz, B. How to prepare an assessment case based on comparison valuation. Journal of Property Management, 43(1) January 1977 pp37-40.
661 Lane, D. E. Comparable sales on trial. Appraisal Journal, 45 July 1977 pp435-441.
662 Market value: law or valuation? Estates Gazette, 270(6186) 26 May 1984 pp751-752.
663 Tchira, A. Comparable sales selection - a computer approach. Appraisal Journal, 47 January 1979 pp86-98.
664 Zerbst, R. H. Caution on the adjustment of comparable sales. Real Estate Appraiser, 43 November 1977 pp28-29.
665 Zerbst, R. H. and Brueggeman, W. B. Adjusting comparable sales for FHA and VA financing. Appraisal Journal, 47 July 1979 pp374-380.

Income approach

666 Akerson, Charles B. Capitalisation theory and techniques study guide. Chicago, American Institute of Real Estate Appraisers, 1984.
667 Akerson, Charles B. Income approach - determining the adequate rates. Appraisal Journal, 48(2) April 1980 pp172-181.
668 American Institute of Real Estate Appraisers. Readings in the income approach to real property valuation. Vol.1. Cambridge,Mass., Ballinger, 1977.
669 Baum, Andrew. The income approach to property valuation. 2nd ed. London, Routledge and Kegan Paul, 1981. (Bibliography pp206-210) (First edition 1979)
670 Beard, B. J. Learning the income approach to value. Journal of Property Management, 42 September 1977 pp237-241.
671 Blackadar, C. G. Dynamic capitalization: an income approach in real dollars at real interest. Appraisal Journal, 52(4) October 1984

pp565-594.
672 Blake, R. L. The interim-income approach to value of improvements no longer suited to highest and best use. _Appraisal Journal_, 46(4) October 1978 pp588-591.
673 Boykin, James H. and Epley, D. R. _Basic income property appraisal_. New York, Addison Wesley, 1982.
674 Burton, J. H. _Evolution of the income approach_. Chicago, American Institute of Real Estate Appraisers, 1982.
675 Cannaday, R. E. and Colwell, Peter F. Unified field theory of the income approach to appraisal. _Real Estate Appraiser and Analyst_, 47 Spring 1981 pp5-9; 47 Summer 1981 pp29-43; 47 Fall 1981 pp25-37.
676 Crean, M. J. Are capitalization rates obsolete? _Appraisal Journal_, 49 April 1981 pp248-257.
677 Dilmore, G. Income property return ratios. _Real Estate Appraiser_, 44 March 1978 pp39-40.
678 Downs, Anthony. Are producing properties over-valued? _National Real Estate Investor_, 22 February 1980 pp26+ .
679 Downs, Anthony. Income properties: are they bound to rise in value? _National Real Estate Investor_, 20 June 1978 pp32 +.
680 Ellwood, L. W. Selection of capitalization rates in today's market. _Appraisal Journal_, 45 July 1977 pp325-330.
681 Farrell, M. D. Valuation of income-producing properties for loan underwriting purposes. _Appraisal Journal_, 48 October 1980 pp576-578.
682 Fiore, J. S. and Knopp, P. J. Remarks on certain problems in mortgage -equity capitalization. _Real Estate Appraiser and Analyst_, 49 Winter 1983 pp32-44; 50 Spring 1984 pp43-52.
683 Fisher, Jeffery D. and Sanders, A.B. Capitalization rates and market information. _Appraisal Journal_, 49 April 1981 pp186-198.
684 Friedman, J. P. _Income property appraisal and analysis_. Reston, Va., Reston, 1981.
685 Gettel, R. Good grief, another method of selecting capitalization rates? _Appraisal Journal_, 45(1) January 1977 pp90-100.
686 Glascock, J. L. and Cunningham, D. The straight-line income capitaliztion model: a special case of present value. _Engineering Economist_, 28(4) Summer 1983 pp311-321.
687 Hardy, C. J. L. Decapitalization - an essential process. _AIM_, 27(2) May 1983 pp13-15.
688 Harris, J. Evaluating participation financing for income properties. _Appraisal Journal_, 52(2) April 1984 pp198-213.
689 Harrison, R. T. Nonmarket income approach to value for HUD-subsidized co-ops. _Appraisal Journal_, 45(2) April 1977 pp180-192.
690 Hemmer, Edgar H. and Fisher, Jeffery D. Dealing with uncertainty in income valuation. _Appraisal Journal_, 46(2) April 1978 pp230-244.
691 Hines, M. A. International income property investment yields and their measurement. _Real Estate Issues_, 8(2) Fall 1983 pp39-46.
692 Hulley, Robert B. Diffusing the information explosion. _Real Estate Issues_, 9(2) Fall/Winter 1984 pp25-29.
693 Jaffe, Austin J. Note on the use of capitalization discount and forward rates. _Appraisal Journal_, 48(1) January 1980 pp24-30.
694 Janssen, C. T. L. Evaluating income property investments. _AIM_, 22(3) August 1978 pp20-24. (Also published in _Education Quarterly: the Journal of the Real Estate Institute of Canada_, 1(3) 1977 and in _New Zealand Valuer_, 24(4) December 1979 pp241-247, 224)
695 Janssen, C. T. L. and Doherty, N. Income captialization and return on investment. _AIM_, 25(2) May 1981 pp18-22.
696 Koelsch, J. P. Discounting projected cash flows. _Appraisal Journal_, 49(4) October 1981 pp522-533.

697 Kurras, J. F. Myth or magic capitalization? Appraisal Journal, 49 April 1981 pp199-204.

698 Lusht, Kenneth. Behavior of apraisers in valuing income property: a status report. Real Estate Appraiser and Analyst, 45 July 1979 pp49-59.

699 Lusht, Kenneth and Zerbst, R. H. Valuing income property in an inflationary environment. Real Estate Appraiser and Analyst, 46(4) 1980 pp11-17.

700 McFadyen, S. Gross rent multiplier reliability in income property appraisal. AIM, 20(2) April 1976 pp20-22, 48.

701 Mackmin, D. H. A study companion to 'The income approach to property valuation': student guides to land management and development: appraisal (V). Reading, University of Reading, College of Estate Management, 1983.

702 Maes, M. A. Market analysis and the income approach. Appraisal Journal, 44 October 1976 pp577-585.

703 Maloney, R. T. Income property illustrated. Cupertino, Cal., Dixon Press, 1975. (Reprint, Santa Monica, Cal., Delphi Information Service Corp., 1979.

704 Martin, R. S. and Noble, L. S. Capitalization rates - the future. Appraisal Journal, 49 July 1981 pp335-352.

705 Martin, W. B. Risk analysis rate-of-return model for evaluating income producing real estate investments. Appraisal Journal, 46 July 1978 pp424-442.

706 Peterson, C. H. Are capitalization rates obsolete? Appraisal Journal, 49 April 1981 pp179-185.

707 Plummer, M. E. The application of the Lusht-Zerbst model for the estimation of value in an income property. AIM, 25(1) February 1981 pp11-12.

708 Plummer, M. E. The gross rent multiplier in income property appraisal. AIM, 23(2) 1979 p21.

709 Reese, L. Decline of the income approach. Real Estate Appraiser and Analyst, 47 Summer 1981 pp48-54.

710 Roulac, Stephen E. Influence of capital market theory on real estate returns and the value of economic analysis. Real Estate Appraiser and Analyst, 44 November 1978 pp62-72.

711 Special issue on income property. Mortgage Banker, 40 November 1979 pp7-55.

712 Sykes, S. G. and Young, Michael S. A differential approach to income property valuation: a new measurement technique. Appraisal Journal, 40(2) 1981 pp214-233.

713 Vatter, R. H. Long-term economic forces affecting non-residential income properties. Mortgage Banker, 41 January 1981 pp28-31.

714 Wofford, Larry E. Simulation approach to the appraisal of income properties. American Real Estate and Urban Economics Association Journal, 6 Winter 1978 pp370-394.

715 Young, Michael S. Capitalization rate adjustments for the valuation of leased real estate. Appraisal Journal, 48 July 1980 pp392-400.

Discounted cash flow

716 Barham, R. Discounting fears. Valuer(ISVA), 50(9) November 1981 pp270-271.

717 Baum, Andrew. Discounting cash flow - the internal rate of return and the cost of borrowing. Estates Gazette, 244(5851) 1 October 1977 pp28-29.

718 Crissey, John C. Discounting a typical real estate sales to cash equivalencies. Valuation, 26(1) November 1980 pp70-73.

Technical topics

719 Discounted cash flow wins followers. Property Investment Review, May 1976 pp8-9. (Greenwell report)
720 Fraser, W. D. YP or DCF? - a question of comparables. Estates Gazette, 272(6209) 3 November 1984 pp492-493.
721 Fung, W. K. H. and Stapleton, R. C. DCF methods of investment appraisal. Managerial Finance, 6(2) 1980 pp32-47.
722 Glew, Seph. Discounted cash flow - valuation technique. New Zealand Valuer, 25(1) March 1982 pp22-25.
723 Hewitt, R. Condominium/developed low discounting concepts again. Real Estate Appraiser and Analyst, 46 January 1980 pp7-12.
724 Koelsch, J. P. Discounting projected cash flows. Appraisal Journal, 49 October 1981 pp522-533.
725 Korpacz, Peter F. and Roth, Mark I. Changing emphasis in appraisal techniques: the transition to discounted cash flow. Appraisal Journal, 51(1) January 1983 pp21-44.
726 Korpacz, Peter and Roth, Mark. Changing emphasis in appraisal techniques: the transition to discounted cash flow. Journal of Valuation, 2(1) 1984 pp19-42.
727 Lane, Denis. Discounted cash flow techniques - a nuts and bolts approach. New Zealand Valuer, 25(8) December 1983 pp455-464.
728 Lipscomb, J. B. Discount rates for cash equivalent analysis. Appraisal Journal, 49(1) January 1981 pp23-33.
729 Miles, M. E. and Esty, Arthur S. Relevant required rate of return. Appraisal Journal, 47 October 1979 pp511-522.
730 Milne, Robert A. Fallacy of discounted cash flow analysis - producing a meaningful measure of return in real estate. Valuer(Australia), 27 April 1983 pp532-535.
731 Robertson, Terry D. and Rufrano, Glenn. Equity yields - a cash flow verification. Real Estate Appraiser, 42(2) March-April 1976 pp42-45.
732 Ruther, Barry. Discounted cash flow and the valuer. Valuer(Australia), 26 July 1980 pp222-223.
733 Stewart, Arthur G. Modern valuation methods DCF and IRR. New Zealand Valuer, 25(2) March 1983 pp271-277.(With comment by W.H. Cairns)
734 Valuing properties on discounted cash flow. Property Investment Review, June 1976 pp30-32. (Arguments for the Greenwell report by Nicholas Stacey and Victor Fieldgrass)

Others

735 Abayagunawardana, D. P. P. Individual worth approach. Estates Gazette, 256(6004) 4 October 1980 pp51-53. (Critique of Sloam below)
736 Barrett, G. V. Appraisal should be market study: techniques of analysis. Appraisal Journal, 47 October 1979 pp538-555.
737 Baum, Andrew. Residual valuations: a cash flow approach. Estates Gazette, 247(5900) 16 September 1978 pp973-977.
738 Baumgarten, J. Market value when there is no market. Appraisal Journal, 46 January 1978 pp79-89.
739 Byrne, P. and Mackmin, D. H. The investment method: an objective approach. Estates Gazette, 234 5 April 1975 pp29,31.
740 Crosby, Neil. The investment method of valuation: a real value approach: 1 and 2. Journal of Valuation, 1(4) 1983 pp341-350: 2(1) 1984 pp48-59.
741 Friedman, J. P. Cash equivalence: market knowledge and judgments. Appraisal Journal, 52 January 1984 pp129-132.
742 Goolsby, W.C. Cash equivalent value of real property. Real Estate Appraiser and Analyst, 49 Fall 1983 pp43-48.
743 Grissom, Terry V. and Kuhle, J. L. An alternative cash flow method

for real estate analysis. Real Estate Appraiser and Analyst, 49 Winter 1983 pp52-58.
744 Martin, R. S. Estimating the effect of existing financing on market value using an after tax approach. Real Estate Appraiser and Analyst, 48 summer 1982 pp67-75.
745 Mason, R. C. Present worth in present dollars. Appraisal Journal,51 July 1983 pp415-421.
746 Sadler, M. The investment method. Estates Gazette, 238(6029) 11 April 1981 pp131-134.
747 Sloam, Nigel S. Investment valuations: individual worth approach. Estates Gazette, 255(5991) 5 July 1980 pp45,47-48.
748 Stapleton, Tim. Capital allowances - the neglected factor. Estates Gazette, 266(6133) 7 May 1983 pp499, 501.
749 Wofford, Larry E. Incorporating uncertainty into the data program. Real Estate Appraiser and Analyst, 45 May 1979 pp30-39.
750 Wofford, Larry E. and others. Using capital market theory in real estate appraisal: evidence from securities markets. Real Estate Appraiser and Analyst, 48 Fall 1982 pp34-39.

Arbitration, law and negligence

751 Adams, J. E. New basis of liability for negligence? Estates Gazette, 270(6179) 7 April 1984 pp27-28.
752 Bergman, B. J. Defending against foreclosure actions. Real Estate Review, 12 Fall 1982 pp57-64.
753 Clemens, D. G. Legal and ethical responsibilities of a valuer. New Zealand Valuer, 25(11) September 1984 pp630-636.
754 Connolly, Robert J. Negligence and professional indemnity insurance. Valuer(Australia), 27 July 1983 pp606-609.
755 Eaton, J. D. Real estate valuation in litigation. Chicago, American Institute of Real Estate Appraisers, 1982.
756 Follows, T. J. Negligence in relation to land valuations. Solicitor's Journal, 126(46) 19 November 1982 pp752-754.
757 Graham, M. L. The 'quasi' arbitrator. New Zealand Valuer, 25(6) June 1983 pp321-324.
758 Heron, R. A. Liability of valuers for professional errors or omissions. New Zealand Valuer, 24(7) September 1980 pp480-485.
759 Heron, R. A. Professional liability of valuers. New Zealand Valuer, 23(9) March 1978 pp477-479.
760 International Association of Assessing Officers. Assessment and Valuation Legal Reporter. Chicago, International Association of Assessing Officers, 1971- . (13th year 1984)
761 International Association of Assessing Officers. Legal problems in property assessment and taxation. Chicago, International Association of Assessing Officers, 1984. (Conference proceedings)
762 Jess, D. C. Damages for negligent surveys and valuations. New Law Journal, 133(6088) 28 January 1983 pp80-83.
763 Jess, D. C. Surveyor's and valuer's negligence. Law Society's Gazette, 81(31) 5 September 1984 pp2362-2363.
764 Kennedy, J. A. Arbitration and conciliation. New Zealand Valuer, 24(6) June 1978 pp394-406, 412.
765 Kerr, R. T. Valuations - professional negligence. Valuer(Australia), 28(4) October 1984 pp304-305.
766 Levy, G. M. Arbitration of real estate valuation and related disputes. Appraisal Journal, 46 April 1978 pp208-222.
767 Levy, G. M. Resolving real estate valuation disputes through arbitration. Appraisal Journal, 52 January 1984 pp92-112.

768 Levy, G. M. Resolving real estate valuation disputes through arbitration. Real Estate Review, 14 Spring 1984 pp38-40; 14 Summer 1984 pp61-66.
769 Lydiard, A. Professional negligence. Company Secretary's Review, 5(17) 4 November 1981 pp134-135.
770 McCardell, F. Outline of the arbitration system. Valuer(Australia), 28(3) July 1984 pp188-195.
771 Mahoney, Peter J. Values - professional negligence. To what extant and to whom is the valuer liable? New Zealand Valuer, 25(2) June 1982 pp71-77.
772 Marling, T. R. Liability for negligence. Valuer(Australia), 27 July 1983 pp592-594, 605.
773 Martin, W. H. Arbitration and the appraiser. Real Estate Appraiser and Analyst, 48 Fall 1982 pp8-13.
774 Martin, W. H. The appraiser - the arbitrator. Real Estate Appraiser and Analyst, 49(2) 1983 pp44-46.
775 Mauleverer, B. ed. Digest of land and property cases. London, Estates Gazette, annual. (Full reports of cases reproduced in Estates Gazette, but not always published elsewhere)
776 Merrick, J. P. Liability for negligent opinions. AIM, 20(3) July 1976 pp9-11.
777 Murdoch, J. R. Negligence in valuations I, II & III. Estates Gazette, 257(6024,6025,6026) 7, 14, & 21 March 1981 pp893-899, 1012-1016, 1129-1132.
778 Murdoch, J. R. The negligent valuer. Estates Gazette, 237 7 February 1976 pp397-399.
779 The negligent valuer and the mortgager. Estates Gazette, 270(6187) 2 June 1984 p853.
780 New Zealand Institute of Valuers. Proceedings of the eighth Pan Pacific congress of real estate appraisers, valuers and counsellors. Wellington, New Zealand Institute of Valuers, 1975.
781 O'Keefe, J. A. B. Liability of sole valuers. New Zealand Valuer, 25(1) March 1982 pp20-21.
782 Pembroke, M. A. Vicarious liability in tort - when is a document genuine. Valuer(Australia), 27 January 1983 pp447-452,460.
783 Pyle, C. R. Letter of opinion: should we or shouldn't we. Real Estate Appraiser and Analyst, 45(4) July/August 1979 pp4-12.
784 Rolle, R. H. Professional indemnity. New Zealand Valuer, 23(1) March 1976 pp25-27.
785 Royal Institution of Chartered Surveyors. Current problems in property law - the Blundell Memorial lectures. London, Royal Institution of Chartered Surveyors, 1981.
786 Royal Institution of Chartered Surveyors. Guidance notes for surveyors acting as arbitrators or as independant valuers. London, Royal Institution of Chartered Surveyors, 1981.
787 Stringer, George E. Professional negligence. Reading, University of Reading, College of Estate Management, 1978.
788 Talbot, E. A. Deceptive trade practices - the new frontier in real estate litigation. Appraisal Journal, 51 January 1983 pp137-141.
789 Todd, E. C. E. Law and the appraiser. AIM, 28(1) February 1984 pp15-16.
790 Wall, J. N. B. Arbitration and the valuer. New Zealand Valuer, 24(3) September 1979 pp151-157.
791 Wendon, J. Responsibilities of third parties for valuation. Law Society's Gazette, 74(20) 1 June 1977 pp490-492.
792 Wilks, H. Precedent submission to an expert/arbitrator. London, Henry Stewart Publications, 1984.

793 Young, R. P. Professional negligence and the valuer. New Zealand Valuer, 24(7) September 1980 pp485-492.

Asset valuation

794 Asset valuation. Chartered Surveyor, 111(8) March 1979 pp308-317; 111(9) April 1979 pp359-363. (Short studies on various aspects, continued in second issue)

795 Asset valuations. Professional Administration, 8(2) February 1978 pp13-22.

796 Asset valuations for property companies. Valuer(ISVA), 50(5) 1981 pp138-139.

797 Assets valuation standards. Estates Gazette, 245(5867) 28 January 1978 pp295-298. (Sets out RICS guidance notes)

798 Australian Institute of Valuers. Guidance notes with background papers of the valuation of fixed assets. Valuer(Australia), 27 October 1982 pp394-395; January 1983 pp472-475; April 1983 pp518-519.

799 Biles, P. Valuation of fixed assets: help yourself by helping the valuer. Accountancy, 93 January 1982 pp62+ .

800 Bowie, N. Setting standards for asset valuation. Chartered Surveyor Weekly, 3(9) 9 June 1983 p565.

801 Bowie, N. Valuation of company property assets. Chartered Surveyor Urban Quarterly, 4(1) Autumn 1976 pp1-3.

802 Carr-Jones, G. Maximising the performance of property assets. Estates Gazette, 272(6205) 6 October 1984 pp20-21.

803 Chapman, J. H. Current cost accounting - the treatment of fixed assets. Rating and Valuation, June 1980 pp169-171.

804 Chapman, J. H. Current cost accounting - the valuation of fixed assets. Rating and Valuation, June 1977 pp163-165.

805 Davey, P. Asset valuations: negotiations should be on a "package deal" basis. Professional Administration, 7(3) March 1977 pp39-40.

806 Draper, D. W. and Findlay, M. Chapman. Capital asset pricing and real estate valuation. American Real Estate and Urban Economics Association Journal, 10(2) 1982. (Pagination not known)

807 Dorchester, John D. The state of the art transcends frontiers. Estates Times, 26 August 1983 p5.

808 Eastaway, N. A. Practical share valuation. London, Butterworth, 1983.

809 Goodwin, R. and Knibbs, R. Valuation of fixed assets - don't just leave it to the valuer. Accountancy, 92 August 1981 pp70-71.

810 How to value pension fund property assets. Chartered Surveyor, 114(1) 1981 p30.

811 Incorporated Society of Valuers and Auctioneers. Asset valuations for reports, accounts, prospectuses and offers of units for sale. London, Incorporated Society of Valuers and Auctioneers, 1979.

812 Incorporated Society of Valuers and Auctioneers. Draft guidance note no. 5. Valuation of land and buildings as fixed assets for financial statements. Valuer(Australia), 27 April 1983 pp520-523.

813 International Asset Valuation Standards Committee. Basis of the valuation of fixed assets and definitions; the Valuation Certificate; Valuation of land and buildings as fixed assets. AIM, 28(1) February 1984 pp17-22. (Guidance notes with background papers published 1983 by IAVSC in London)

814 Jones, Rod and Finn, M. Property too often neglected in the assets reckoning. Accountancy, 95(1094) October 1984 pp84-85.

815 Jones Lang Wootton. Valuation of fixed assets under current cost accounting. London, Jones Lang Wootton, 1977.

816 Langendoen, G. Growing field of asset management. Journal of

Property Management, 43(1) January/February 1978 pp43-47.

817 Levy, H. The capital asset pricing model: theory and empiricism. Economic Journal, 93(369) 1983 pp145-165.

818 Meloy, R. G. An asset management framework for corporate real estate. Real Estate Review, 12 Spring 1982 pp99-103.

819 Murza, Adam. Check your assets - you could miss out. Chief Executive, March 1981 p41.

820 Myers, J. Valuation of assets. New Law Journal, 127(2818) 8 September 1977 p899.

821 New guidance on current cost accounting. Chartered Surveyor, 111(10) May 1979 pp424-427. (On treatment of assets)

822 Norton, C. L. and Porter, G. A. Measuring real estate assets: an accounting controversy. Real Estate Review, 11 Winter 1982 pp90-93.

823 Now's the time to get tough on asset valuation. Estates Times, 9 September 1983 p9. (Editorial)

824 Pearce, D. N. Idris. Valuation standards. Estates Gazette, 252(5954) 6 October 1979 pp49-51. (History of developing role of Assets Valuation Standards Committee of the Royal Institution of Chartered Surveyors)

825 Powell, G. Asset valuation across frontiers is coming. Estates Times, 620 6 November 1981 pp12-13.

826 Rayner, M. The valuation of 'no-market' property assets. Journal of Valuation, 1(2) 1983 pp136-139.

827 Rayner, M. Valuation of property assets for which no market exists. Estates Gazette, 238(5781) 22 May 1976 pp550-552.

828 Royal Institution of Chartered Surveyors. Background papers on the valuation of assets. London, Royal Institution of Chartered Surveyors, 1979.

829 Royal Institution of Chartered Surveyors. Guidance notes for the valuation of assets prepared by the Assets Valuation Standards Committee. 2nd ed. London, Royal Institution of Chartered Surveyors, 1981.

830 Sachar, R. A. Maximising property value through an asset management plan. Journal of Property Management, 44(1) January/February 1979 pp20-24.

831 Sassi, W. V. Asset management January 1970 - August 1980. Storrs, New England Research Application Center, 1980. (Citation from NTIS database)

832 Sober, P. Depreciation and ED 18: the impact on property investment companies. Estates Gazette, 242(5836) 18 June 1977 pp949-951.

833 Sober, P. ED 18 and property investment companies. Accountant, 176 (5335) 14 April 1977 pp417-419.

834 Studdy, J. B., Punch, J. A. and Howes, J. S. Valuation of property assets - implications of current trends in company reporting and accounting practices. Valuer(Australia), 25(1) January 1978 pp7-17.

835 Valuation of company property assets. Estates Gazette, 235(5746) 13 September 1975 p228. (Sandilands Committee)

836 Valuers and the City Code. Valuer(ISVA), 45(9) November 1976 pp271-276.(RICS Assets Valuation Standards Committee and the City Code on Takeovers and Mergers)

837 Yorke, D. EEC legislation and asset valuations. Chartered Surveyor, 111(7) February 1979 pp288-289.

Compensation

838 Brennan, J. F. Digest of cases on compensation for resumption of land. Chatswood, Australia, Butterworth, 1977.

839 Compensation - valuation date on purchase notice. W & S (Long Eaton) Ltd v Derbyshire County Council. Rating and Valuation Reporter, 15(32-35) August 1975 pp343-347.

840 Cullingworth, J. B. Land values and compensation, in Environmental planning 1939-1969. vol.IV. London, HMSO, 1980.

841 Davies, K. Law of compulsory purchase and compensation. 4th edition London, Butterworths, 1984.

842 Davies, K. Slum clearance and site value. Local Government Chronicle, 5777 4 November 1977 pp889-890.

843 Denyer-Green, Barry. Compulsory purchase and compensation. 2nd edition. London, Estates Gazette, 1984. (Changed title from first edition above)

844 Denyer-Green, Barry. Eminent domain: a comparative discussion on the assessment of compensation in the United States and England. Appraisal Journal, 50 April 1982 pp212-219.

845 Denyer-Green, Barry. How to evaluate CPO compensation? Chartered Surveyor Weekly, 6(6) 9 February 1984 p377.

846 Denyer-Green, Barry. An outline of the law of compulsory purchase and compensation. London, Estates Gazette, 1980.

847 Fogarty, E. D. Compensation under the Public Works Act. New Zealand Valuer, 24(1) March 1979 pp33-37; 24(2) June 1979 pp79-90.

848 Fricke, G. L. Compensation, especially in relation to town planning. Valuer(Australia), 26 October 1980 pp337-344.

849 Green belt planning assumptions in the 'no scheme world'. Rating and Valuation Reporter, 17(1) January 1977 pp5-7.

850 Groover, W. K. Market value and just compensation. Real Estate Appraiser, 42 November 1976 pp39-41.

851 Lewsley, C. Compensation - part of eight building plots. Rating and Valuation Reporter, 24(9) September 1984 pp1761 .

852 Orchard, A. R. Valuation of a Part 1 claim under the Land Compensation Act 1973. Estates Gazette, 247(5892) 22 July 1978 pp291-294.

853 O'Sullivan, R. E. Compensation principles and practice for valuers. New Zealand Valuer, 23(4) December 1976 pp195-201.

854 Sheehan, J. B. Towards a new theory of planning compensation. Valuer (Australia), 28(2) April 1984 pp110-112.

855 Speedy, S. L. Recent problems in valuations for compensation for land taken and severed. Valuer(Australia), 27 April 1982 pp181-186.

856 Speedy, S. L. Severance compensation under the doctrine of eminent domain. AIM, 21(4) October 1977 pp18-28. (Extensive bibliography)

857 Speedy, S. L. Special aspects of compensation. New Zealand Valuer, 24(3) September 1979 pp194-202.

858 Todd, E. C. E. Compensation for the taking of partial interests in Canada. AIM, 26(1) February 1982 pp14-19.

Computers and their applications

859 Allan, K. M. The valuer, the computer, the situation. New Zealand Valuer, 25(4) December 1982 pp191-192.

860 Benedict, H. M., Herman, G. D. and Kinnard, W. N. Calculator Techniques for real estate. Chicago, Realtors National Marketing Institute, 1977.

861 Bowcock, Philip and Rose, J. J. Valuing with a pocket calculator. Oxford, Technical Press, 1982.

862 Brandon, P. S. with Moore, G. R. Microcomputers in building appraisal. New York, Nichols Publishing Company, 1983. (Also London, Granada, 1983)

863 Burns, G. Computer in a valuation practice. New Zealand Valuer, 25(8)

December 1983 pp453-454.
864 Butler, J. Q. and Henderson, G. V. Computerized exchange evaluation model. *Appraisal Journal*, 45 July 1977 pp383-395.
865 *CAAS News*. Chicago, International Association of Assessing Officers, Computer Assisted Appraisal Section, quarterly. (Newsletter)
866 Calculating value (VALPAC). *Chartered Surveyor Weekly*, 3(7) 19 May 1983 p372.
867 Camporini, J. A. Computerized rental listings. *Journal of Property Management*, 43 March 1978 pp101-104.
868 Carbone, R. and Longini, R. L. Feedback model for automated real estate assessment. *Management Science*, 24 November 1977 pp241-248.
869 Church, Albert M. and Gustafson, Robert H. *Statistics and computers in the appraisal process*. Chicago, International Association of Assessing Officers, 1976.
870 Computer program keeps property values current. *Business Insurance*, 32 24 July 1978 p18.
871 Computerized real estate analysis. *Valuer*(Australia), 28(3) p223.
872 Computers and their valuation. *Valuer*(ISVA), 48(9) November 1979 pp293-300.
873 Computers in property management. *Estates Gazette*, 271(6193) 14 July 1984 p208.
874 Computers: the readout for real estate. *Real Estate Today*, 10 November 1977 pp4-32.
875 Cooper, J. M. Calculator applications in valuation practice: the usefulness of programmable and pre-programmable calculators. *Valuer* (Australia), 26(5) 1981 pp360-365. (Bibliography)
876 Dasso, H. and Vernor, J. D. Computer applications in real estate brokerage. *Real Estate Today*, 13 May 1980 pp14-20.
877 Davis, J. M. and Donald, E. M. Using personal computers to analyse real estate investment decisions. *Real Estate Appraiser and Analyst*, 45 May 1979 pp5-15.
878 Denne, Robert C. *Computer-assisted appraisal and assessment systems*. Chicago, International Association of Assessing Officer, 1977. (Bibliography series)(Supplement no.1 by Robert M. Clatanoff, 1983)
879 Dilmore, G. Program to generate, test, and select land size adjustment factors. *Appraisal Journal*, 49 April 1981 pp290-296.
880 Dixon, T. J. Word processing for appraisers. *Real Estate Appraiser and Analyst*, 46(5) 1980 pp7-9.
881 Dorchester, John D. Small computers for the real estate industry. *Appraisal Journal*, 48(4) October 1980 pp599-611; 49(1) January 1981 pp119-126.
882 Dum, M. J. Using an electronic spreadsheet in the appraisal office. *Appraisal Journal*, 50(3) July 1982 pp457-463.
883 Dum, M. J. and Dum, T. E. Microcomputer in the typical appraisal office. *Appraisal Journal*, 49(1) January 1981 pp126-130.
884 Elliott, D. and Cameron, J. G. An overview of computer applications in the appraisal process. *AIM*, 24(1) February 1980 pp36-40.
885 Featherstone, J. B. Computer corner. *Appraisal Journal*, 48(2) April 1980 pp275-279.
886 Fraser, R. R. Some new developments in computer assisted mass valuation. *Valuer*(Australia), 28(2) April 1984 pp118-121.
887 Glen, J. T. and Bailey, R. R. A computer-assisted appraisal system for income-producing properties. *Aspects of Assessment in Ontario*, 22 August 1977 pp31-39.
888 Gonzales, L. *Computers for realtors*. New York, Ballantine Books, 1984.
889 Granger, F. and Crunkleton, J. R. Advice on the selection of a

computerized property management system. Journal of Property Management, 48(5) September/October 1983 pp43+ .
890 Greater London Council, Valuation and Estates Department. Information processing for Valuation and Estates Department: current position and future plans. London, Greater London Council, Technical Services Committee, 1983.
891 Grempler, D. D. Hiring the computer for a real estate office. Real Estate Today, 10 January 1977 pp22-27.
892 Griffin, G. Conventional appraisal techniques can be computerized. Appraisal Journal, 47(2) April 1979 pp253-262.
893 Hahn, William and Marlene. Evaluating real estate software: an overview. Realtor, 61(5) 1984 pp26-31.
894 Hargreaves, R. V. Computer assisted valuations using weighted ratings. New Zealand Valuer, 24(12) December 1981 pp949-952.
895 Hargreaves, R. V. A computer usage survey of valuers in New Zealand. Wellington, New Zealand Institute of Valuers, 1982. (New Technology Committee Publication no.1)
896 Hargreaves, R. V. Does the computer have a place in your office? I. New Zealand Valuer, 25(9) March 1984 pp522-524.
897 Hargreaves, R. V. Does the computer have a place in your office? II Computer programming considerations. New Zealand Valuer, 25(10) June 1984 pp584-587.
898 Hargreaves, R. V. Some microcomputer applications to the valuation process. Palmerston North, Massey University, Department of Agricultural Economics and Farm Management, 1981. (Occasional paper no. 10)
899 Harmon, C. Using computers in asset management. Journal of Property management, 47 May-June 1982 pp12-13. (Interview with Michael S. Young)
900 Harris, J. Evaluating participation financing for income properties. Appraisal Journal, 52(2) April 1984 pp198-213.
901 Hartigay, S. Application of computer systems to property portfolio management. Bristol, Bristol Polytechnic, Department of Surveying, 1984. (Summarised in Estates Times, 15 June 1984 p11)
902 Henneberry, J. Computers: the impact of microtechnology on landed property. Estates Gazette, 262(6089) 19 June 1982 pp1151-1152.
903 Hewlett Packard Co. HP-81 real estate investment and analysis handbook. Loveland, Cal., Hewlett Packard Co., 1975.
904 Hodges, M. B. Value is a computer-assisted number. Real Estate Review, 13 Fall 1983 pp82-86.
905 Hunt, G. The changing world of John Foord. Chartered Surveyor Weekly, 7(12) 21 June 1984 p800.
906 Hunt, G. How does the Sun Alliance manage? Chartered Surveyor Weekly, 7(7) 27 May 1984 p430.
907 International Association of Assessing Officers. Computer-assisted appraisal and assessment systems: an annotated bibliography:Supplement 1. Chicago, International Association of Assessing Officers, 1983. (Original not traced)
908 Jaffe, Austin J. Computer-assisted instruction and real estate investment analysis. Real Estate Appraiser, 42 November 1976 pp21-28.
909 Jensen, D. L. The role of cluster analysis in computer assisted mass appraisal. Cambridge, Mass., Institute of Land Policy, 1977.
910 Johnston, K. J., Elliott, D. and Cameron, J. G. Restricted interest deductibility: a treatment using the computer-based discounted cash flow approach to valuation. AIM, 26(2) May 1982 pp10-14,19.
911 Kaimann, R. A. and Heintz, T. J. MIS for MLS. Real Estate Today, 10 May/June 1977 pp24-27.

912 Kell, L. A. Selection of a word processing system for the appraiser's office. Real Estate Appraisaer and Analyst, 48 Fall 1982 pp32-33.
913 Kinnard, W. N., Boyce, B. N. and Rocca, F. A. HP-22 operations and procedures for use by real estate appraisers and analysts. Storrs, University of Connecticut, Center for Real Estate and Urban Economic Studies, 1976.
914 Kirkwood, J. Information technology and land administration. London, Estates Gazette, 1984.
915 Kirkwood, J. Programmable calculators for appraisal. Estates Gazette, 260(6060) 14 November 1981 pp671-674.
916 Kirkwood, J. Report highlights estate agent's ignorance of computers. Estates Gazette, 271(6195) 28 July 1984 p350.
917 Land, Howard G. and Maxted, William M. Valuations...or calculations? Estates Gazette, 259 29 August 1981 pp683-684.
918 Levi, Atoun. Appraisal files management - retrieval system. Valuation, 25(1) July 1978 pp38-47.
919 Lewis, S. E. Computers and real estate: new technology is essential competitive tool in increasingly sophisticated real estate industry. National Real Estate Investor, 24 December 1982 pp36+.
920 Lincoln Institute of Land Policy. Computer assisted mass appraisal /assessment ratios bibliography. Cambridge, Mass., Lincoln Institute of Land Policy, 1977. (Lincoln Institute Monograph no. 77-4)
921 Maxwell, B. Small computer systems big boon for small business. Journal of Property Management, 44 May 1979 pp102-105.
922 Needham, M. Getting the most from micros. Estates Times 22 June 1984 p15.
923 Needham, M. A simpler route to property valuation. Estates Times, 29 June 1984 p9.
924 Newman, C. Property and technology. London, Estates Gazette, 1983.
925 Opelka, F. Gregory. New calculators aid appraising. Savings and Loan News, 102 June 1981 pp120-121.
926 Ordway, N. Controlling for uncertainty through computer applications of PERT/CPM to real estate project analysis. American Real Estate and Urban Economics Association Journal, 4 Fall 1976 pp33-55.
927 Peltzer, Kenneth E. Computerized analysis of a joint-venture-investment office building. Appraisal Journal, 50(4) October 1982 pp537-563.
928 Penman, Wilson A. Ellwood plus computer equals property investment analysis. New Zealand Valuer, 25(12) December 1984 pp689-691.
929 Perkins, D. Look before you quantum-leap. Chartered Surveyor Weekly, 8(11) 20 September 1984 p725.
930 Plummer, M. E. The minicomputer in the real estate and appraisal fields. AIM, 26(2) May 1982 pp28-31.
931 Robertson, W. F. Computerized property management tasks. Canadian Builder, 28(10) October 1978 pp22-23.
932 Rushton, J. and Lawton, J. Computers: an appreciating asset for valuers. Chartered Surveyor Weekly, 5(1) 6 October 1983 pp27-28.
933 Ryan, T. Refurbishment valuations handled by a micro. Building, 244(7289) 29 April 1983 pp49-51.
934 Seltzer, Mac C. Your pocket calculator contains all the interest tables. New Zealand Real Estate, 34(4) August 1983 pp82-87.
935 Smith, David A. Real estate professionals need personal computers. Real Estate Review, 14 Spring 1984 pp16-17.
936 Special report: computer and office equipment. Chartered Surveyor Weekly, 5(8) 24 November 1983 pp484-495.
937 Spiegel, R. J. The appraiser, the computer and the 1981 economic recovery tax act. Real Estate Appraiser and Analyst, 49(1) 1983 pp43-50

938 Sykes, S. Computers in property. Estates Times, 12 November 1982 p17. (Investment analysis)
939 Tchira, A. Comparable sales selection - a computer approach. Appraisal Journal, 47 January 1979 pp86-98.
940 Tenzer, G. M. and Tarantello, R. A. FMRR: a programmable calculator implementation. Real Estate Appraiser and Analyst, November-December 1979 pp11-16.
941 Tilson, P. The practical use of computers in estate agency. Estates Gazette, 270(6187) 2 June 1984 p807; 270(6189) 16 June 1984 p1016; 270(6191) 30 June 1984 pp1256,1258; 271(6200) 1 September 1984 p773; 272(6206) 13 October 1984 p142.
942 Toro, T. A. Data processing and computer technology in real estate appraising. Real Estate Appraiser and Analyst, 44 September 1978 pp50-51.
943 Touche Ross & Co. and Berkery, M .J. Real estate software guidelines: property management. Chicago, Institute of Real Estate Management in cooperation with the National Association of Realtors, 1984.
944 Wall, J. N. B. Future supply of property sales - technology progress. New Zealand Valuer, 25(4) December 1982 pp192-194.
945 Whiting, P. M. The role of computers in general practice estate agency. Reading, University of Reading, College of Estate Management, Centre for Advanced Land Use Studies, 1984.
946 Young, Michael S. Differentiating between computer-based property management and asset management systems. Journal of Property Management, 48(5) September/October 1983 pp6+ .

Expert witness

947 Brugger, George A. A short course in survival techniques for expert witnesses. Valuation, 27(1) November 1981 pp10-21.
948 Camp, M. R. The valuer and cross examination. New Zealand Valuer, 25(6) June 1984 pp569-571.
949 Cordier, Henry K. 'Neutral' appraisers. Valuation, 27(1) November 1981 pp126-129.
950 Dorram, Peter B. The expert witness. Chicago, APA Planners Press, 1982.
951 Foster, W. F. Accidental misrepresentations: the problems of liability and its avoidance. AIM, 25(4) November 1981 pp16-21.
952 Hyam, A. A. Statements of evidence. Valuer(Australia), 26 October 1981 pp656-658.
953 Johnson, J. R. The legal ramifications of stating an opinion of value. AIM, 24(4) November 1980 pp25-27.
954 Klaasen, R. L. Expert testimony. AIM, 22(2) April 1978 pp9-12.
955 Klaasen, R. L. The letter of opinion. AIM, 27(3) August 1983 pp30-32.
956 Lysaght, C. The expert witness - the legal framework. Arbitration, 50(2) November 1984 pp191-194.
957 McKim, Samuel J. III. Prehearing preparation for valuation expert witness - some points to consider. New Zealand Valuer, 25(6) June 1984 pp574-578.
958 McLachlan, R. J. The court and the valuer as an expert witness. New Zealand Valuer, 23(11) September 1978 pp556-561.
959 McLachlan, R. J. The valuer as a witness. New Zealand Valuer, 25(6) June 1984 pp571-573.
960 Mollica, A. F. Appraiser and videotape testimony. Appraisal Journal, 47(3) July 1979 pp438-442.
961 Parkinson, K. J. Valuer as expert witness. Valuer(Australia),

28(2) April 1984 p90.
962 Pyle, C. R. Letters of opinion: should we or shouldn't we? Real Estate Appraiser and Analyst, 45 July 1979 pp4-12.
963 Shank, J. N. Hearsay and the valuer as expert witness. Valuer(Australia), 27 July 1983 pp613-614.
964 Sheehan, A. J. The valuer as witness. New Zealand Valuer, 25(1) March 1982 pp18-20.
965 Sinclair, Mr Justice. The Court's expectations of the role of a registered valuer. New Zealand Valuer, 25(11) September 1984 pp627-629.
966 Smith, W. F. G. Valuer as a witness. Valuer(Australia), 26 January 1980 pp36-39, 42.
967 Watson, J. A. F. Nothing but the truth: or expert evidence in principle and practice for surveyors, valuers and others, London, Estates Gazette, 1975.
968 Williams, S. S. Preparation and presentation of evidence-in-Chief. New Zealand Valuer, 25(6) June 1984 pp563-567.

Highest and best use

969 Albritton, H. D. Testing highest and best use. Appraisal Journal, 47(3) July 1979 pp406-411.
970 American Institute of Real Estate Appraisers. Readings in highest and best use. Chicago, American Institute of Real Estate Appraisers of the National Association of Realtors, 1981.
971 Archer, W. R. Valuation under uncertainty: will the real highest and best use please stand up? Real Estate Appraiser, 43 May 1977 pp32-40.
972 Barrett, G. V. Restatement of highest and best use. Real Estate Appraiser and Analyst, 45 November 1979 pp4-9.
973 Bounds, F. P. A highest and best use approach to valuation. Appraisal Journal, 50(3) July 1982 pp434-439.
974 Carn, N. G. Is highest and best use a justification for zoning? Appraisal Journal, 52(2) April 1984 pp177-182.
975 Derbes, M. J. Highest and best use - what is it? Appraisal Journal, 49(2) April 1981 pp166-178.
976 Goodheim, Brian. Decision-tree pay off: a graphic approach to highest and best use. Appraisal Journal, 50(4) 1982 pp522+.
977 Grissom, Terry V. The semantics debate: highest and best use vs. most probable use. Appraisal Journal, 51(1) January 1983 pp45-57.
978 McMahon, M. Concept of highest and best use. Valuer(Australia), 28(4) October 1984 pp291-303.
979 North, L. W. The concept of highest and best use. Winnipeg, Manitoba, Appraisal Institute of Canada, Research and Development Fund, 1981.
980 Opelka, F. Gregory. Highest and best use: case study explains appraisal technique. Savings and Loan News, 99 May 1978 pp106-107.
981 Ordway, N. and Harris, J. Dynamic nature of highest and best use. Appraisal Journal, 49(3) July 1981 pp325-334.
982 Scribner, D. Key to value estimation: highest and best use to more probable use. Real Estate Appraiser, 44 May 1978 pp23-28.
983 Siebuhr, R. W. Determining highest and best use by S.149 certificate. Valuer(Australia), 28(4) October 1984 pp285-6.
984 Smith, H. C. and Maurais, M. R. Highest and best use in the appraisal profession. Real Estate Appraiser and Analyst, 46 March 1980 pp27-40.
985 Spencer, M. H. Obtaining consent for highest and best use. Valuer (Australia), 28(4) October 1984 pp287-290.

986 Webb, J. R. Highest and best use: a critical re-examination. Appraisal Journal, 48(1) January 2980 pp57-63.

Insurance valuation

987 Emeny, R. Valuation of real property for insurance purposes? or could you be sued for negligence? Estates Gazette, 246(5886) 10 June 1978 pp903-907.
988 Reavis, M. W. Property insurance values and coverage problems. Journal of Property Management, 43 July 1978 pp228-229.
989 Robertson, D. How to value for insurance. Chartered Surveyor Weekly, 9(5) 1 November 1984 pp345-347.
990 Royal Institution of Chartered Surveyors. Re-instatement assessment for insurance purposes. London, Surveyors Publications, 1980. (Practice note 3)

Leasehold

991 Amies, F. A. Surveyor's valuation of lease-surrender value. Rating and Valuation Reporter, 16(4) April 1976 pp108-109.
992 Analysis of leasehold investments. Estates Gazette, 270(6188) 9 June 1984 pp959-960.
993 Arnison, C. Masters and tenants: leasehold tenure as a mechanism for moral governance, in Chiddick, David and Millington, Alan F. Land management: new directions. London, Spon, 1984. pp136-143.
994 Athanasopoulos, P. J. and Bacon, P. W. The evaluation of leverages leases. Financial Management, 9(1) 1980 pp76-80.
995 Baum, Andrew. The analysis of short leasehold investments: exposing the implicit, in Chiddick, David and Millington, Alan F. Land management: new directions. London, Spon, 1984. pp88-98.
996 Baum, Andrew. The enigma of the short leasehold. Journal of Valuation, 1(1) 1983 pp5-8.
997 Boucher, D. S. Tenant rights: the hidden leasehold. Appraisal Journal, 50(1) January 1982 pp113-115.
998 Brand, C. M. and Williams, D. W. Implied obligations in business leases and licences. Estates Gazette, 268(6164) 10 December 1983 pp1099,1101.
999 Changes to commercial leasehold arrangements: Canberra. Valuer(Australia), 26 October 1980 pp280-285.
1000 Christiansen, W. K. S. Whence the 'Glasgow' lease? New Zealand Valuer, 25(7) September 1983 pp369-370.
1001 Colam, M. The single rate valuation of leaseholds. Journal of Valuation, 2(1) 1984 pp14-18.
1002 Dilmore, G. How to value leasehold estates. Real Estate Review, 8(3) Fall 1978 pp94-96.
1003 Fineman, Stanley J. Rent revaluation under an existing lease. Appraisal Journal, 5(2) April 1984 pp307-309.
1004 Fraser, W. D. The valuation and analysis of leasehold investments in times of inflation. Estates Gazette, 244(5853) 15 October 1977 pp197-199, 201, 203.
1005 Freedman, P. Problems with mixed user lettings. Property Management, 1(1) Autumn 1982 pp37-40.
1006 Furbur, J. D. Clear leases - a challenge to the valuer's skill. Estates Gazette, 269(6172) 18 February 1984 pp603-607.
1007 Gaines, James P. and Schnee, Edward J. Tax implications of leasing rehabilitated real estate. Journal of Property Management, 45(6) November/December 1980 pp320-324.

1008 Gerhardt, Robert H. Valuing the "nemesis" lease. Journal of Property Management, 45(3) May/June 1980 pp180-185.
1009 Greenwood, K. Commercial leases. New Zealand Valuer, 24(7) September 1980 pp555-561.
1010 Halper, E. B. People and property: to buy or not to buy? Real Estate Review, 13 Summer 1983 pp78-87.
1011 Herring Son & Daw. A tenant's guide to lease renewals and rent reviews. London, Herring Son & Daw, 1982.
1012 Kelley, L. Basics of lease negotiation. Real Estate Today, 13 August 1980 pp28-32.
1013 Keys, D. Commercial leases. New Zealand Valuer, 24(7) September 1980 pp543-555.
1014 Kirk, D. C. Recent trends in the market for standard residential leases in A.C.T. Valuer(Australia), 28(3) July 1984 pp183-187.
1015 Leaseholds: a time for a change: a report by a working group of the Building Societies Association as adopted by the Council of the Association on residential long leaseholds in England and Wales. London, Building Societies Association and Law Commission, 1984.
1016 Leasing: space for success (broker's role: special report). Real Estate Today, 11 August 1978 pp19-47.
1017 Leslie Lintott & Associates. The cost and consequences of signing a full repairing and insuring lease. London, Leslie Lintott & Associates, 1976.
1018 Luscombe, Wendy. Leaseholds - do we depreciate them or do they depreciate us? Estates Gazette, 246(5888) 24 June 1978 pp1101-1103.
1019 Lyster, Guy. Sale and leaseback for the owner/occupier. London, Strutt and Parker, 1980. (Property Trends no 3)
1020 McIntosh, A. P. J. The rational approach to reversionary leasehold property investment valuations, in Chiddick, David and Millington, Alan F. Land management: new directions. London, Spon, 1984. pp59-68.
1021 McIntosh, A. P. J. Valuing leasehold interests. Estates Gazette, 265(6126) 19 March 1983 pp939-941.
1022 Mackmin, D. H. The analysis of leasehold transactions. Valuer(ISVA), 48(9) November 1979 pp287-288.
1023 Marriage value. Estates Gazette, 267(6148) 20 August 1983 p690.
1024 Meaney, C. Leasehold Reform Act 1967. Property Management, 2(3) 1984 pp230-262.
1025 Messer, Jay M. Leasebacks: smart buys. Pensions and Investment Age, 9(12) 8 June 1981 pp34,41.
1026 Millington, Alan F. Sinking fund theory: its application and use in today's market. Estates Gazette, 266(6134) 14 May 1983 pp595-599.
1027 Nicholls, A. D. Valuation commentary - leasehold enfranchisement. Rating and Valuation Reporter, February 1976 pp35-36.
1028 Raison, B. V. Land tenure in the Australian Capital Territory:changes in land use, planning processes and the leasehold system. Valuer (Australia), 26 April 1981 pp479-482.
1029 Ratzka, A. D. Sixty years of municipal leasehold in Stockholm: an econometric and cost-revenue analysis. Stockholm, Swedish Council for Building Research, 1979.
1030 Reynolds, N. Residual value leasing. Accountant, 191(5720) 22 November 1984 pp13-14.
1031 Rhoads, T. J. Valuing the expired property interest: long term residential leaseholds. Valuer,(Australia), 28(2) April 1984 pp116-117.
1032 Rosenberg, A. S. and Weinstein, H. T. Sale-leasebacks: an analysis of

these transactions after the Lyon decision. Journal of Taxation, 45 September 1976 pp146-151.

1033 Royal Institution of Chartered Surveyors. Leasehold enfranchisement 1979-1983. RICS Abstracts and Reviews, 20(1) January 1984 Review 501. (Bibliography)

1034 Schloss, Nathan. Rental adjustment clauses in commercial leases: choosing an inflation indicator. Journal of Property Management, 43(6) November/December 1978 pp295-300.

1035 Schloss, Nathan. Should CPI be used for lease indexation? Journal of Property Management, 46(5) September/October 1982 pp40+ .

1036 Shenkel, W. M. Net leases: a critical review. Journal of Property Management, 45(3) May/June 1981 pp146+ .

1037 Stapleton, Tim. Lease term bargaining, in Chiddick, David and Millington, Alan F. Land management: new directions. London, Spon, 1984. pp152-159.

1038 The tenant's bid and marriage value in leasehold reform valuations. Rating and Valuation Reporter, 16(6) June 1976 pp170-172.

1039 Totman, E. Leases must cope with changed property needs. Property Business, December 1983 p68.

1040 University of Reading, Centre for Advanced Land Use Studies. A commentary on a commercial lease. Reading, University of Reading, College of Estate Management, Centre for Advanced Land Use Studies, 1983.

1041 Ward, C. W. R. Financial analysis of leasing decisions and property investment. Journal of Valuation, 1(1) 1983 pp32-38.

1042 Ward, C. W. R. Property lease-or-buy decisions. Accountancy and Business Research, 13(50) Spring 1983 pp143-149.

1043 Wilson, D. J. The valuation of pre-paid residential building leases. Canadian Appraiser, 28(4) November 1984 pp28-33.

1044 Wood, Ernest. Deterministic models of leasehold investment value, in Chiddick, David and Millington, Alan F. Land managment: new directions. London, Spon, 1984. pp69-87.

1045 Young, Michael S. Capitalization rate adjustments for the valuation of leased real estate. Appraisal Journal, 48(3) July 1980 pp392-401.

1046 Young, Michael S. Rental rate adjustments for multi-year leases. Journal of Property Management, 45(6) November/December 1980 pp326-328.

Models and modelling

1047 Colwell, Peter F. and others. The analytical foundations of adjustment grid methods. Journal of the American Real Estate and Urban Economics Association, 11 Spring 1983 pp11-29.

1048 Lusht, Kenneth M. and Fisher, Jeffery D. Anticipated growth and the specification of debt in real estate value models. Journal of the American Real Estate and Urban Economics Association, 12 Spring 1984 pp1-11.

1049 McIntosh, A., Sykes S. G. and Sykes S. Towards a standard property income valuation model: rationalisation or stagnation? Journal of Valuation, 1(2) Winter 1982 pp117+ .

1050 Moore, J. S. and others. Analyzing the temporal stability of appraisal model coefficients: an application of ridge regression techniques. Journal of the American Real Estate and Urban Economics Association, 12 Spring 1984 pp50-71.

1051 Sirmans, C. F. and Newsome, B. After-tax mortgage equity valuation. Appraisal Journal, 52 April 1984 pp250-269.

Technical topics

1052 Sykes, S. G. Property valuation: a rational model. Investment Analyst, 61 January 1981 pp20-26.
1053 Sykes, S. G. Property valuation: a rational model. Journal of Valuation, 2(3) 1984 pp258-270.
1054 Sykes, S. G. Valuation models: action or reaction. Estates Gazette, 267(6153) 24 September 1983 pp1108,1110,1112. (Also criticised in issues of 8 October 1983 p111 and 19 November 1983 p751)
1055 Trinh, Hieu Nghia. Developing real estate valuation models: a new simplified approach. AIM, 26(4) November 1982 pp24-27.

Multiple regression

1056 Bruce, R. W. and Sundell, D. J. Multiple regression analysis: history and applications in the appraisal profession. Real Estate Appraiser, 43(1) January 1977 pp37-44. (Bibliography 3 pages)
1057 Dick, G. W. MRA analysis applied to property valuation in Colombia. Real Estate Appraiser, 42 July 1976 pp13-19.
1058 Janssen, C. T. L. Confidence and prediction intervals in regression appraisal. Real Estate Appraiser, 43 September 1977 pp25-33.
1059 Jason, T. T. C. Taking the mystique out of multiple regression analysis. New Zealand Valuer, 24(20) June 1981 pp817-820.
1060 Kung, Ong Ann. An introduction to the application of multiple regression analysis to property valuation. Surveyor(Journal of the Institution of Surveyors, Malaysia), 18(2) 1983 pp69-72.
1061 Morgan, G. Valuation prediction, forecasting and regression analysis. Nottingham, Trent Polytechnic, Department of Surveying, 1984. (Seminar paper given at Sheffield, May 1984)
1062 Morton, T. Narrow versus wide stratification of data in the development of regression appraisal models. American Real Estate and Urban Economics Association Journal, 4 Fall 1976 pp7-18.
1063 Richey, C. W. and Hendrick, T. E. Multiple regression: a listing tool. Real Estate Today, 10 February 1977 pp4-9.
1064 Robertson, Terry D. and Rufrano, Glenn. Pooled samples, regression analysis and the appraiser. Real Estate Appraiser, 42 September 1976 pp39-43.
1065 Smith, D. V. An appraiser looks at multiple regression. Appraisal Journal, 47(2) April 1979 pp248-252.
1066 Weaver, William C. To regress or not to regress: that is the question. Real Estate Appraiser, 42 November 1976 pp31-38.
1067 Westwick, C. Problems in valuing property for annual accounts. Chartered Surveyor, 113(1) 1980 pp18-19.
1068 Woolford, W. A. and Cassin, S. G. Multiple regression: a valuable tool for mass-land appraisal. Appraisal Journal, 51(2) 1983 pp213-224.

Rating

1069 Amies, F. A. Completion of an unoccupied building. Rating and Valuation Reporter, 15(8) September/October 1975 pp367-370.
1070 Amies, F. A. Is the Layfield Report the last word? Rating and Valuation Reporter, 16(7) July/August 1976 pp193-205.
1071 Amies, F. A. Local Tax scheme in the Layfield Report. Rating and Valuation Reporter, 16(5) May 1976 pp134-162.
1072 Amies, F. A. Recovery on Valuation Officer's proposed assessment. Rating and Valuation Reporter, 16(8) September 1976 pp226-228.
1073 Baker, D. W. The role of the rating authority in valuation. Rating and Valuation, April 1984 pp107-108.
1074 Beaton, W. The non-market on Valuation Day. AIM, 21(2) April 1977

pp28-30,32+.(Corrected reprint 21(3) July 1977 pp26-29) (Valuation Day of 1971 for public valuations)

1075 Bucknall, B. Rating from artificiality to artificiality. *Local Government Chronicle*, 5751 17 June 1977 pp496-497.

1076 Charman, J. Obstacles that can frustrate a simple valuation. *Estates Times*, 667 15 October 1982 pp10-11.

1077 Cheshire, P. and Evans, A. Reforming the rates. *Estates Gazette*, 268(6160) 12 November 1983 pp646-649.

1078 Completion of a building for the unoccupied rate. *Rating and Valuation Reporter*, 16(4) April 1976 pp109-111; 16(10) November 1976 pp285-288.

1079 Cooper, Kenneth G. and Weinberg, Robert M. *Simulating the economic impacts of revaluation in Boston*. Boston, Federal Reserve Bank of Boston, 1975.

1080 Crosby, W. B. The new Valuation Panels in Scotland - their work and their problems. *Rating and Valuation*, March 1977 pp81-84.

1081 Daines, D. R. Some thoughts on land value rating. *Valuer*(Australia), 26 April 1980 pp122-125.

1082 Domestic rating evaluation: consideration document planned. *Municipal Journal*, 30 March 1984 p446.

1083 Duncan, A. Rating in England and Wales - where are we going? *Rating and Valuation Reporter*, 24(9) September 1984 pp170-173.

1084 Emeny, R. and Wilks, H. *Principles and practice of rating valuation*. 4th ed. London, Estates Gazette, 1984. (3rd edition, 1972)

1085 Greater London Council, Valuation and Estates Department. *Analysis of rateable value and number of hereditaments in the valuation lists in force on 1 April 1984: compiled from Valuation Officer's returns*. London, Greater London Council, Valuation and Estates Department, 1984.

1086 Griffiths, R. A. Rating and the extractive industries. *Quarry Management and Products*, 3(5) May 1976 pp117-120.

1087 Guy, R. An eye on the rent. *Local Government Chronicle RVA Supplement*, 6019 1 October 1982 pp10-11.

1088 Herring Son & Daw. *A client's guide to rating*. London, Herring Son & Daw, 1982.

1089 Hill, B. The new Domesday Book will improve efficiency. *Municipal Journal*, 87(17) 27 April 1979 p438.

1090 Hillman, J. High rates: a deterrent to development? *Estates Gazette*, 265(6120) 5 February 1983 pp369-370, 372.

1091 Hubbard, C. Enfranchisement or extension in the higher rateable value bands. *Estates Gazette*, 268(6162) 26 November 1983 pp876,878,880; 268(6163) 3 December 1983 p978,980.

1092 Hyam, A. A. Valuation for rating and taxing purposes. *Valuer*(Australia), 27 October 1982 pp364-366.

1093 Hyam, A. A. Valuations for rating and taxing purposes. *Valuer*(Australia), 26 October 1981 pp601-608.

1094 Jewell, R. E. C. Rateability of empty property - office blocks and showrooms. *Law Society's Gazette*, 74(23) 29 June 1977 pp569+.

1095 Lacey, R. Green for danger? *Public Finance and Accountancy*, 4(6) June 1977 pp194-195.

1096 Law, H. The land question - an alternative approach. *Planning Outlook*, 25(1) 1982 pp28-34.

1097 Lee, J. The intricacies of section 25. *Rating and Valuation*, June 1977 pp175-176.

1098 Lewsley, C. Alternative uses in rating valuation. *Rating and Valuation Reporter*, 23(4) April 1983 pp74.

1099 Lewsley, C. Exemptions from unoccupied rate. *Rating and Valuation*

Reporter, 23(9) September 1983 pp170-171.

1100 Lewsley, C. Fairness in rating valuation. Rating and Valuation Reporter, 24(7/8) July/August 1984 pp151-152.

1101 Lewsley, C. Rating valuation moves closer to the market. Rating and Valuation Reporter, 24(4) April 1984 pp75-76.

1102 McGlade, Adrian. Rating valuations: available aids to cost restraint. Valuer(Australia), 27 July 1982 pp234-236.

1103 Malley, J. C. Local Government Finance Bill - effect of valuation panels. Rating and Valuation, April 1979 pp111-112.

1104 Mander, Murray S. New Zealand rating valuation systems. Valuer(Australia), 27 July 1982 pp239-241.

1105 Markson, Henry E. Rating valuation: economic aspects of the hypothetical tenancy: or, measure for measure. Journal of Planning and Environment Law, June 1976 pp346-353.

1106 Nicholls, A. D. Disrepair and gross value. Rating and Valuation, October 1976 pp267-268.

1107 Nicholls, A. D. Ups and downs - proposals and appeals. Rating and Valuation, October 1981 pp269-271.

1108 Nicholls, A. D. Valuation commentary. Rating and Valuation. Regular column in each issue.

1109 Othick, F. Ability to pay. Local Government Chronicle, 5786 17 March 1978 p300.

1110 Othick, F. Hardship relief. Local Government Chronicle, 5846 4 May 1979 p478-479.

1111 Othick, F. The hole in the doughnut. Local Government Chronicle, 5741 8 April 1977 pp297-298.

1112 Othick, F. Prospects for revaluation. Local Government Chronicle, 12(1) 5 January 1979 n.p.

1113 Pearce, G. Rating appeals to the local Valuation Court. Rating and Valuation, April 1977 pp120-121.

1114 Petherick, J. Peter. Rating on capital and site values. Valuer(Australia), 27 July 1982 pp253-254, 260.

1115 Rabinowitz, A. Town planning and capital valuation. Town and Country Planning, 46(1) January 1978 pp18-21.

1116 Rating and Valuation Association. Contractor's basis of valuation: report of a research group. London, Rating and Valuation Association, 1982.

1117 Roberts, D. F. Rating-problems peculiar to seaside resorts. Telescope, 2(4) January 1978 pp78-80.

1118 Royal Institution of Chartered Surveyors. Site value rating. RICS Abstracts and Reviews, March 1974 Review R321. (Bibliography)

1119 Smith, K. The domestic hereditament and other problems. Estates Gazette, 272(6214) 6 December 1984 pp1139,1141.

1120 Snow, Alan. The rateability of unoccupied premises. Valuer(ISVA), 45(4) May 1976 p93.

1121 Stapleton, Tim. Relief from empty rates. Estates Gazette, 270(6191) 30 June 1984 pp1252, 1254.

1122 Strachan, B. Rates: who is liable? New Law Journal, 127(5797) 14 April 1977 pp355-357.

1123 Street, J. W. F. The philosophy of empty property rates. Rating and Valuation, January 1984 pp5-8.

1124 Syms, P. The rates exemption incentive. Estates Gazette, 270(6188) 8 June 1984 pp914, 918.

1125 Thornhill, W. Overrated system. Local Government Chronicle RVA Supplement, 6019 1 October 1982 pp20-21.

1126 Unoccupied rate - completion when ready for occupation as a building. Post Office v Nottingham County Council. Rating Appeals, Part 3

1976 pp49-63.

1127 Valuation aspects of the Layfield report. Estates Gazette, 240 6 November 1976 pp443, 445, 447.

1128 Wheaton, William C. The statewide impact of full property revaluation in Massachusetts. Boston, Federal Reserve Bank of Boston, 1975.

1129 Wilkins, I. Land based rates and taxes. Valuer(Australia), 27 April 1983 pp540-542.

1130 Wilkinson, C. J. Current rating and taxing practice in Tasmania 1982. Valuer(Australia), 27 October 1982 pp372-375,380.

1131 Wilks, H. Rating paper 1: General and introductory. Law Society's Gazette, 81(18) 16 May 1984 pp1352-1353.

1132 Wilks, H. Rating paper 2: Elements of rating valuation. Law Society's Gazette, 81(22) 13 June 1984 pp1669-1673.

1133 Wilks, H. Rating paper 3: Local valuation courts. Law Society's Gazette, 81(26) 11 July 1984 pp1987-1988.

Rented property and rents

1134 Amies, F. A. Market rent of hereditament not conclusive evidence of its gross value. Rating and Valuation Reporter, 16(6) June 1984 pp167-169.

1135 Arbitrator's rent review decision receives sanction. Estates Times, 6 January 1984 p9.

1136 Aylwin, R. Comparing like with like in rent reviews. Estates Times, 26 June 1983 p9.

1137 Banks, P. L. Rent reviews. London, Strutt and Parker, 1979. (Property Trends no. 5)

1138 Baum, Andrew. Comparable evidence in rent reviews:1 - the choice. Rent Review and Lease Renewal, Spring 1983 3(3) pp215-220.

1139 Bernstein, R. and J. Hill. Valuing the incomparable: valuing the comparable. Estates Gazette, 251(5942) 14 July 1979 pp147-149; 251(5943) 21 July 1979 pp245-247.

1140 Brenner, J. F. Rent control in North America and four European countries. Washington, D. C., Council for International Urban Liaison, 1977.

1141 Carless, D. G. More than rents and repairs. Real Estate Today, 11 May 1978 pp22-29.

1142 Christiansen, W. K. S. Naming rights and naming rents - a first survey. New Zealand Valuer, 25(4) December 1982 pp197-206.

1143 Christiansen, W. K. S. Rent for naming rights: a formula for two-storey building. New Zealand Valuer, 25(5) March 1983 pp267-268.

1144 Clarke, D. N. and Adams, J. E. Rent reviews and variable rents. 2nd ed. London, Oyez Longman, 1984.

1145 Clarke, P. H. Rent reviews: a framework for valuers. Journal of Planning and Environment Law, September 1980 pp565-577.

1146 Cunningham, F. M. Government rental policy -is it fair? AIM, 24(3) August 1980 pp27-31.

1147 Debenham, J. Turnover rents. Law Society's Gazette, 72(43) 3 December 1975 pp1199.

1148 Diamond, D. D. and others. In search of a landlord symposium. Town and Country Planning, 47 1979 pp72-74, 76-81.

1149 Doling, John. Developments in fair rent determinations. Journal of Valuation, 3(1) 1984 pp42-52.

1150 Doling, John and Davies, M. Fair rents and capital values. Estates Gazette, 260 14 November 1981 p677.

1151 Dyson, Henry. Rent control in France. Estates Gazette, 271(6199) 25 August 1984 pp690+.

1152 Eames, Gary. Rent pricing for maximising revenue. Journal of Property Management, 42(1) January/February 1977 pp47-50.
1153 Economic analysis and rental growth. Estates Gazette, 267(6150) 3 September 1983 pp861-863.
1154 Farino, D. Rental valuation aspects of business leases. Estates Gazette, 236(5758) 6 December 1975 pp717-722.
1155 Finch, Robert. ISVA model rent review clauses. Estates Gazette, 272(6205) 6 October 1984 pp57,59-60.
1156 Finch, Robert. ISVA model rent review clauses. Valuer(ISVA), 53(8) October 1984 p238.
1157 Finch, Robert. ISVA recommended rent reivew clauses - were those first impressions right? Estates Gazette, 272(6215) 15 December 1984 p1274.
1158 Fine, B. Landed property and the distinction between royalty and rent. Land Economics, 58(3) 1982 pp338-350.
1159 Fineman, S. J. Rent revaluation under an existing lease. Realtor, 61(5) 1984 pp24-25.
1160 Flanagan, R. J. Gross income estimates: market rent versus contract rent. AIM, 26(2) May 1982 pp32-35. (Reprint from Assessment Digest, January/February 1982)
1161 Freedman, P. and Fogel, S. ISVA recommended rent-review clauses - some first impressions. Estates Gazette, 272(6209) 3 November 1984 pp496,498; 272(6210) 10 November 1984 pp618, 620.
1162 Glover, T. Rent and rate reviews. Accountant, 189(5658) 8 September 1983 pp13-14.
1163 Hallett, Michael and Schiller, R. The problems and possibilities of a property rent index. Estates Gazette, 245 21 January 1978 pp209, 211.
1164 Harker, N. Inflation-proof rent reviews. Estates Gazette, 250(5930) 21 April 1979 pp233-235.
1165 Harris, Diane. An investment for rent. Money, 13(4) April 1984 pp87-90.
1166 Hill, A. C. Rent control in Hong Kong. Valuer(Australia), 26 July 1981 pp542-545, 549.
1167 Hunt, J. N. and Greaves, M. J. An algebraic comparison of valuing varying profit rents. Reading, University of Reading, College of Estate Management, Centre for Advanced Land Use Studies, 1978. (Occasional Paper no.11)
1168 Investors Chronicle/Hillier Parker Rent Index. London, Hillier Parker May & Rowden. 1977- . (annual)
1169 Investors Chronicle Hillier Parker Research. Average yields. London, Hillier Parker May & Rowden, 1984 - . (quarterly)
1170 Jaffe, Austin J. Using a simple model to estimate market rents. Appraisal Journal, 45(1) 1977 pp7-13.
1171 Kenny, P. Investing in the assured tenancy. Estates Gazette, 269 (6170) 4 February 1984 pp395-396.
1172 King & Co. Rental growth. London, King & Co., occasional.
1173 Koo, H. Y. C. Land market distortion - tenure reform. Ames, Iowa, Iowa State University Press, 1982.
1174 Lyons, R. Theory and malpractice. Estates Gazette, 264 12 February 1983 pp451, 455, 457.
1175 McCarthy, D. M. City rental valuations and rental reviews. Valuer (Australia), 28(4) October 1984 pp270-280.
1176 McLeister, D. Market changes enhance rentals' potential. Professional Builder and Apartment Business, 47 July 1982 pp22-23.
1177 Mander, M. R. Valuations for rental purposes in terms of the Land Amendment Act, 1979. New Zealand Valuer, 24(10) June 1981 pp810

-816, 819.

1178 Miller, E R. Real estate cycle: an argument for raising rents. Journal of Property Management, 43(6) November/December 1978 pp306-308.

1179 Murdoch, S. Rent review notices. Estates Gazette, 269(6169) 28 January 1984 pp297-298, 300.

1180 Olmo, Ralph J. The paradox of inflation and rents. Journal of Property Management, 45(1) January/February 1980 pp31-32.

1181 Pollock, R. L. Valuations under the Rent Appeal Act. New Zealand Valuer, 23(1) March 1976 pp15-18.

1182 Rees, M. H. B. Rent reviews: the model clauses. Estates Gazette, 272(6213) 1 December 1984 p1005.

1183 Repairing obligations: I - implied terms. Estates Gazette, 271(6194) 21 July 1978 pp296-297.

1184 Repairing obligations: II - express terms. Estates Gazette, 271(6196) 4 August 1978 pp465-466.

1185 Roberts, N. Record rents can only serve as a pointer towards trends. Estates Times, 9 December 1983 pp8-9.

1186 Rosenberg, L. Landlord rights - they are necessary. AIM, 21(4) October 1977 pp7-9.

1187 St Quintin. Tables of rent adjustment factors to a 5-year rent review pattern. London, St Quintin, 1981.

1188 Serruya, L. M. and Chau, T. M. Effects of rent control on the decision to invest in residential construction: some empirical evidence. AIM, 21(3) July 1977 pp33-35.

1189 Shulman, D. Real estate valuation under rent control: the case of Santa Monica. American Real Estate and Urban Economics Association Journal, 9(1) 1981 n.p.

1190 Smith, D. Ground rents. New Zealand Valuer, 24(9) March 1981 pp738-752.

1191 Smith, Lawrence. Rent controls in Ontario: roofs or ceilings? Berkeley, Cal., University of California, Institute of Business and Economic Research, 1981. (Publication 81-39)

1192 Sonstelle, J. C. and Portney, P. R. Gross rents and market values: testing the implications of Tiebout's hypothesis. Journal of Urban Economics, 7 January 1980 pp102-118.

1193 Stafford, B. and Doling, John. Rent control and rent regulation in England and Wales 1915-1980. Birmingham, University of Birmingham, Centre for Urban and Regional Studies, 1981.(Occasional Paper no.2)

1194 Stagen, Thomas. Rent indexing: a rent control alternative. Journal of Property Management, 43(6) November/December 1978 pp302-303.

1195 Stapleton, Tim. Options to renew. Estates Gazette, 269(6178) 31 March 1984 pp1232-1233.

1196 Teale, M. Sorting out tenant's needs. Property Business, June 1984 p38.

1197 Tenancies with part II of the Landlord and Tenant Act 1954. Estates Gazette, 269(6172) 18 February 1984 p644; 269(6174) 3 March 1984 p864.

1198 Valuation and premiums. Estates Gazette, 241(5818) 12 February 1977 pp476-477.

1199 Ward, C. The capitalisation of negative profit rents. Journal of Valuation, 2(2) 1984 pp205-208.

1200 West, W. A. The law of dilapidations. London, Estates Gazette, 1979. (First ed. 1974)

1201 Williams, D. W. Interpreting the interim rent provisions. Estates Gazette, 271(6203) 22 September 1984 pp1058, 1060, 1062.

1202 Williams, D. W. Landlord and tenant casebook. London, Estates Gazette, 1984.

Technical topics

1203 Williams, D. W. Recent trends in rent review. Estates Gazette, 271 (6192) 7 June 1984 pp18, 20.

1204 Wolfe, Marion F. Economic behavior and attitudes of rental property owners. Berkeley, Cal., University of California, Institute of Business and Economic Research, 1983. (Publication 83-67)

Reports

1205 Allan, K. M. Professional standards - valuation reports. New Zealand Valuer, 25(11) September 1984 pp654-657.

1206 Boyd, K. J. Decision writing. Canadian Appraiser, 28(3) August 1984 pp23-28.

1207 Foreman, R. L. Communicating the appraisal: a guide to report writing. Chicago, American Institute of Real Estate Appraisers, 1982.

1208 Heinrich, R. J. Candidate's guide to writing a passing MAI demonstration appraisal report. Appraisal Journal, 47(4) October 1979 pp561-573.

1209 Lomax, D. A. A guide to narrative demonstration appraisal reporting. Chicago, Society of Real Estate Appraisers, 1976.

1210 Luscombe, W. Content of valuation reports. Estates Gazette, 245(5865) 14 January 1978 pp117-119.

1211 McIntosh, M. J. G. Expectations of a valuer's reporting standards. New Zealand Valuer, 25(11) September 1984 pp616-624.

1212 Marrison, Andrew M. Professional standards - what do the public require and expect? New Zealand Valuer, 25(9) March 1984 pp485-490.

1213 Northrup, C. Van. The writing of appraisal reports and the Internal Revenue Service. Valuation, 28(1) November 1982 pp52-62.

1214 Rose, J. J. and Marshall, Philip J. L. Marshall's valuation proformas for real property appraisals including a 'typical' valuation report. Beckenham, Kent, P. J. Marshall, 1976.

1215 Society of Real Estate Appraisers. A guide to narrative demonstration appraisal reporting: a detailed analysis of the technical and theoretical appraisal of real estate. Chicago, Society of Real Estate Appraisers, 1976.

1216 Society of Real Estate Appraisers. A guide to narrative demonstration appraisal reporting. Chicago, Society of Real Estate Appraisers, 1978.

1217 Stapleton, Tim. Pleased to report. London, Estates Gazette, 1983.

1218 Trowbridge, C. R. Office guide to real estate appraisal reporting, with model specimens. Englewood Cliffs, N.J., Prentice-Hall, 1974.

Tables

This section relates mainly to tables produced for valuation purposes, not those building cost indices produced regularly in journal format, as in Building Economist or Building Cost Information Service (Royal Institution of Chartered Surveyors) or any other tables produced as calculation aids.

1219 Barham, Ronald. The client's true interests? Estates Gazette, 261 16 January 1982 pp129-130.

1220 Bowcock, Philip. Property valuation tables. London, Macmillan, 1979.

1221 Bowcock, Philip, and Rose, J. J. High-speed quarterly in advance. Estates Gazette, 245(5870) 18 February 1978 pp551-554.

1222 Building Cost Information service. Guide to rebuilding costs for insurance purposes. 7th edition. London, Building Cost Information Service, 1984.

1223 Colwell, Peter F. and Rushing, P. J. To Ellwood and beyond. Appraisal

Journal, 47 July 1979 pp352-358.

1224 Davidson, A. W. *Parry's valuation and conversion tables*. 10th edition London, Estates Gazette, 1978.

1225 Dial, J. L. *Dial's equity yield tables: a Dow Jones-Irwin professional guide to appraising and financing real estate*. Homewood, Ill., Dow Jones-Irwin, 1979.

1226 Ellwood, L. W. *Ellwood tables for real estate appraising and financing*. 4th ed. Chicago, American Institute of Real Estate Appraisers, 1978. (1st edition 1959)

1227 Enever, Nigel. The valuation of investments - which tables? *Estates Gazette*, 238(5785) 19 June 1976 pp864-868.

1228 Fisher, Jeffrey D. Ellwood after tax - new dimensions. *Appraisal Journal*, 45(3) July 1977 pp331-342.

1229 Goebel, P. and Miller, Norman. *Handbook of mortgage mathematics and financial tables*. Englewood Cliffs, Prentice-Hall, 1981.

1230 Harris, J. C. Applying Ellwood in an era of persistent inflation. *Real Estate Appraiser and Analyst*, 49 Spring 1983 pp15-21.

1231 Incorporated Society of Valuers and Auctioneers. *The construction of valuation tables*. London, Incorporated soceity of Valuers and Auctioneers, 1981. (Revised reprint)

1232 Johnson, Irwin, E. *Instant mortgage-equity: extended tables of overall rates*. Lexington, Mass., Lexington for National Association of Independant Fee Appraisers, 1980.

1233 Mackmin, D. H. How effective are tables? *Estates Gazette*, 259(6041) 4 July 1981 pp23-24, 26.

1234 Marshall, Philip. *Equated yield tables*. Beckenham, Kent, the author, 1975.

1235 Marshall, Philip. *Donaldson's investment tables*. 2nd edition. London, Donaldson & Sons, 1979. (1st edition 1976)

1236 Martin, Robert S. Ellwood: the language of appraisers. *Real Estate Appraiser and Analyst*, 47 Summer 1981 pp5-18.

1237 Martin, Robert S. Ellwood: the language of appraisers. *Real Estate Appraiser and Analyst*, 48 Spring 1982 pp38-44.

1238 Martin, Robert S. Using AIREA's new financial tables to find income adjustment constants in Ellwood. *Appraisal Journal*, 50(3) July 1982 pp440-445.

1239 Mason, James J. *AIREA tables for financial analysis and valuation*. Chicago, American Institute for Real Estate Appraisal, 1981.

1240 Nelson, R. D. Market testing of Ellwood. *Appraisal Journal*, 44 April 1976 pp262-268

1241 Nelson, R. D. and Allen, L. G. Market testing of Ellwood. *Appraisal Journal*, 45 January 1977 pp56-64.

1242 Noton, N. H. Valuation tables - a new look. *Estates Gazette*, 252(5963) 8 December 1979 pp999-1001.

1243 Parry, Bowcock and Rose. *Estates Gazette*, 252(5960) 17 November 1979 pp724-725.

1244 Percentage lease tables. *Buildings*, 70 December 1976 pp55-57.

1245 Rose, J. J. *The construction of valuation tables*. 4th edition. London, Incorporated Society of Valuers and Auctioneers, 1981. (3rd edition 1974)

1246 Rose, J. J. *Rose's property valuation tables*. Oxford, The Freeland Press, 1976.

1247 Rose, J. J. The single rate years purchase table. *Valuer*(ISVA) 45(9) November 1976 p277.

1248 Rose, J. J. *Tables of constant rent*. Oxford, Technical Press, 1979.

1249 St Quintin. *Tables of initial yields adjusted to compensate for non-standard rent review patterns*. London, St Quintin, 1983.

Technical topics

1250 St Quintin. *Tables of rent adjustment factors to a five-year rent review pattern*. London, St Quintin, 1981.
1251 Steele, R. A. DCR/R capitalization rate tables for today's financing. *Appraisal Journal*, 49(1) January 1981 pp15-22.
1252 Steele, R. A. J factor: a valuable Ellwood legacy. *Appraisal Journal*, 46(4) October 1978 pp581-587.
1253 Wiley, T. Equity risk analysis by Ellwood graph technique. *Appraisal Journal*, 45 October 1977 pp541-549.
1254 Young, F. S. C. An introduction to the mortgage equity concept and Ellwood tables. *AIM*, 22(1) January 1978 pp20-36.
1255 Young, Michael S. Ellwood: at last, the final word. *Appraisal Journal*, 48(2) April 1980 pp287-288.

Taxation

1256 Achour, D. A micro-simulation of the new tax rules on the profitability of a real estate investment. *AIM*, 27(2) May 1983 pp7-12.
1257 Applications for reductions of real estate assessed valuations. *CPA Journal*, 54 April 1984 pp68-69.
1258 Bentick, B. L. The impact of taxation and valuation practices on the timing and efficiency of land use. *Journal of Political Economy*, 87(4) 1979 pp859-868.
1259 Black, D. E. Property tax incidence: the excise-tax effect and assessment practices. *National Tax Journal*, 30 December 1977 pp429-434.
1260 Bloom, H. S. and Ladd, H. F. Property tax revaluation and tax levy growth. *Journal of Urban Economics*, 11 January 1982 pp73-84.
1261 Brodie, Ronald ed. *Real Estate Tax Planning Newsletter*. Miami, Fl., Tax Plan Inc., quarterly.
1262 Carlton, Dennis W. The spatial effects of a tax on housing and land. *Regional Science and Urban Economics*, 11(4) November 1981 pp509-527.
1263 Carmean, Patricia A. *Property tax incentives for alternative energy devices*. Chicago, International Association of Assessing Officers, 1980. (Research and Information Series)
1264 Carmean, Patricia A. *Site value taxation*. Chicago, International Association of Assessing Officers, 1980. (Research and Information Series)
1265 Cebula, R. J. Property taxation and prices: an exploratory note. *Review of Business and Economic Research*, 17 Winter 1981-1982 pp85-87.
1266 Clatanoff, Robert M. *Valuation and property taxation of nonrenewable resources: an annotated bibliography*. Chicago, Council of Planning Librarians, 1983. (CPL Bibliography no.99)
1267 Coin, B. J. Valuing real estate subject to tax-free financing. *Appraisal Journal*, 48(2) April 1980 pp261-268.
1268 Colborne, A. Premiums: tax payments and savings as they affect the valuation of premiums with particular referencce to the tenant. *Estates Gazette*, 247(5901) 23 September 1978 pp1065-1067.
1269 Cracking the land values question: complex issues. *Surveyor*, 153 (4528) 22 March 1979 p22.
1270 Denne, Robert C. *Property taxation in the United States: an annotated bibliography*. Part.I. Alabama-Maine; Part.II. Maryland-North Carolina; Part.III. North Dakota-Wyoming and All States. Chicago, International Association of Assessing Officers, 1978. (Bibliography Series) (Supplement no. 1. 1979 by Stuart W Miller)
1271 Eastwood, K. W. Taxation matters as they affect a valuation practice.

Valuer(Australia), 28(3) July 1984 pp178-182.
1272 Englebrecht, T. D. and Goggans, T. P. Reporting gain from condominium conversions: cost apportionment vs. cost recovery. Real Estate Review, 10 Fall 1980 pp16-18.
1273 Falk, C. E. and Singer, W. S. Planning for real estate condemnation awards in light of recent favorable rulings. Journal of Taxation, 59 December 1983 pp400-403.
1274 Fineman, S. J. Caveat appraiser: the risks associated with rendering appraisals in connection with real estate tax shelters. Appraisal Journal, 52(3) July 1984 pp462-469.
1275 Fisher, Jeffrey D. and others. Tax incentives for investment in non-residential real estate. National Tax Journal, 37 March 1984 pp376+ .
1276 Gehan, R. F. How the accelerated cost recovery system affects property. Financial Executive, 50(3) 1982 pp12-15.
1277 Gibson, J. Taxation and the home - the valuer's view. Accountant 184 14 May 1981 pp539-541.
1278 Goldstein, G. S. and Pauly, M. V. Effect of revenue and tax limitation on property values. National Tax Journal, 32 June 1979 Suppt. pp97-102.
1279 Goldstein, M. Property and the businessman - benefit in kind aspects. Accountant, 15 March 1984 pp11-13.
1280 Great Britain. Inland Revenue, Valuation Office. Ryde's scale 1984. London, Inland Revenue, 1984. (Reprinted in Chartered Surveyor Weekly, 9(8) 22 November 1984 pp590-592.
1281 Gress, R. E. The relationship of reappraisal frequency and the equitable distribution of the property tax. Santa Barbara, Cal., University of California, Urban Economics Program, 1978.(Research reports in public policy no. 19)
1282 Grey, Francis J. The impact on real estate of the Tax Reform Act of 1976. Real Estate Review, 7(1) Spring 1977 pp22-28.
1283 Hamilton, B. W. Capitalization of intrajurisdictional differences in local tax prices. American Economic Review, 66 December 1976 pp742-753.
1284 Harrison, J. G. Handbook on taxation of land. London, Institute of Chartered Accountants of England and Wales, 1983.
1285 Hendershott, P. H. and Ling, D. C. Trading and the tax shelter value of depreciable real estate. National Tax Journal, 37 June 1984 pp213-223.
1286 Higgins, J Warren. Impact of federal taxation on real estate decisions. Rev. ed. Storrs, Connecticut, University of Connecticut, Center for Real Estate and Urban Economics Studies, 1979.
1287 Higgins, J Warren. IRS approach to valuation of real estate. Real Estate Appraiser and Analyst, 45 November 1979 pp44-46.
1288 Hill, B. The property tax revolt: it could not happen here. Municipal and Public Services Journal, 86(35) 8 September 1978 pp893-894.
1289 Howard, Dick and Wead, James K. Periodic reappraisal of real property: the Utah approach. Washington, D.C., Council of State Governments, 1976. (RM 581)
1290 Hoyes, Tom. Development Land Tax: the bases of value. Journal of Valuation, 1(2) 1983 pp153-159.
1291 Inglis, Michael W. New Land and Environment Court: and taxation of real estate. Valuer(Australia), 26 July 1980 pp196-198.
1292 International Association of Assessing Officers. Analyzing assessment equity: techniques for measuring and improving the quality of property tax administration. Chicago, International Association of Assessing Officers, 1977.

1293 International Association of Assessing Officers. Property assessment valuation. Chicago,International Association of Assessing Officers, 1977. (For tax purposes)
1294 International Association of Assessing Officers. Property taxation and the preservation of historic properties. Chicago, International Association of Assessing Officers, 1977. (Research and Information series)
1295 International Association of Assessing Officers. Property tax incentives for preservation: use-value assessment and the preservation of farmland, open space, and historic sites. Chicago, International Association of Assessing Officers, 1976.
1296 International Association of Assessing Officers. Property tax legislation in the United States. Chicago, International Association of Assessing Officers, annually in February.
1297 International Association of Assessing Officers. Urban property tax incentives. Chicago,International Association of Assessing Officers, 1978. (Research and Information series)
1298 Jackson, H. F. How assessment tax rates and equalization rates affect real estate values. Real Estate Appraiser and Analyst, 45 March 1979 pp15-22.
1299 Jarchow, S. P. Tax risks of condominium conversion. Real Estate Review, 10 Winter 1981 pp28-30.
1300 Jensen, H. L. Current use valuations of real property for federal estate tax purposes. Appraisal Journal, 48(3) July 1980 pp423-427.
1301 Jones, I. G. Improvements in CGT. Estates Gazette, 268(2159) 5 November 1983 pp546,548.
1302 Kindahl, James K. Tax limits and property values. Land Economics, 59(3) August 1983 pp315-323.
1303 Kramer, H. Z. Assessment for real property tax purposes. Garden City, N.J., Adelphi University Press, 1975.
1304 Lightman, S. The Value Added Tax and real property transactions in the United Kingdom. International Property Investment Journal, 1(1) 1982 pp1-38.
1305 Long, Mark H. Real estate partnerships under the new tax law. Real Estate Review, 7(1) Spring 1977 pp30-32.
1306 McDaniel, J. C. Economic Recovery Tax Act of 1981 - boom or bust for appraisers? Appraisal Journal, 51(3) July 1983 pp376-391.
1307 Mackie, J. Municipal taxation and the assessed value. AIM, 22(11) November 1978 pp16-18.
1308 Mellows, J. R. Taxation of land transactions. London, Butterworths, 1982.
1309 Mitchell, B. A. and Rosen, S. M. Tax planning for a condominium or cooperative conversion. Practical Accountant, 13 September 1980 pp41-47.
1310 Morris, Douglas and others. Use value assessment and taxation rates in New Hampshire. Assessors Journal, 10 July 1975 pp27-37.
1311 Natbony, W. Depreciating dealer real property. Taxes, 62 June 1984 pp363-372.
1312 Organisation for Economic Cooperation and Development. Taxes on immoveable property: report by the Committee on fiscal affairs and the ad hoc Group on urban problems. Paris, Organisation for Economic Cooperation and Development. 1983.
1313 Pearson, T. D. Assessment ratios and property tax burdens in Norfolk, Virginia, 1974-1975. American Real Estate and Urban Economics Association Journal, 7 Summer 1979 pp190-203.
1314 Plaut, T. The real property tax, differential assessment and the loss

of farmland on the rural urban fringe. Philadelphia, Regional Science Research Institute, 1977.

1315 Pollock, R. L. and Shoup, D. Effect of shifting the property tax base from improvement value to land value: an empirical estimate. Land Economics, 53 February 1977 pp67-77.

1316 Prest, A. R. The taxation of urban land. Manchester, Manchester University Press, 1981. (Bibliography pp190-201)

1317 Ragas, W. R. and Miestchovich, I. J. Historic preservation and the 1976 Tax reform act. Appraisal Journal, 46(1) January 1978 pp44-52.

1318 Ralston, S. W. A. Land value for taxation. AIM, 22(2) April 1978 pp32-38.

1319 Ralston, S. W. A. Land value for taxation. New Zealand Valuer, 23(9) March 1978 pp465-475.

1320 Real estate taxes and the review process. CPA Journal, 51 August 1981 pp52-54.

1321 Roddewig, Richard J. and Schlaes, Jared. Appraising the best tax shelter in history. Appraisal Journal, 50(1) January 1982 pp25-42.

1322 Rose, Louis A. The development value tax: reply. Urban Studies, 13 February 1976 pp71-73. (Reply to comments on an article of 1973)

1323 Silver, Ian R. Effect of taxation on property values. New Zealand Valuer, 25(4) December 1982 pp207-217. (Followed by commentary by Roger E. Hallinan, pp218-220)

1324 Sirmans, C. F. and Newsome, B. After-tax mortgage equity valuation. Appraisal Journal, 52(2) April 1984 pp250-269.

1325 Soares, P. C. Land and tax planning. London, Longmans, 1982.

1326 Thompson, M. S. Valuation of real estate tax shelters. Trusts and Estates, 122 July 1983 pp40-43.

1327 UK tax system. Estates Gazette, 269(6170) 4 February 1984 pp421-422.

1328 United States. Bureau of the Census, Governments Division, Taxation Branch. State and local ratio studies and property assessment. Washington, D.C., Superintendant of Documents, 1975. (State and Local Government, Special studies, no. 72)

1329 Valuing an undivided share. Taxation, 112(2913) 8 October 1983 pp21-23.

1330 Weatherall, A. D. Tax on property: industrial and commercial aspects. Kluwer-Harrap, 1976.

1331 Weinstein, Marvin W. Real estate under the Tax Reform Act of 1976. Real Estate Law Journal, 5(4) Spring 1977 pp370-373.

1332 Welch, R. B. Property tax developments: modernization, classification site value taxation. National Tax Journal, 29 September 1976 pp322-327.

1333 Williford, J. S. The unique tax characteristics of partnerships. Real Estate Review, 13(2) Summer 1983 pp28-34.

1334 Winslow, E. C. Cyclical and continuous reassessment of real property for ad valorem taxation. Chapel Hill, N.C., University of North Carolina, Institute of Government, 1975.

1335 Wood, Ernest. Tax on freehold investments. Estates Gazette, 269(6176) 17 March 1984 pp1012-1013, 1016, 1018.

Industrial land and buildings

As valuation techniques are adjusted to value different types of property according to their salient features, property categories have been divided by broad property types. Since valuation also depends on markets and development activity, specific data on these have been included in each chapter. Theoretical studies have not been separately identified. Only those items which relate purely to one country's interests - most often to markets - have been isolated into geographical sub-sections. This is only done where the quantity of information justifies a subdivision. At times this has meant taking a decision as to the dominant features represented in an article or book in order to categorise it most effectively. Indexing will cover other aspects. This first chapter covers industrial property, land and buildings. The definition of industrial property used here includes most general studies of industrial and commercial property. Where there is doubt the item is most usually included in this chapter.

1336 Adams, B. Financing commercial/industrial properties. Realtor, 61(6) 1984 pp24-28.

1337 Banyard, C. A tenant's check list? Estates Gazette, 269(6171) 11 February 1984 p495.

1338 Boleat, Mark and Williams, H. Property investment decisions taken by manufacturing and distributive industry. Birmingham, Joint Unit for Research in Urban Economics, Aston University, 1979. (Working paper no.23)

1339 Bradford, G Michael. Appraisal of oil and gas production companies. Valuation 29(1) December 1983 pp6-11.

1340 Cleaveley, Edward S. The marketing of industrial and commercial property, 1984.

1341 Conway, H. M. Marketing industrial buildings and sites: the M.I.B.S. strategy for area economic development. Atlanta, Georgia, Conway Publications, 1980. (Bibliography pp181-189)

1342 Conway, H. M., Liston, L. L. and Saul, R. J. Industrial park growth: an environmental success story. Atlanta, Conway Publications, 1979.

1343 Cullis, J. Alternative ways of valuing industrial premises. Chartered Surveyor, 113(1) 1980 pp20-21.

1344 Derry, C. J. C. How much is industrial plant and machinery worth? Chartered Surveyor, 111(7) February 1979 pp256-259.

1345 Derry, C. J. C. Valuation of plant and machinery. Chartered Surveyor, 112(11) June 1980 pp509-510.

1346 Desmond, Glenn M. and Kelley, Richard E. Business valuation handbook. Chicago, Appraisal Institute, 1981.

1347 Doel, J. A checklist for valuing industrial premises. Chartered

Surveyor, 113(3) 1980 p196.

1348 Dolman, J. P. Special factors in the appraisal of large industrial plants. Appraisal Journal, 47(1) January 1979 pp8-15.

1349 Duffy Eley Giffone Worthington. Taking stock: a technical study of an approach to the undertaking of feasibility studies for the re-use of vacant industrial buildings. London, Duffy Eley Giffone Worthington, 1980.

1350 Eikmeyer, L. J. Appraising the industrial property: an old problem revisited. AIM, 22(2) April 1977 pp13-17.

1351 Fitzgerald, W. F. Valuation of a miniwarehouse. Appraisal Journal, 49 July 1981 pp353-360.

1352 Fitzwilliam, William F. Valuation of a miniwarehouse. Appraisal Jo-urnal, 49(3) July 1981 pp353-360.

1353 Fong, C. O. Planning for industrial estate development in a developing economy. Management Science, 26 October 1980 pp1061-1067.

1354 Gadd, J. L. Industrial appraisal procedures and problems. Industrial Development, 150 1981 pp33-35.

1355 Gaines, James. P. Industrial land valuation. Real Estate Appraiser and Analyst, 47 1981 pp5-9.

1356 Girard, W. How to make big money selling commercial and industrial property. Englewood Cliffs, N.J., Prentice Hall, 1977.

1357 Girard, W. Profit opportunities in commercial and industrial real estate. Englewood Cliffs, N.J., Prentice Hall, 1979.

1358 Gribb, R. C. Release provisions in office and industrial park development loans. Real Estate Review, Winter 1979 n.p.

1359 Hartman, Donald J. Industrial real estate: cost-approach with caution. Appraisal Journal, 45(3) July 1977 pp444-449.

1360 Hartman, Donald J. Industrial real estate: estimating value in use. Appraisal Journal, 47(3) July 1979 pp340-350.

1361 Haymes, Alan. Making the most of an industrial investment. Real Estate Review. 6 Fall 1976 pp14-17.

1362 Haymes, Alan. Real estate dealing: increasing cash flow in an industrial investment. Real Estate Review. 6 Summer 1976 pp18-21.

1363 Hazell, T. High-tech firms produce definition for science parks. Estates Times, 4 November 1983 p7.

1364 Henneberry, John. The impact of microtechnology on landed property. Estates Gazette, 262 19 June 1982 pp1151-1152.

1365 Henneberry, John. Property for high-technology industry. Land Development Studies, 1 1984 pp145-168.

1366 Henneberry, John. Some aspects of technological change and its impact on the demand for industrial accommodation. in Chiddick, David and Millington, Alan. Land management: new directions. London, Spon, 1984. pp161-170.

1367 Hillier, Jean. The advance factory market. Planner, 70(10) October 1984 p15.

1368 Hillier Parker May & Rowden. The effect of motorways on industrial rents. London, Financial Times Business Publications, 1979. (ICHP Index Research Reports no.2)

1369 Hillier Parker May & Rowden. M25 motorway map. London, Hillier Parker May & Rowden, 1983.

1370 How to value commercial or industrial property. Chartered Surveyor, 112(6) 1980 pp201-202.

1371 Hyde, J. V. Appraiser's approach to noise damage. Real Estate Appraiser. 42 April 1977 pp280-283.

1372 Jefferies, R. L. The problem of annual rent revaluation of commercial and industrial property. New Zealand Valuer, 24(4) December 1979 pp262-282.

1373 Jenkins, J. W. Valuation of a business: an overview. Appraisal Journal, 48(1) January 1980 pp64-77.

1374 Jensen, B. R. Building efficiency - cost and value. The Valuer.(Australia) 28(3) July 1984 pp217-222.

1375 Jones, D. Property - the neglected factor in takeovers and mergers. Chartered Surveyor Weekly, 1(6) 2 December 1982 p406.

1376 Karslake, H. H. and Nicholls, A. D. Industrial valuations. London, Estates Gazette, 1974.

1377 Kay, T. V. Plant and machinery appraisals - the UK experience. Valuation, 26(1) 1980 pp2-10.

1378 Kyle, R. C. Evaluating industrial properties. Journal of Property Management. 44(6) November/December 1979. pp321-323.

1379 Lewsley, C. Valuing an aircraft maintenance base. Rating and Valuation Reporter, 19(9) September 1979 pp209-210.

1380 Lomdardelli, H. P. Random thoughts on the predictability of industrial real estate. Appraisal Journal, 46 January 1978 pp34-43.

1381 McCarthy, P. Managed industrial parks: participating for profit. Estates Gazette, 253(5968) 19 January 1980 pp237-239.

1382 McIntosh, A. P. J. An institutional approach to high technology industrial property development. in Chiddick, David and Millington, Alan F. Land management: new directions. London, Spon, 1984. pp171-181.

1383 Martin, David. Public transport provision and property values. in Chiddick, David and Millington, Alan F. eds. Land management: new directions. London, Spon, 1984. pp189-197.

1384 Mixed-use development: new looks at an old idea. Buildings, 77 July 1983 pp72-76.

1385 Nathaniel Lichfield & Partners and Goldstein Leigh Associates. M25 London orbital, property market effects: January 1981. London, Goldstein Leigh Associates, 1981.

1386 Palmer, D. Is the inner city land overvalued? European Industrial and Commercial Review, 4(1) 1978 pp23-25.

1387 Prychidny, W. Business valuation and the appraiser. AIM, 21(2) April 1977 pp14-17.

1388 Ratcliffe, J. The valuation of development properties. Reading, Department of Land Management and Development, University of Reading, 1983. (Student guides to land management and development appraisal no. 1)

1389 Real Estate Education Council. Successful industrial real estate brokerage. 2nd ed. Chicago, Real Estate Education Council, 1980. (with Grubb & Ellis Commercial Brokerage Co.)

1390 Recommended guide for the floor measurement of commercial and industrial buildings. New Zealand Valuer, 25(1) March 1982 pp8-10. (Joint publication of Building Owners and Managers Association and Property Management Institute Inc.)

1391 Research and development parks. Business Facilities, 17(6) June 1984 pp33-38.

1392 Roberts, Joe and others. Building goes on, though at reduced levels; wait-and-see outlook pervades market. National Real Estate Investor, 23(11) October 1981 pp59-82.

1393 Roberts, N. Floorspace-worker ratios: a determinant of demand. Estates Times, 16 March 1984 pp12-14.

1394 Robinson, P. C. Complete guide to appraising commercial and industrial properties. Englewood Cliffs, N.J., Prentice Hall, 1977.

1395 Root-Reed, M. The disposable age approaches fast. Chief Executive(UK), November 1983 pp89-90. (Throwaway commercial buildings)

1396 Royal Institution of Chartered Surveyors. General Practice Division.

Plant and machinery valuation. London, Surveyor's Technical Services, 1981.
1397 Schiller, R. How society has changed its properties. Management Today, July 1982 pp85-96.
1398 Seymour, C. F. Appraising industrial parks. Appraisal Journal, 47(2) April 1979 pp165-175.
1399 Skogstad, Tor. Valuing industrial real estate in use. Appraisal Journal. 44(3) July 1976 pp328-334.
1400 Spink, F. H. ed. Industrial development handbook. Washington, D.C., Urban Land Institute, 1975.
1401 University of Reading, College of Estate Management, Centre for Advanced Land Use Studies. Buildings for industry. Reading, Centre for Advanced Land Use Studies, 1979.
1402 Valuation and disposal of plant and machinery. Valuer(ISVA), 53(1) January/February 1984 ppi-viii.
1403 Valuation of plant and machinery, in Strathan, R. N. ed. Property valuation handbook, Reading, College of Estate Management, University of Reading, 1984.
1404 Wasylenko, M. J. Evidence of fiscal differentials and intrametropolitan firm relocation. Land Economics, 56 August 1980 pp339-349.
1405 Webb, N. V. and Kay, T. V. Plant and machinery valuation. Valuer (ISVA), 47(9) November 1978 pp273-277.
1406 Williams, B. The economics of industial property development. Industrial Development Officer, 1(4) June 1975 pp30-32.
1407 Wiseman, Michael and Varaiya, Pravin. Reindustrialization and the outlook for declining areas. Research in Urban Economics, 3 1983 pp167-190. (Also available as Berkeley, University of California, Institute of Business and Economic Research, report RP32)

International

1408 Hillier Parker May & Rowden. International property bulletin. London, Hillier Parker May & Rowden, 1983.

Australia

1409 Jones Lang Wootton. The Australian industrial property report. Sydney, Jones Lang Wootton, 1984.

France

1410 Crowther, R. Industrial and office development in France. Estates Gazette, 224(5063) 9 December 1972 pp1659-1663.

Great Britain

1411 Aslin, Nigel. Hi-tech buildings: a brave new world. London, Strutt & Parker, 1979. (Property trends no.6)
1412 At last the surplus is falling as the bulldozers plunge in. Property Confidential, 338 October 1983 pp11-14. (Trends from 1978-1983)
1413 Badminton, C. and Edinburgh, B. Industrial obsolescence. Planner, 62(6) September 1976 pp180-181.
1414 Bailey, A. The chase for industrial space. Director, 38(5) December 1984 p30. (King & Company's Floorspace survey)
1415 Bernard Thorpe & Partners. Industrial floorspace: a major survey of vacant buildings in Greater London. London, Bernard Thorpe and Partners, 1982.
1416 Bernard Thorpe & Partners. Industrial property markets in Greater London and the South-East: a study by Bernard Thorpe and Partners. London, Bernard Thorpe & Partners, no date.
1417 Bewers, P. Review 1983: industrial market starts to recover. Estates

Gazette, 269(6168) 21 January 1984 pp61-69. (Supplement)
1418 Bond, R. Dramatic slump in industrial development. Surveyor, 160(4710) 30 September 1982 pp14-15. (Manchester)
1419 Bowie, N. The institutional drift to freehold ownership. Estates Gazette, 270(6179) 7 April 1984 pp20, 22.
1420 Brennan, J and others. Industrial property. Financial Times, regular reports and surveys, particularly, 27 September 1977 p15; 15 February 1978 p17; 3 July 1978 p13; 27 September 1978 p17.
1421 Burrows, B. C. Information technology - its impact on property development. Long Range Planning, 17(4) August 1984 pp60-73.
1422 Campbell Gordon. Industrial property: report on the Heathrow market. London, Campbell Gordon, 1982.
1423 Carter, Norma and Watts, Chris. The Cambridge Science Park. London, Surveyor's Publications, 1984. (Royal Institution of Chartered Surveyors, Planning and Development Case Study no. 4)
1424 Castle, G. Industrial and commercial property in London and the South East. Commerce International, October 1983 pp41, 43.
1425 Catalano, A. Review of UK Enterprise zones. London, CES Ltd, 1983.
1426 Cheshire, P. and Evans, A. The future demand for industrial property. Estates Gazette, 259(6053) 26 September 1981 pp1045-1046.
1427 Cochrane, W. and others. Industrial property. Financial Times, 4 November 1983 Section 4, p1.
1428 Cockhill, R. Best prospects for property investors. Chartered Surveyor Weekly, 2(10) 10 March 1983 p567.
1429 Commercial and industrial property. Accountant, 183(5501) 17 July 1980 pp89-109.
1430 Conrad Ritblat & Co. A research document on advanced industrial unit user requirements in South East England. London, Conrad Ritblat & Co., 1982.
1431 Cook, A. The industrial property market in Birmingham and the West Midlands. Birmingham, Aston University, Joint Unit for Research in Urban Economics, 1980. (Working paper 17)
1432 Coopers & Lybrand Associates Ltd. and Drivas Jonas. Provision of small industrial premises. London, Small Firms Division, Department of Industry, 1980.
1433 Cozens, D. G. Rates: the unexpected tax on unoccupied property. Accountant, 183 25 September 1980 pp510-511.
1434 Datafile: facts and figures for property. Property Business, monthly.
1435 De Zoete & Bevan. The industrial property market annual review. London, De Zoete and Bevan, annual.
1436 Debenham Tewson & Chinnocks. Economics of industrial development. London, Debenham Tewson & Chinnocks, 1979.
1437 Debenham Tewson & Chinnocks. High tech myths and realities: a review of developments for knowledge-based industries. London, Debenham Tewson & Chinnocks, 1983. (Reviewed Chartered Surveyor Weekly, 4(5) 4 August 1983 pp248-249, 251, 253.
1438 Debenham Tewson & Chinnocks. Industrial rent and rates 1973-1981. London, Debenham, Tewson & Chinnocks, 1981. (annual - usually covers a 7-10 year period)
1439 Drivers Jonas. Aberdeen commercial and industrial property survey no. 9. September 1978- . London, Drivers Jonas, semi-annual.
1440 Drivers Jonas. East Anglia industrial property survey. (1978-1982) London, Drivers Jonas, semi-annual.
1441 Drivers Jonas. East London and Essex industrial property survey. London, Drivers Jonas, 1981.
1442 Drivers Jonas. Review of science parks and high technology developments. London, Drivers Jonas, 1982.

1443 Edward Erdman. Property comment: industrial. London, Edward Erdman, 1979 - . (annual)
1444 Ellacombe, A. Report details low institutional voids. Chartered Surveyor Weekly, 2(7) 17 February 1983 p361.
1445 Evans, Peter and Plumb, Craig. The property requirements of knowledge-based industries. London, Debenham, Tewson & Chinnocks, 1984.
1446 Flanagan, I. Industrial property feels the breeze. Management Today, March 1981 pp98,100,102,104,106,110,112.
1447 Focus on industrial development. Property Business, November 1984 pp78-90.
1448 Fothergill, Stephen and others. Changes in industrial floorspace and employment in cities, towns and rural areas. Cambridge, University of Cambridge, Department of Land Economy, 1983.
1449 Fothergill, Stephen and others. Industrial land availability in cities, towns and rural areas. Cambridge, University of Cambridge, Department of Land Economy, 1983.
1450 Frank Innes Bonfield Commercial. Derby sees demand for small works units. Chartered Surveyor Weekly, 9(8) 22 November 1984 p583.
1451 Goldstein, M. Disposal of industrial buildings. Accountant, 190 (5681) 23 February 1984 pp15-17.
1452 Goodman, M. Management and property. Management Today, June 1979 p113.
1453 Grant & Partners. Industrial building allowance and small manufacturing business. London, Grant and Partners, 1981.
1454 Grant & Partners. A report on the industrial property market. London, Grant & Partners, 1977 - . (annual)
1455 Great Britain, Department of Industry. Small workshop scheme - effects of 100% industrial building allowance. London, Department of Industry, 1982.
1456 Great Britain, Department of the Environment. Commercial and industrial floorspace statistics 1978-81. London, HMSO, 1982.
1457 Great Britain, Department of the Environment. New industrial development. London, Department of the Environment,1979.
1458 Greater Manchester: industrial. Estates Times, 2 June 1984 pp21-30.
1459 Guirdham, Q. and others. Industrial property. Financial Times, 5 October 1976 p17; 10 February 1977 p17.
1460 Healey & Baker. Industrial guide Summer 1980. London, Healey & Baker, 1980 - .
1461 Herring Son & Daw. Property technology - the needs of modern industry. London, Herring Son & Daw, 1982.
1462 Herring Son & Daw. Property technology - the needs of modern industry: a further survey of the electronics industry. London, Herring Son & Daw, 1983. (supplement to above)
1463 High-tech development. Estates Times, 2 October 1982 pp17-36.
1464 High technology: an ET survey. Estates Times, 21 October 1983 pp15-27.
1465 High-tech property. Chartered Surveyor Weekly, 7(13) 28 April 1984 pp880-893.
1466 Hill, Martin P. Industrial and commmercial uses in Housing Action Areas: an exploratory study in the West Midlands. Birmingham, University of Birmingham, Centre for Urban and Regional Studies, 1980. (Research memorandum no. 81)
1467 Hillier Parker May & Rowden. A forecast of industrial rents. London, Hillier Parker May & Rowden, 1982 - . (annual)
1468 Hillier Parker May & Rowden. Industrial contour map: rents and yields. London, Hillier Parker May & Rowden, 1982.
1469 Hillier Parker May & Rowden. Industrial rent contours. London, Hillier Parker May & Rowden, 1980.

1470 Hillier Parker May & Rowden. Second survey of industrial voids. London, Hillier Parker May & Rowden, 1984. (Discussed in Estates Times, 30 March 1984 p4)
1471 Home, R. K. Wood Green Shopping City. London, Surveyor's Publications, 1984. (Royal Institution of Chartered Surveyors, Planning and Development Case Study no. 2)
1472 Huntley, J. The new factory - or is it? Property Business, December 1983 pp49-50.
1473 Industrial and commercial property Investor's Chronicle, 10 November 1977 supplement; 9 November 1979 pp 5+ ; 28 October 1983 pp5-103; 2 November 1984 pp1-103. (regular supplement)
1474 Industrial development. Chartered Surveyor, 111(9) April 1979 pp349-356.
1475 Industrial property. in Estates Times, annual.
1476 Industrial property market review. in Estates Gazette, annual.
1477 Investment institutions discriminate against small industrial units. Chartered Surveyor, 111(10) May 1979 pp422-423.
1478 Investor's Chronicle Hillier Parker Research. IC/HP Rent index. London, Hillier Parker May & Rowden, annual. (no.10 1982)
1479 Investor's Chronicle Hillier Parker Research. Survey of industrial voids. February 1983. London, Hillier Parker May & Rowden, 1983. (annual)
1480 Kenneth Ryden & Partners. Scottish industrial and commercial property review. Edinburgh, Kenneth Ryden & Partners, 1980 - . (semi-annual)
1481 King & Co. Graphs showing regional trends in the availability of industrial floorspace. April 1975 - December 1982. London, King & Co., 1982.
1482 King & Co. Industrial floorspace survey. London, King & Co., 1978- . (quarterly)
1483 King & Co. Industrial property. London, King & Co., annual.
1484 Langton, Robert C. Industrial floorspace: a major survey of vacant buildings in Greater London. London, Bernard Thorpe & Partners, 1982.
1485 London Borough of Southwark, Planning Division. Office industrial and commercial monitoring report. London, London Borough of Southwark, 1982. (Research report 82/1)
1486 McEachern, W. A. Large-lot zoning in Connecticut. Storrs, Conn., University of Connecticut, School of Business Administration, Center for Real Estate and Urban Economic Studies, 1979. (Real Estate report no. 29)
1487 McIntosh, A. P. J. Funding hi-tech industrial property. Estates Gazette, 269(6173) 25 February 1984 pp710,712.
1488 Mann, E. Theme parks. Building, 2 December 1983 pp29+ .
1489 Neale, C. South Woodham Ferrars: the Essex design guide in practice, London, Surveyor's Publications, 1984. (Royal Institution of Chartered Surveyors, Planning and Development Case Study no. 3)
1490 New breed of industrials begin to set rental trends. Estates Times, 731 3 February 1984 pp12-13.
1491 Ogden, C. Buildings for industry, Reading, University of Reading, College of Estate Management, Centre for Advanced Land Use Studies, 1979.
1492 Organ, J. New breed of industrials begin to set rental trends. Estates Times, 3 February 1984 pp12-13.
1493 Page, R. W. High technology property survey December 1984. London, Healey & Baker, 1984.
1494 Prognosis: healthy in 12 months. Property Investment Review, July

1976 pp8-11.
1495 Roger Tym & Partners. Enterprise zones. London, Roger Tym and Partners, 1982.
1496 Royal Institution of Chartered Surveyors, Planning and Development Division. Discrimination against small industrial units. London, Royal Institution of Chartered Surveyors, 1979.
1497 Royal Institution of Chartered Surveyors. Enterprise zones:a memorandum of observations. London, Royal Institution of Chartered Surveyors, 1984.
1498 'Showpiece' site for West Midlands. British Business, 12(6) 23 September 1983 p214.
1499 Slough Estates Ltd. Industrial investment: a case study in factory building. London, Slough Estates Ltd., 1978.
1500 Strohm, P. 'Hi-tech' - the tenants talk. Estates Gazette, 269(6178) 31 March 1984 p1226.
1501 Sullom Voe. Town and Country Planning, 48(3) June 1979 pp95-97. (investment study)
1502 Sun-Alliance's Swindon high-technology centre. Estates Gazette, 270(6182) 28 April 1984 p274.
1503 Symonds, Barry and Newhall, Mary. Mini-factories at Peterborough. London, Surveyors Publications, 1983. (Royal Institution of Chartered Surveyors Planning and Development Case Study, prepared for the Royal Institution of Chartered Surveyors by School of Construction and Surveying, Chelmer Institute of Higher Education)
1504 Taylor, A. and others. Industrial property. Financial Times, 21 September 1979 Section III p1; 4 February 1980 Section III p1; 1 November 1982 Section III p1.
1505 Teale, M. Hazy role for Aztec west. Property Business, December 1983 p63.
1506 Teale, M. High technology pipe-dream - but what about the future? Property Business, December 1983 pp56-57.
1507 Teale, M. Uniform high tech needs impossible to define. Property Business, July 1984 pp22-28.
1508 Thomas, D. England's golden west. New Society, 1068 5 May 1983 pp177-178.
1509 The truth about high-tech. Chartered Surveyor Weekly, 4(5) 4 August 1983 pp248-253; 11 August 1983 pp292-295.
1510 United Kingdom: economic ills create tenant's market in warehouse sector. National Real Estate Investor, 23 January 1981 pp46+ .
1511 University of Reading. Centre for Advanced Land Use Studies. Development for high technology. Reading, University of Reading, College of Estate Management, Centre for Advanced Land Use Studies, 1984. (Papers from 3 conferences)
1512 University of Reading. College of Estate Management. Property and information technology: the future for the offices market. Reading, University of Reading, College of Estate Management, 1983.
1513 Vickers da Costa Ltd. A review of the UK industrial property market. Property Quarterly Review, 12 May 1979 pp19-29.
1514 West Midlands - industrial. Chartered Surveyor Weekly, 6(8) 23 February 1984 pp503-528.
1515 Whaler, V. G. See how they grow: a survey of industrial park development trends. Industrial Development Handbook, 147 July 1978 pp13-14.
1516 Whelan, C. and Parker, G. Wandsworth. Chartered Surveyor Weekly, 7(10) 7 June 1984 pp655-661.
1517 Williams, James F. D. A review of science parks and high technology developments. London, Drivers Jonas, 1982.

Industrial land and buildings

1518 Worthington, J. High-tech low-tech. Building, 244(7282) 11 March 1983 pp30-33.

Hong Kong

1519 Roberts, P. J. Valuation of development land in Hong Kong. Hong Kong Hong Kong University Press, 1975.

United States

1520 Associations in real estate. National Real Estate Investor, 25 June 1983 p28.

1521 Braun, T. Las Vegas: more industrial space planned as existing inventory shrinks. National Real Estate Investor. 19 May 1977 pp77-78.

1522 Coldwell Banker. United States industrial vacancy index. London, Coldwell Banker, quarterly.

1523 Crim, S. K. Industrial parks reel from recession, interest rates, environmentalists. Mortgage Banker. 36 September 1976 pp11-14.

1524 Dorvillier, Deanna. Puerto Rico industrial development takes lead in overall recovery: confidence replaces caution as economy resumes upswing. National Real Estate Investor. 19 March 1977 pp35-40.

1525 Industrial expansion concentrated in park sites: master-planned projects attracting major investors. National Real Estate Investor, 19 October 1977 pp58-60.

1526 Lewis, S. E. Industrial real estate: market is mixed....National Real Estate Investor, 22 April 1980 pp31-32.

1527 Lewis, S. E. Industrial real estate: money woes affect construction, sales activity, but inventories are on the rise in many areas. National Real Estate Investor, 23 April 1981 pp39-40.

1528 Martin, Thomas J. Urban sites proving attractive for new industry. National Real Estate Investor, 25(2) February 1983 pp30,34,106.

1529 Melaniphy, J. C. Commercial and industrial condominiums. Washington, D.C., Urban Land Institute, 1976.

1530 O'Donnell, J. D. Industrial development to be more dollar intensive. National Real Estate Investor, 25 April 1983 pp58-59.

1531 O'Leary, SIR tracks the changing industrial market. Real Estate Today 14 March 1981 pp22-24.

1532 Peters, J. Jacksonville: upturn in mood and market spurred by growing demand: major industrial developments underway or in talking stage. National Real Estate Investor. 18 November 1976 pp69-70.

1533 Roberts, Joe and others. Construction and leasing activity severely curtailed: adaptable high-tech projects in strong demand. National Real Estate Investor, 24(11) October 1982 pp64-98.

Commercial property

The commercial market has been taken to mean the office market and the central commercial market when discussed as such. Shop or retail property is usually discussed separately. Many studies clearly indicate that office property is the subject although the title may suggest the wider commercial market. The many regular surveys appearing in the real estate press are not listed separately.

1534 Barras, Richard. The returns from office development and investment. London, Centre for Environment Studies, 1979. (Research series no. 35)

1535 Basie, J. P. Saving energy and money in office building management. Real Estate Appraiser. 42 July 1976 pp5-9.

1536 Beitler, J. and Randall, B. The case for the office condominium. Real Estate Review, 13(3) Fall 1983 pp99-102.

1537 Bible, Douglas S. and Whaley, John. Projecting an urban office market: a source of information for appraisers. Appraisal Journal. 51(4) October 1983. pp515-523.

1538 Birkeland, B. R. Multi-tenant office/industrial park. Journal of Property Management, 44 November 1979 pp302-304.

1539 Boddy, M. Land property and finance. Bristol, University of Bristol School for Advanced Urban Studies, 1978. (Working Paper 2)

1540 Bridel, J. The commercial mortgage market - a review of insurance company lending terms. Estates Gazette, 244(5852) 8 October 1977 pp113-117.

1541 Campbell, I. R. Business valuation, a non-technical guide for business people. Don Mills, Ontario, CCH Canadian, 1985.

1542 Coopman, R. The future for commercial property development. Chartered Surveyor Urban Quarterly, 4(3) 1977 pp41-44.

1543 Cymrot, Allen and others. How to invest in office buildings and shopping centers. Real Estate Review, 12 1982 pp75-82.

1544 Davies, R. Retail and commercial planning. London, Croom Helm, 1984.

1545 Davis, J. A. New life for aging commercial property. Mortgage Banker, 43 November 1982 pp72-76.

1546 Desmond, Glenn M and Kelley, Richard E. Business valuation handbook. Llano, California, Valuation Press, 1980.

1547 Donnelly, J. C. Investor attitudes and the appraisal of the major urban center office building. Appraisal Journal, 49 January 1981 pp61-73.

1548 Economists Advisory Group Ltd. Factors influencing the location of offices of multinational enterprises. London, Economists Advisory Group Ltd., 1980.

1549 Finch, R. G. and Broadhurst, R. S. Co-ownership schemes for commercial property investment. *Law Society's Gazette*, 76(9) 7 March 1979 pp234-235.

1550 Freedman, P. *Checklist for commercial lettings: reminders for surveyors and solicitors on the negotiation and drafting of business leases*. London, Henry Stewart Publications, 1983.

1551 Furbur, J. D. Office service charges data: analysis of landlord's costs. *Estates Gazette*, 272(6213) 1 December 1984 p1036; 272(6214) 8 December 1984 p1142; 272(6215) 15 December 1984 p1242. (See also tables published in *Estates Gazette*, 272(6208) 27 October 1984 p413)

1552 Furbur, J. D. The real cost of renting an office. *Chartered Surveyor Weekly*, 5(4) 27 October 1983 p215.

1553 Gauldin, T. A. Developing a suburban office building. *Mortgage Banker*, 40 November 1979 pp43-45.

1554 Gonczy, S. I. Office building manager: a jack of all trades! *Journal of Property Management*. 41 November 1976 pp267-271.

1555 Gordon, E. S. *How to market space in an office building*. Boston, Warren, Gorham and Lamont, 1976.

1556 Henderson, R. Designed for a purpose or purpose-designed? *Estates Gazette*, 267(6152) 17 September 1983 pp1018-1020.

1557 Hillier Parker May & Rowden. *The effect of air conditioning on office rents*. London, Financial Times Business Publications, 1978. (Investor's Chronicle Hillier Parker Index Research Reports no.1)

1558 Hillier Parker May & Rowden. *The effect of air conditioning on office rents*. London, Financial Times Business Publications, 1982. (Investor's Chronicle Hillier Parker Index Research Reports no.5)

1559 Hubbard, S. Searching for new offices - a checklist. *Company Secretary's Review*, 5(14) 23 September 1981 pp110-111.

1560 Hyman, M. A. A dilemma for property managers: assessment of personal property as real property. *Journal of Property Management*, 48 1983 pp18-20.

1561 *Income/expense analysis: suburban office buildings*. Chicago, Institute of Real Estate Management, National Association of Realtors, 1980.

1562 Jones Lang Wootton. *A guide to trends in international office rents*. London, Jones Lang Wootton, 1984 - . (annual)

1563 Kau, James B. and Sirmans, C. F. Changes in urban land values 1836-1970. *Journal of Urban Economics*, 15(1) 1984 pp18-25.

1564 Lehari, R. A. The best way to value a real estate company. *CA Magazine*, 116 July 1983 pp38-42.

1565 Linacre, V. T. Commercial property management. *Estates Gazette*, 239(5792) 7 August 1976 pp413-417.

1566 McKinnon, A. Effect of investment tax credit on commercial real estate values. *Real Estate Appraiser and Analyst*, 47(1) 1981 pp12-15.

1567 McQuillan, P., Doherty, P. and Donald, G. *Valuation of businesses: a practitioner's guide*. 2nd ed. Don Mills, Ontario, CCH Canadian, 1984. (First ed. 1978)

1568 Meagher, J. P. Syndicating office construction. *Barrons*, 62 13 December 1982 pp60-61.

1569 Meaney, C. Developments in business tenancies. *Estates Gazette*, 268(6159) 5 November 1983 pp538, 540. 542; 268(6160) 12 November 1983 pp640, 642; 268(6161) 19 November 1983 pp780, 782.

1570 Nilges, David. Leasing office space in a competitive market. *Journal of Property Management*. 46(6) November/December 1982 pp8+ .

1571 Office design: interior and exterior. *Real Estate Today*, 13 July 1980 pp33-48.

1572 Peltzer, Kenneth E. Computerized analysis of a joint-venture-invest-

ment office building. Appraisal Journal, 50 October 1982 pp537-563.
1573 Piper, J. B. Office condominium economics. Appraisal Journal, 49(1) January 1981 pp34-44.
1574 Pittenger, W. L. Value considerations in bank real estate. Real Estate Appraiser and Analyst, 48 1982 pp15-22.
1577 Ratcliffe, J. The valuation of development properties. Journal of Valuation, 1(1) 1982 pp24-31.
1578 Real Estate Education Council with Grubb and Ellis Commercial Brokerage. Successful leasing and selling of office property. Chicago, Real Estate Education Council, 1980.
1579 Real estate office reflections. Real Estate today, 13 July 1980 pp49-53.
1580 Richard Ellis. Changing demand and locational trends for offices. London,Richard Ellis, 1982.
1581 Richard Ellis. Going places - relocating offices. London, Richard Ellis, 1982.
1582 Richard Ellis. The impact of the microchip on the demand for offices. London, Richard Ellis, 1982.
1583 Richard Ellis. World rental levels: offices. London, Richard Ellis, 1982 - . (semi-annual)
1584 Roberts, D. F. Salesmanship and the office leasing process. Journal of Property Management. 44(6) November/December 1979 pp305-308.
1585 Ronson, Howard. Office development comparisons: London, Paris, New York. Appraisal Journal, 51(4) October 1983 pp509-514.
1586 Rosenthal, R. New directions in medical office building development. Real Estate Appraiser, 44 March 1978 pp5-12.
1587 Russell, Michael P. Opportunities in suburban office development. Real Estate Review, 9(3) Fall 1979 pp100-102.
1588 Salata, Anthony. Do office developers face redundancy in the microchip age? Estates Times, 15 December 1980 p11.
1589 Salata, Anthony. Offices today and tomorrow. University of Reading, College of Estate Management, 1983. (Property Development Library v.1)
1590 Sellars, M. A. Office rental valuations. New Zealand Valuer, 24(10) June 1981 pp821-825.
1591 Shop talk. Real Estate Today, 13 November/December 1980 pp35-42.
1592 Speyer, Jerry I. Future of highrise office buildings. Journal of Property Management. 41(1) January/February 1976 pp191-193.
1593 University of Reading, College of Estate Management, Centre for Advanced Land Use Studies. Property and information technology - the future for the office market. Reading, University of Reading, College of Estate Management, Centre for Advanced Land Use Studies, 1983.
1594 Urban disinvestment, redlining and the appraiser. New Zealand Real Estate, 34(4) August 1983 pp137-229. (Bibliography)
1595 Wall, J. N. B. Land valuation techniques. New Zealand Valuer, 23(4) December 1976 pp208-211.
1596 Wall, J. N. B. Valuing land with redevelopment potential. New Zealand Valuer, 23(7) September 1977 pp362-366.
1597 Weatherall Green & Smith. International survey of the costs of renting prime office accommodation in the financial centres of London, New York, Paris and Frankfurt. London, Weatherall Green & Smith, 1981.
1598 Weaver, William C. Forecasting office space demand and conjoint measurement techniques. Appraisal Journal, 52(3) July 1984 pp389-398.
1599 Wheatcroft, Patience. Why you should look after your office. International Management(UK), 34(12) December 1979 pp45-47.

Commercial property

1600 White, John R. How to plan and build a major office building. Real Estate Review, 10 Spring 1980 pp87-82.
1601 Why some tenants prefer a building without guts. Property Confidential, 348 August 1984 pp12-16.
1602 Wimberly, Brooks. True office values. Journal of Property Management. 43(5) September/October 1978 pp240-246.
1603 Woodward, L. N. Scientific way to locate an office. Real Estate Today. 10 August 1977 pp46-49.
1604 Wurtzebach, Charles H. Major factors affecting selection of office facilities. Journal of Property Management. 41(5) September/October 1976 pp221-224.
1605 Zoning ordinances and professional offices. Real Estate Today, 13 June 1980 pp59-60.

International

1606 Cunnew, T. Reduced demand, political uncertainty limit building: high-tech sparks an otherwise dull industrial market. National Real Estate Investor, 26(1) January 1984 p41.
1607 Europe scores well in office costs. Vision, 115 July/August 1981 pp11-12.
1608 Firmer foundations for commercial property. Economist, 293(7373-4) 22 December 1984 pp85-87.
1609 Richard Ellis. World rental levels: offices. Journal of Valuation, 2(4) 1984 pp324-327. (Reproduces the tables as published by Richard Ellis)
1610 Ronson, H. Office development comparisons: London, Paris, New York. Appraisal Journal, 51(4) October 1983 pp509-514.
1611 The troubles have been international. Investor's Chronicle, 21 May 1976 pp7-9.

Australia

1612 Cairns, W. H. City real estate investments: the immediate future. Valuer(Australia), 26 April 1980 pp114-117.
1613 Huntley, J. Offices boost confidence. Property Business, May 1984 p35.
1614 Jones Lang Wootton. Outlook 1984 - a summary of the 1984 office market. Sydney, Jones Lang Wootton, 1984.
1615 Sydney: office absorption expected to remain strong for years. National Real Estate Investor, 25 January 1983 pp43-44.
1616 Whipple, R. T. M. Regularities in the vertical arrangement of land uses in Sydney's central area. Land Development Studies, 1 1984 pp3-22.

Great Britain

The office market is usually summarised in the main journals in the January issues, for example Estates Gazette has run a survey each year in January entitled Office review, Office market or similarly. These have sometimes appeared as supplements as they have increased in size. Such surveys are not listed separately, users are referred to the January issues of the main journal titles given in the Appendix.

1617 Abrams, J. Up-market garden bears fruit for media-men and property developers alike. Estates Times, 569 31 October 1980 p11.
1618 Brett, M. Property past its prime. Investor's Chronicle, 65(819) 15 July 1983 pp12-13.
1619 Business premises handbook. London, Gower, 1981.
1620 Cassell, M. and others. Office property. Financial Times, 20 March

1981 Section III p1; 19 March 1982 Section III p1;

1621 Catalano, A. and Barras, Richard. Office development in central Manchester. London, Centre for Environment Studies, 1980. (Research series 37)

1622 Cochrane, W and others. Office property. Financial Times, 25 May 1984 Section IV p1.

1623 Commercial marketing. Valuer(ISVA), 53(4) May 1984 pp93-99.

1624 Commercial property: special report. Times, 26 November 1980 pp19-23.

1625 De Zoete & Bevan. The offices property market. London, De Zoete and Bevan, annually. (with Jones Lang Wootton)

1626 Debenham Tewson & Chinnocks. Office rent and rates 1973-1981. London, Debenham, Tewson and Chinnocks,1981. (Annual covering the years 1973-1982, 1973-1983 etc.)

1627 Debenham Tewson & Chinnocks. Office floorspace surveys. London Debenham Tewson & Chinnocks, quarterly.

1628 Dron & Wright. Office rents and rates April 1983. London, Dron & Wright, 1983.

1629 Dron & Wright. Rent and rates: a comparative study. London, Dron & Wright, 1984. (Office study: to be annual)

1630 Flanagan, I. Industrial property feels the breeze. Management Today, March 1981 pp98,100+.

1631 Focus on city offices. Property Business, September 1984 pp49-65.

1632 Frost, D. Office property in the South East. Commerce International, March 1978 pp15, 17, 19.

1633 Furbur, J. D. A comparison of office rents and rates. Estates Gazette, 272(6213) 1 December 1984 pp1008-1009.

1634 Furbur, J. D. How the market views real cost. Chartered Surveyor Weekly, 4(12) 22 September 1983 p6006.

1635 Furbur, J. D. Office service charges data. Estates Gazette, 272(6208) 27 October 1984 p413.

1636 Government's office rent bill soon to be £200m. Chartered Surveyor, 111(6) January 1979 p215.

1637 Great Britain, Department of the Environment. Commercial and industrial property statistics. London, HMSO, annual.

1638 Great Britain, Department of the Environment. The office location review. London, Department of the Environment, 1976.

1639 Great Britain, Inland Revenue. Valuation office property market report. London, Surveyor's Publications, annual from 1983. (Previously published internally, surveys the market for the previous 6-12 months in a range of markets)

1640 Harris, M. Commercial property investment: the next five years. London, Strutt & Parker, 1979. (Property trends 1)

1641 Healey & Baker. Analysis of selected UK office centres. London, Healey and Baker, 1983.

1642 Healey & Baker. Graph of prime commercial property yields. London, Healey & Baker, 1979-1984. (quarterly: incorporated into Investment report from 1985)

1643 Healey & Baker. Office guide Summer 1979. London, Healey & Baker, 1979 - .

1644 Healey & Baker. Prime commercial property yields and rental growth 1972-1981. London, Healey & Baker, 1981.

1645 Hillier Parker May & Rowden. Office rent contours. London, Hillier Parker May and Rowden, 1981.

1646 Hillier Parker May & Rowden. Offices in Britain: survey of office market activity. London, Hillier Parker May & Rowden, 1981 - . (semi-annual: nos. 1-5 titled Survey of office market activity.)

1647 Huntley, J. Blue-chip demands. Property Business, January 1984

pp40-45.
1648 Huntley, J. and Teale, M. Outer London office boom. Property Business, February 1984 pp42-44.
1649 Investors Chronicle Hillier Parker Research. Office rent contours. London, Hillier Parker May & Rowden, 1981.
1650 Jones Lang Wootton. The decentralisation of offices from Central London. London, Jones Lang Wootton, 1983. (Technical paper)
1651 Jones Lang Wootton. Office development in Greater London outside the central area. London, Jones Lang Wootton, 1983. (Technical paper) (Reviewed in Estates Gazette, 4 February 1984 p371)
1652 Jones Lang Wootton. Provincial offices. London, Jones Lang Wootton, 1978.
1653 Jones Lang Wootton. 50 centres: a guide to office and industrial rental trends in England and Wales. London, Jones Lang Wootton, 1983. (semi-annual)
1654 Knight Frank & Rutley. Office development in the M25 Corridor: north. London, Knight Frank & Rutley, 1984.
1655 Knight Frank & Rutley. Office development in the M25 Corridor: south. London, Knight Frank & Rutley, 1985.
1656 Knight Frank & Rutley. Office development in the Western Corridor. London, Knight Frank & Rutley, 1982 and 1983.
1657 London estates. Valuer(ISVA), 53(2) March 1984 pp50-51. (The ancient London estates, Cadogan, Portman, Grosvenor, Howard de Walden)
1658 Mallett, Lee and others. M4 offices move into the fast lane. Chartered Surveyor Weekly, 9(10) 6 December 1984 pp714-5. (first of several articles on property along the M4)
1659 Matthews Goodman and Postlethwaite. Commercial property market report. London, Matthews Goodman & Postlethwaite, 1982.
1660 Michael Laurie & Partners. An analysis of commercial property values. 1962-1975. London, Economist Intelligence Unit, 1976. (annual)
1661 Office review. Estates Times, October 1979 Special supplement. (Items listed in RICS Abstracts and Reviews, 15(11) November 1979 R433)
1662 Offices: an Estates Times review survey. Estates Times Review, 1981 pp31-50.
1663 Pickford, C. The UK office market: the way ahead. Valuer(ISVA), June 1982 pp80-81.
1664 Property Agents International. Property: the UK office factory and warehouse directory, including UK shops directory. London, Property Agents International,1984/5 - . (quarterly)
1665 Richard Ellis. Changing demand and locational trends for offices. London, Richard Ellis, 1982.
1666 Richard Ellis. The impact of the microchip on the demand for offices. London, Richard Ellis, 1982.
1667 Richard Ellis. The prime office market. London, Richard Ellis, 1980. (with update to 1981)
1668 Rowe & Pitman. Market report: the property market. Journal of Valuation, 2(4) 1984 pp435-443.
1669 Royal Institution of Chartered Surveyors. RICS/Institute of Actuaries City office rent indices. London, Royal Institution of Chartered Surveyors. (Issued as a Press Release and printed in several journals including the Chartered Surveyor Weekly. Being revamped in 1985)
1670 St Quintin. Office development outside Central London. Vol.I Summary report. Vol.II A comparative study of 13 office locations. London. St Quintin, no date.

1671 Savills. Commercial property investment market report 1979. London, Savills, 1979.
1672 Strutt & Parker. Survey of office supply. London, Strutt & Parker, quarterly.
1673 University of Reading, College of Estate Management, Centre for Advanced Land Use Studies. Property and information technology: the future for the office market. Reading, University of Reading, College of Estate Management, Centre for Advanced Land Use Studies, 1983.

Aberdeen
1674 Kenneth Ryden & Partners. Aberdeen office market. Edinburgh, Kenneth Ryden & Partners, 1980.

Belfast
1675 Adair, Alastair. Influences on office development in Belfast. in Chiddick, David and Millington, Alan F. eds. Land management: new directions. London, Spon, 1984. pp198-209.

Birmingham
1676 Elliott Son & Boyton. Office survey of West Midlands County. Autumn 1979. Birmingham, Elliott Son & Boyton, annual.
1677 Laing Properties Ltd. The future of office accommodation in Edgbaston and Birmingham: a survey and report. Bristol, Laing Properties Ltd, 1980.
1678 Welch, L. A Brum deal of Birmingham offices. Chartered Surveyor Weekly, 6(7) 16 February 1984 pp426-427.

Glasgow
1679 Jones Lang Wootton. Offices in Glasgow and Edinburgh: a report. London, Brian Mitchell Associates on behalf of Jones Lang Wootton, 1982.
1680 Kenneth Ryden & Partners. The Edinburgh and Glasgow office markets. Edinburgh, Kenneth Ryden & Partners, 1979 - . (annual)
1681 Lambert Smith & Partners. Report on the Glasgow office market. No. 1. London, Lambert Smith & Partners, 1981 - . (quarterly)
1682 Richard Ellis. Office development Central Glasgow. Glasgow, Richard Ellis, 1982.

Leeds
1683 St Quintin. A report on the Leeds office and industrial property market April 1980. London, St Quintin, 1980.

London
1684 Barras, Richard ed. The office boom in London. London, CES Ltd., 1981
1685 Barras, Richard. The office development cycle in London. London, Centre for Environmental Studies, 1979. (Research series 35)
1686 Barras, Richard. The office development cycle in London. Land Development Studies, 1 1984 pp35-50.
1687 Bernard Thorpe & Partners. Development in London 1967-1980. London, Bernard Thorpe and Partners, 1981.
1688 Blundell, G. Decentralisation: putting the finger on fluctuations. Estates Times, 763 14 September 1984 p11.
1689 Blundell, G. Decentralisation: is the city under threat? Estates Times, 764 21 September 1984 pp11-13.
1690 City of London. City of London Information report: offices. London,

City of London Corporation, 1982.

1691 Daniels, P. Office policy problems in Greater London. *Planner* 63(4) July 1977 pp102-105.

1692 Debenham Tewson & Chinnocks. *Central London office floorspace survey* London, Debenham Tewson & Chinnocks, quarterly.

1693 Debenham Tewson & Chinnocks. *Office rents and rates*. London, Debenham Tewson & Chinnocks, annual. (Usually covers a 7-10 year period)

1694 Debenham Tewson & Chinnocks. *A review of office market floorspace movement: EC and WC districts*. London, Debenham Tewson & Chinnocks, 1982. (London)

1695 Drivers Jonas. *Mayfair and St James property survey 1977*. London, Drivers Jonas, 1977.

1696 Dron & Wright. *Effect of the micro-chip on office demand in London*. London, Dron & Wright, 1982.

1697 Dron & Wright. *A survey of available city office space*. London, Dron & Wright, 1983. (London EC postal districts)

1698 Goddard & Smith. *Slough: market comment*. London, Goddard & Smith, 1983. (Comparison between office rents in Slough and London's West End)

1699 Greater London Council. *Office development and employment in Greater London*. London, Greater London Council, 1979.

1700 Greater London Council. *Office policy review: the GLDP preferred locations*. London,Greater London Council, 1981. (Greater London Development Plan)

1701 W Greenwell & Co. *London office property*. London, W Greenwell, 1983.

1702 Headley, R. *Victoria offices report*. London, Tuckerman Chartered Surveyors, 1983.

1703 Hillier Parker May & Rowden. *City of London office map*. London, Hillier Parker May and Rowden, 1982.

1704 Hillier Parker May & Rowden. City of London office map. Review. *Chartered Surveyor Weekly*, 7(5) 3 May 1984 pp296-297.

1705 Hillier Parker May & Rowden. *Office developments in the City of London area with a gross floor area of over 100,000 sq feet completed between 1961-1981 together with planned developments*. London, Hillier Parker May & Rowden, 1982.

1706 Humberts. *A survey of office space available in the Holborn area*. London, Humberts, 1979 - .

1707 Jones Lang Wootton. *The analysis of available space and take-up*. London, Jones Lang Wootton, 1983. (CLOR Technical paper no. 2)

1708 Jones Lang Wootton. *Central London offices research*. London, Jones Lang Wootton, semi-annual. (CLOR)

1709 Jones Lang Wootton. *The decentralisation of offices from Central London special survey*. London, Jones Lang Wootton, 1983.

1710 Jones Lang Wootton. *The derivation of the total office stock in Central London*. London, Jones Lang Wootton, 1982 (CLOR Technical paper no. 1)

1711 Jones Lang Wootton. *Office development in Greater London outside the central area*. London, Jones Lang Wootton, 1983. (annual)

1712 Jones Lang Wootton. *Offices in the City of London*. London, Jones Lang Wootton, 1980.

1713 Kerr, D. *An assessment of development potential in London's commercial property sector*. London, Greater London Council, 1977. (Research memorandum 505)

1714 Leslie Lintott & Associates. *Survey of Greater West End area: air-conditioned office accommodation*. Leslie Lintott & Associates, 1978 - . (semi-annual)

1715 London office developments: red-lined. *Economist*, 280 18 July 1981

pp78-79.
1716 London offices: cheap at twice the space. Economist, 289(7309) 1 October 1983 pp83-84.
1717 Oswald, P. Challenge facing offices in inner London. Accountant, 182 10 April 1980 pp548-549.
1718 Richard Ellis. London SW1 office accommodation market annual review and outlook: the market in 1980. London, Richard Ellis, 1981.
1719 Richard Ellis. Office market review: City of London. London, Richard Ellis, January 1984 - . (quarterly with various earlier titles, since 1980)
1720 Richard Ellis. SW1 office accommodation market. London, Richard Ellis 1980. (quarterly)
1721 Richard Ellis. West Central office accommodation market. London, Richard Ellis, 1980 - . (quarterly)
1722 Richard Ellis. West Central office accommodation market annual review: the market in 1980. London, Richard Ellis, 1981.
1723 Richard Ellis. West End office report: Autumn 1983. London, Richard Ellis, 1983.
1724 Richard Saunders & Partners. City floorspace survey. London, Richard Saunders, 1978 - . (annual)
1725 Richard Saunders & Partners. City of London floorspace survey. London, Richard Saunders & Partners, monthly.
1726 Rigbey, L. No offices ban for City or West End? Chartered Surveyor, 114(2) September 1981 pp60-64.
1727 St Quintin. London commercial office floorspace survey: a survey and analysis of office development. London, St Quintin, 1982.
1728 Saunders, A. and Ward, C. Index of the UK commercial property market. Applied Economics, 10 September 1978 pp251-262.
1729 Savills. City office demand survey London 1983. London, Savills, 1983. (annual)
1730 Sherman, Paul. London commercial office floorspace survey: a survey and analysis of office development. London, St Quintin, 1982.
1731 Sherman, Paul. London commercial office space survey: a survey and analysis of office development. Journal of Valuation. 1(2) 1983 pp160-177.
1732 Teale, M. Improvement apathy in London's West End 'villages'. Property Business, October 1984 pp42-48.
1733 Weatherall Green & Smith. Holborn office report. London, Weatherall Green & Smith, 1978 - . (annual)

Manchester
1734 Richard Ellis. Central Manchester office survey. Manchester, Richard Ellis, 1984.
1735 Richard Ellis. South Manchester office survey. Manchester, Richard Ellis, 1984.

Reading
1736 Mallett, Lee. Bright prospects for Reading offices - reports from Richard Ellis and Chilvers. Chartered Surveyor Weekly, 289(7309) 1 October 1983 pp83-84.
1737 Richard Ellis. Central Reading office market review September 1983. London, Richard Ellis, 1983.
1738 Richard Ellis. Central Reading office market review September 1984: an update. London, Richard Ellis, 1984.
1739 Teale, M. Reading aims to top office investment table. Property Business, October 1984 pp61,64,67-68.
Jersey

Commercial property

1740 Gothard & Trevor. Graph of office rental growth, St Helier, 1970-1984. St Helier, Gothard & Trevor, 1984. (Exact title not known)

Hong Kong

1741 Hong Kong: tightening office sector leading on higher rents. National Real Estate Investor, 24 January 1982 pp42-43.

1742 Jones Lang Wootton. Office space survey. London, Jones Lang Wootton, 1984.

1743 Richard Ellis. Hong Kong property report, 1982. London, richard Ellis, 1983. (Offices)

Netherlands

1744 Commercial property in the Netherlands. In Touch, September 1979 p85.

1745 Savills. Commercial property investment market of the Netherlands. Autumn 1978. London, Savills, 1978.

New Zealand

1746 Jefferies, R. L. Analysis of urban leasehold land sales: case studies: Papakura commercial leaseholders. New Zealand Valuer, 24(3) September 1979 pp167-185.

Nigeria

1747 Knight Frank & Rutley. The Lagos office market. London, Knight Frank & Rutley Research, 1983.

Spain

1748 Richard Ellis. Barcelona office market 1982/83. London, Richard Ellis, 1983.

United States

Regular surveys appear in the same resources as for industrial property.

1749 '83 office leasing sets record: Dallas heads list. Appraiser, 40(5) May 1984 pp4-5.

1750 Austin, Gene. Philadelphia: commercial building expected to drag. National Real Estate Investor, 21 February 1979 p40.

1751 Barker, R. Commercial leasing market Washington. The Valuer.(Australia) 28(2) April 1984 pp126-127.

1752 Battle, Bob and others. Business park trends. National Real Estate Investor, 26(12) 1984 pp104-156.

1753 Bergsman, S. The Denver office market: soft or overbuilt? Barrons, 64 20 August 1984 pp56-57.

1754 Bergsman, S. The ground floor. Barron's, 64(34) 20 August 1984 pp56-57.

1755 Brennan, Robert F. Cleveland: offices continue, brokers optimistic about filling space. National Real Estate Investor, 24 November 1982 pp109-110+ .

1756 Coldwell Banker. United States office vacancy index. London, Coldwell, Banker, quarterly.

1757 Derven, Ronald. The Northeast: scene is improving as economy keeps picking up steam. National Real Estate Investor, 25 October 1983 pp86+ .

1758 Dole, Charles E. Boston: cash box loosens and office space demands grow large. National Real Estate Investor, 25 February 1983 p36+.

1759 Dole, Charles E. Boston: healthy climate prevails as office vacancies remain low; hotel building boom continues, and financing is plentiful. National Real Estate Investor, 25(11) October 1983 pp257-270, 290-292, 372.

1760 Dole, Charles E. Boston: observers fear 1983-84 may bring office space glut. National Real Estate Investor, 24 June 1982 p36+.

1761 End of the office boom. Business Week, 4 October 1982 pp94-98.

1762 Ginsberg, B. The coming collapse in Manhattan commercial rentals. Real Estate Review, 12 Fall 1982 pp24-26.

1763 W Greenwell & Co. The New York office market. New York, W Greenwell, no date.

1764 Hemmerick, Steve. 'Overpricing' sparks dispute. Pensions and Investment Age, 12(21) 15 October 1984 pp51,54.

1765 Isaacs, Charles S. The effects of foreign ownership on American office leases. Journal of Property Management. 45(6) November/December 1981 pp315-319.

1766 Jones Lang Wootton. Downtown Manhattan office building market analysis. New York, Jones Lang Wootton, 1980/1.

1767 Jones Lang Wootton. Office building markets in the United States and in three United States cities: New York, Los Angeles, and Houston. New York, Jones Lang Wootton, 1980 - . (irregular)

1768 Karsian, Dillon. North Jersey strong office market, meadowlands projects foster hope for broader recovery and controlled growth during 1977. National Real Estate Investor, 19 January 1977 pp55-56.

1769 Kevenides, Herve. Office market: ascertain economic forces affecting office demand to provide framework for development decisions. National Real Estate Investor, 26(10) September 1984 pp80, 89-92 196-198.

1770 Kinchen, D. M. Los Angeles: apartment, office markets exhibit contrasting styles. National Real Estate Investor, 18 November 1976 pp41-42.

1771 Kroll, Cynthia. Employment growth and office space along the 680 corridor: booming supply and potential demand in a suburban area. Berkeley, Cal., University of California, Institute of Business and Economic Research, 1984.

1772 Levy, R. Commercial rents: the sky's the limit. Dun's Review, 117(6) June 1981 pp42-45, 49-50.

1773 Lewis, S. E. Levy: office development offers great opportunities. National Real Estate Investor, 23 June 1981 pp58+ .

1774 Lovejoy, G. M. Funding commercial development. Valuer(Australia), 28(3) July 1984 pp211-225.

1775 Lyst, John. Indianapolis: increasing demand observed for office and industrial space. National Real Estate Investor, 19 May 1977 pp85-86.

1776 Meagher, J. P. Area forecasts: global office rents. Barrons, 62 15 February 1982 pp16+ .

1777 Meagher, J. P. Office glut? a time to build. Barrons, 62 11 October 1982 pp16+ .

1778 Nelson, Kristin. San Francisco office space inventory. Berkeley, Cal., University of California, Institute of Business and Economic Research, 1980.

1779 New England office space: what's available, where and for how much. New England Business, 5(2) 7 February 1983 pp28-31.

1780 New realities: a survey of the commercial real estate market in the United States. Economist, 278 7 February 1981 supplement p3+.

1781 Nicholson, S. New York: office absorption leads mild revival for coming year. National Real Estate Investor, 19 February 1977 pp34-35.

1782 Nilges, D. Leasing office space in a competitive market. Journal of

Property Management, 77 October 1983 pp72-73.
1783 Now office buildings are going condo. Business Week, 2865 22 October 1984 pp141.
1784 Office parks are lush market. Engineering News Record, 213(9) 30 August 1984 pp28-29.
1785 Office space survey 1982. Buildings, 76 January 1982 pp56-59. (annual)
1786 Overbuilding is not permanent but part of a cycle. National Real Estate Investor, 25 July 1983 pp23+ .
1787 Parker, Joel. The outlook for commercial real estate in the Southeast. Economic Review(Federal Reserve Bank of Atlanta), 69(8) September 1984 pp30-43.
1788 Peeks, E. Charleston, W. Va.: office space in very short supply, with no relief in sight. National Real Estate Investor, 19 December 1977 pp59-64.
1789 Roberts, J. The Midwest: tenant's market continues as norm due to over building. National Real Estate Investor, 25 October 1983 pp67-68.
1790 Ruehl, P. Baltimore: office space surplus affects downtown business district. National Real Estate Investor, 19 April 1977 pp59-60.
1791 Schultz, G. L. The West: softness remains but experts see room for growth. National Real Estate Investor, 25 October 1983 pp105-106.
1792 Spatter, Samuel L. and others. Office market outlook: tenants calling the shots in many cities. National Real Estate Investor, 25(6) June 1983 pp45-76.
1793 Speyer, Jerry I. Future of highrise office buildings. Journal of Property Management, 41 July 1976 pp191-193.
1794 Squeeze on office market profit continues. Buildings, 76 December 1982 pp56-57.
1795 Tamarkin, B. Forget the past, let's mortgage the future. Forbes, 127(6) 16 March 1981 pp33-34.
1796 Tschirchart, Don. Detroit: office and retail sectors overbuilt: construction slow. National Real Estate Investor, 8 November 1976 pp34-35.
1797 Tully, S. The bashful billionaires of Olympia and York. Fortune, 105(12) 14 June 1982 pp86-87, 89+ .
1798 Weiss, Gary. Towering trouble: office building vacancy rates rising sharply. Barron's, 65(20) 20 May 1985 pp26-30.
1799 Welch, Randy. Denver: developers hesitant to start projects as office market cools. National Real Estate Investor, 25 February 1983 pp58+ .
1800 Whitley, T. Richmond: area sees commercial building boom in first half of the year; developers begin to view it as secondary growth market. National Real Estate Investor, 26(8) July 1984 pp109-110, 112+ .
1801 Willmann, John B. Washington D. C.: office and apartment markets very tight. National Real Estate Investor, 19 June 1977 pp69-70.
1802 Willmann, John B. Washington D. C.: office leasing escapes doldrums of election year. National Real Estate Investor, 18 November 1976 pp37-38.
1803 Wilmore, E. and others. Office market review. National Real Estate Investor, 23(6) June 1981 pp39-56.

Retail property

In addition to the studies of the market and property trends in the real estate press, quarterly and annually, the many studies of the Unit for Retail Planning Information in the United Kingdom provide valuable background studies assisting with the location of comparables. The Urban Land Institute provide some similar information for the United States.

1804 Alexander, Alan. Evaluating the first-time retail tenant. Journal of Property Management, 46(5) September/October 1982 pp38+ .

1805 Alexander, Alan. Leasing opportunities in the full shopping center. Journal of Property Management, 49(1) January/February 1984 pp12+ .

1806 Analysis of shop rents. Estates Gazette, 269(6169) 28 January 1984 p333.

1807 Antill, L. The shopping centre. Estates Gazette, 268(6158) 29 October 1983 pp428,430,432,434.

1808 Beddington, N. Design for shopping centres. London, Butterworth Design Services, 1982.

1809 Bershad, L. Why public developers face extinction. Chain Store Age Executive, 55 May 1979 pp27-30.

1810 Brueggeman, W. B. and others. Federal income taxes, inflation and holding periods for income-producing property. American Real Estate and Urban Economics Association Journal, 9 Summer 1981 pp148-164.

1811 Cars, drivers and parking. The Fitch & Company Shopping Centre Consortium Shopping Centre Report, 5 Autumn 1984 p4.

1812 Cunnew, T. Swollen European real estate bubble bursts. National Real Estate Investor, 25 March 1983 p32.

1813 Darlow, Clive and Embling, J. 'Off-price' brings new life to old centres. Estates Gazette, 271(6202) 15 September 1984 pp956,960,962.

1814 Davis, J. M. and Wyndelts, R. W. Component depreciation for a shopping center. Appraisal Journal, 47 April 1979 pp204-217.

1815 Debenham Tewson & Chinnocks. Shop rents and rates 1978-1983. London, Debenham Tewson & Chinnocks, 1983.

1816 Farber, L. L. Checks and balances make shopping centers attractive investments. Mortgage Banker, 38 December 1977 pp34-37.

1817 Graham, M. L. Shop rental analysis. New Zealand Valuer, 25(5) March 1983 pp244-246.

1818 Guy, Clifford M. The estimation of retail turnover for planning purposes. Planner, 70(5) May 1984 pp12-14.

1819 Harris, M. Investment in shops. London, Strutt & Parker, 1979. (Property trends 2)

1820 Harris, M. and Heselgrave, A. P. W. Retail property: a good investment London, Strutt & Parker, 1982. (Property trends 8)

1821 Hillier Parker May & Rowden. The effect of town centre size on shop rental growth. London, Financial Times Business Publications, 1979. (ICHP Index Research Report no.3)
1822 Hillier Parker May & Rowden. The relationship between shop rents and town centre size. London, Financial Times Business Publications, 1979. (ICHP Index Research Report no.4)
1823 Hillier Parker May & Rowden. Secondary shop rent index. London, Financial Times Business Publications, 1984. (ICHP Index Research Report no.6)
1824 Jensen, S. A. Valuing a real estate brokerage. Real Estate Today, 11 September 1978 pp42-46.
1825 Luedes, D. R. A current view of automobile dealership facilities. Real Estate Appraiser and Analyst, 49(2) 1983 pp55-60.
1826 Lyons, R. Rent reviews in shopping developments - II. Estates Gazette, 271(6198) 18 August 1984 pp602,604,608. (No I by Marples)
1827 McKenzie, R. Sites for supermarkets. Retail Britain, 1 January 1984 pp6-7.
1828 McTigue, S. Regional shopping plazas. The Valuer(Australia), 28(3) July 1984 pp164-169.
1829 Marples, J. Rent reviews in shopping developments - I. Estates Gazette, 271(6197) 11 August 1984 pp515-516, 519. (No II by Lyons) (Also published as Blundell lectures 1984 by Surveyor's Publications, 1984, for the Royal Institution of Chartered Surveyors)
1830 Martin, P. G. Shopping centre management. London, E. & F. N. Spon, 1982.
1831 Muller, T. The fiscal impact of regional malls on central business districts in small cities. Washington, D.C., Urban Land Institute, 1978. (Prepared for the Economic Development Administration, U.S. Bureau of Commerce)
1832 Netting, Roger. Shopping development research. in Chiddick, David and Millington, Alan. eds. Land management: new directions. London, Spon, 1984. pp189-197.
1833 North, L. W. Current problems in the valuation of shopping centres. AIM, 19 1975 pp39-42.
1834 Northern, R. Ian. Shopping centre development. Reading, University of Reading, College of Estate Management, 1984. (Property Development Library Vol. 2)
1835 Northern, R. Ian and Haskell, Michael. Shopping centres: a developer's guide to planning and design. Reading, University of Reading, College of Estate Management, 1977.
1836 Patricios, N. N. Human aspects of planning shopping centers. Environment and Behaviour, December 1979 pp511-538.
1837 Paul, Barry. Future of shopping centres. Valuer(Australia), 27 October 1982 pp388-392.
1838 Peiser, Richard B. and Andrus, S. G. Phasing of income-producing real estate. Interfaces, 13 October1983 pp1-9.
1839 Royal Institution of Chartered Surveyors, General Practice Division. The retailing revolution. One day conference, 13 December 1984. London, Surveyor's Technical Service, 1984.
1840 Rubenstein, J. L. and Brooks, R. A. Two shopping centers - a comparison. Real Estate Today, 15 March 1982 pp13-17.
1841 Ruttenberg, Roger. Management's role in shopping center renovation. Journal of Property Management, 46(6) November/December 1982 pp38+.
1842 Ryan, Frank E. and Muhlebach, Richard F. The retail tenant in the office building. Journal of Property Management, 46(2) March/April 1982 pp18+ .
1843 Schiller, R. Shopping trends as they affect the investor. Estates

Gazette, 267(6145) 30 July 1983 pp420-422.

1844 Shopping center outlook: small centers lead the way as activity picks up. *National Real Estate Investor*, 20 May 1978 pp38-40.

1845 Siegelaub, H. and Meistrich, H. A. How professional shopping center developer obtains a mortgage. *Real Estate Review*, 9 Sprin 1979 pp50-58.

1846 Stambaugh, D. Evolution of a shopping center lease. *Real Estate Today*, 11 August 1978 pp20.

1847 Stambaugh, D. Regional mall from the ground up. *Real Estate Today*, 11 August 1978 pp24-28.

1848 Taking the mall approach to outdoor centers. *Chain Store Age Executive* 59 October 1983 pp68-69.

1849 Tomlinson, Wayne E. Strip-style shopping centers: problems and opportunities. *Journal of Property Management*, 44(6) November/December 1979 pp298-300.

1850 Trippi, R. R. and Spiegel, R.J. Computer assisted appraisal of the regional shopping mall. *Real Estate Appraiser and Analyst*, 44 September 1978 pp23-27.

1851 Unit for Retail Planning Information. *Hypermarkets and superstores bibliography*. 6th edition. Reading, Unit for Retail Planning Information, 1980. (Bibliography 2) (Updated by Information sheet 1 and Supplement 1)

1852 Unit for Retail Planning Information. *Manage shopping centres: a bibliography*. Reading, Unit for Retail Planning Information, 1979. (Bibliography 4) (Updated by Information sheet 12: Studies of managed shopping schemes. 1983)

1853 Unit for Retail Planning Information. *Retail planning methods bibliography*. Reading, Unit for Retail Planning Information, 1980. (Bibliography 5)

1854 Unit for Retail Planning Information. *Retailer's costs: rents as a percentage of turnover*. Reading, Unit for Retail Planning Information, 1978. (Information brief 78/9)

1855 Unit for Retail Planning Information. *Shopping centre turnover to floorspace ratios: variations between the 1971 Census of Distribution major centres*. Reading, Unit for Retail Planning Information, 1979. (Information brief 79/4)

1856 Unit for Retail Planning Information. *Small shops and local shopping bibliography*. 4th edition. Reading, Unit for Retail Planning Information, 1978. (Bibliography 3)

1857 Unit for Retail Planning Information. *Trading characteristics of retail warehouse operators*. Reading, Unit for Retail Planning Information, 1982. (Publication U 23)

1858 Unit for Retail Planning Information. *Turnover to floorspace ratios of leading retail companies*. Reading, Unit for Retail Planning Information, 1979. (Information brief 79/5)

1859 University of Reading, College of Estate Management, Centre for Land Use Studies. *Shopping centres*. Reading, University of Reading, College of Estate Management, Centre for Advanced Land Use Studies, 1977.

1860 University of Reading, College of Estate Management, Centre for Land Use Studies. *Shops for shopkeepers - tenant's requirements in modern shopping development*. Reading, University of Reading, College of Estate Management, Centre for Advanced Land Use Studies, 1977.

1861 Zavislake, R. J. and Jackson, A. J. P. The problems of food stores locations. *AIM*, 22(3) 1978 pp11-13.

Retail property

Australia

1862 Heydon, G. Valuation of small shopping centres. Valuer(Australia), 23(4) October 1974 pp284-291.

Canada

1863 Ircha, Michael C. Shopping centres: their development and impact in Atlantic Canada. Plan Canada, 22(2) December 1982 pp35-44.

Great Britain

1864 Crock of gold in Britain's High Streets. Economist, 271 7 April 1979 pp111-112.

1865 Davies, Ross L. and Bennison, David L. British town centre shopping schemes: a statistical digest. Reading, Unit for Retail Planning Information, 1979.

1866 Debenham Tewson & Chinnocks. Shop rents and rates, 1978-1983. London, Debenham Tewson & Chinnocks, 1982.

1867 Donaldsons & Sons. Shopping centre data. London, Donaldsons & Sons, 1977. (Research notes)

1868 Drivers Jonas. City of Bath shopping study 1977. London, Drivers Jonas, 1978.

1869 Guy, Clifford M. Retail location and retail planning in Britain. London, Gower, 1980.

1870 H & B take prime shop yields down. Estates Gazette, 267(6151) 10 September 1983 p914.

1871 Hillier Parker May & Rowden. British shopping developments 1965-1982. London, Hillier Parker May & Rowden, 1983. (annual supplements 1983-1984)

1872 Hillier Parker May & Rowden. Central London shops survey. London, Hillier Parker May & Rowden, 1979 and 1983.

1873 Hillier Parker May & Rowden. A forecast of shop rents. Journal of Valuation, 2(4) 1984 pp312-320. (Reproduced in full)

1874 Hillier Parker May & Rowden. Hypermarket impact study. London, Hillier Parker May & Rowden, 1979. (Neasden, Brent)

1875 Hillier Parker May & Rowden. London Docklands Development Corporation: report on shopping. London, Hillier Parker May & Rowden, 1983.

1876 Hillier Parker May & Rowden. Survey of Building Society branches. London, Hillier Parker May & Rowden, 1976 - . (annual)

1877 Hillier Parker Research. Multiple shop branch numbers February 1981. London, Hillier Parker May & Rowden, 1981.

1878 Jones Lang Wootton. Property investment in supermarkets and superstores. London, Jones Lang Wootton, 1977.

1879 Lambert Smith & Partners. Supermarket, superstores and retail warehouses, rents and investment, February 1983. London, Lambert Smith & Partners, 1983.

1880 Lee, Michael. Brent Cross study. London, Donaldsons & Sons, 1977. (Research report no. 4)

1881 Lee, Michael, Jones, Peter & Leach, Catriona. Caerphilly hypermarket study. London, Donaldson & Sons, 1973.

1882 Lee, Michael, Jones,Peter, & Leach, Catriona. Caerphilly hypermarket study. Year 2. London, Donaldsons & Sons, 1975.

1883 Lee, Michael & Kent, Elizabeth. Caerphilly hypermarket study. Year 5. London, Donaldsons & Sons, 1979. (Research report no.6)

1884 Osborne King & Megram. Movements of prime shop rental values in Belfast. Belfast, Osborne King & Megram, no date.

1885 Palser, B. Fast food beefing up rents. Property Business, 3 1984 pp18,20.

1886 Parker, Anthony. Planned shopping developments. Estates Gazette,

272(6206) 13 October 1984 pp131, 134-136.
1887 Penfold, D. DIY keeps booming. Estates Gazette, 269(6177) 24 March 1984 p1093.
1888 Property Agents International. Property: the UK office, factory and warehouse directory including UK shops directory. london, Property Agents International, 1984/5 - . (quarterly)
1889 Retail world. Property Business, regular feature in each issue.
1890 Schiller, R. Shop rents. Shop property, July 1983 pp12-13.
1891 Strohm, P. Tesco say shops can help. Estates Gazette, 269(6168) 21 January 1984 p181. (Paper submitted to the House of Commons Environment Committee 1984)
1892 Unit for Retail Planning Information. List of UK hypermarkets and superstores. Reading, Unit for Retail Planning Information, annual.
1893 Unit for Retail Planning Information. Register of managed shopping schemes. Reading, Unit for Retail Planning Information, 1980. (Publication P3: lists developers in Appendix)
1894 Unit for Retail Planning Information. Retail trends and developments. Reading, Unit for Retail Planning Information, 1978. (Information brief 78/7)
1895 Unit for Retail Planning Information. Retailing in the inner cities: report of two URPI workshops. Reading, Unit for Retail Planning Information, 1980. (Publication U18)
1896 The UK shop property market. Vickers da Costa Ltd's Property Quarterly Review, 11 February 1979 pp16-26.
1897 Wilson, J. Retail warehousing in Greater London. Estates Gazette, 272(6207) 20 October 1984 pp244-246.

Hong Kong

1898 Takada, Hishashi. Vertical utilisation of land in a subcentre of Tokyo high-rise buildings and the underground shopping malls in Shinjuku. Valuer(Australia), 27 January 1982 pp43-55.

Singapore

1899 Jones Lang Wootton. Talking shop - Quarterly newsletter on the retail market. London, Jones Lang Wootton, no dates.

United States

1900 Haymes, Alan. Real estate dealing: the rise and fall of an urban mall. Real Estate Review, 6 Winter 1977 pp16-17.
1901 Monroe, L. K. Shopping center forecast 1984. Buildings, 78 January 1984 pp54-55.
1902 Shopping center development to change in '80s. National Real Estate Investor, 26 May 1984 pp38+ .
1903 Shopping center industry: a middle aged giant. Buildings, 73 January 1979 pp69-72.
1904 Shopping center outlook: modest gains seen as recovery begins. National Real Estate Investor, 25 May 1983 pp37-62.
1905 Shopping center outlook: ringing registers bring music to developer's ears. National Real Estate Investor, 21 May 1979 pp39-58.
1906 Urban Land Institute. Dollars and cents of shopping centers: a study of receipts and expenses, prepared under the auspices of the Shopping Center Study Committee of the Community Builders Council of the Urban Land Institute. Washington, D.C., Urban Land Institute, date uncertain.

Residential property

Surveys of the markets in particular locations are numerous and usually to be found in the sources already given for industrial and commercial property. However so many studies of housing mobility, development and prices have been made that it is impossible to list everything. Those that are listed here represent a selection closely related to the valuation of residential property. Housing bibliographies should be consulted for other aspects of the housing market. The geographical subdivisions have not been used where articles discuss a principle in relation to case studies, only where the whole item relates only to that area. Sub-sections have been defined only for distinct categories of residential property having sufficient literature of their own. These are: apartments, residential homes, i.e. for the elderly and nursing homes, mobile homes, hotels, motels and restaurants.

1907 Abelson, P. W. A study of property valuations in relation to market prices and the characteristics of properties. *Economic Record*, 55(151) 1979 pp328-338.

1908 Alberts, W. W. and Kerr, H. S. Rate of return from investing in single -family housing. *Land Economics*, 57 May 1981 pp230-242.

1909 Alcaly, Roger E. Transportation and urban land values: a review of the theoretical literature. *Land Economics*, 52 February 1976 pp42-53.

1910 Allen, Patrick. *Shared ownership: a stepping stone to home ownership: report on a survey of local authority shared ownership schemes*. London, H.M.S.O., 1982.

1911 American Institute of Real Estate Appraisers. *Appraising the single family residence*. See Bloom, G. F. and Harrison, H. S.

1912 Amies, F. A. Dwelling house valuations on rental value. *Rating and Valuation Reporter*, 18(4) April 1978 pp93-94.

1913 Amies, F. A. House assessments in the green paper. *Rating and Valuation Reporter*, 17(5) May 1977 p117.

1914 Anas, A. *Residential location markets and urban transportation: econmic theory, econometrics, and policy analysis with discrete choice models*. New York, Academic Press, 1982.

1915 Anderson, P. and Smith, A. The private housing developer. *Planner*, 65 March 1979 pp49-51.

1916 Andreassi, Michael and others. *The impact of residential energy conservation standards on households*. Washington, D.C., Urban Institute, 1980. (Report 1344-05:HUD-0001661)(Sponsored by United States Department of Housing and Urban Development, Office of Policy Development and Research)

1917 App, F. J. Appraising for the employee relocation company. Real Estate Appraiser and Analyst, 45 January 1979 pp5-12.
1918 Armfield, W. A. Investment in subsidized housing: opportunities and risks. New York, Pilot Books, 1979.
1919 Arthur, F. and Janssen, C.T.L. Estimating selling prices of homes. AIM, 24(4) November 1980 pp28-32. (Bibliography)
1920 Bandyopadhyay, J. K. and B. Algorithm for setting the list price of a residential real estate property. Interfaces, 1981 pp55-61.
1921 Barcal, J. and Sliskovich, J. V. Considerations in allocating residential real property in a three-trust estate plan. Journal of Taxation, 59 August 1983 pp90-93.
1922 Barnes, M. N. Strategy for residential rehabilitation. Real Estate Review, 6 Fall 1976 pp40-45.
1923 Barrow, M. M. and O'Sullivan, A. J. The empirical determination of house prices, error correction mechanisms and the correction of errors. Urban Studies, 21(1) February 1984 pp89-92.
1924 Bartlein, R. H. Income tax and home sales. Real Estate Today, 14 April 1981 pp14-17.
1925 Bassett, K. and Stout, J. R. Housing and residential structure: alternative approaches. London and Boston, Routledge Kegan Paul, 1980.
1926 Bather, N. J. The speculative residential developer and urban growth. Reading, University of Reading, Department of Geography, 1976. (Geographical papers 47)
1927 Bednarz, R. S. The effect of air pollution on property value in Chicago. Chicago, University of Chicago, Department of Geography, 1975.
1928 Belkin, J. and others. Empirical study of time on market using multidimensional segmentation of housing markets. American Real Estate and Urban Economics Association Journal, 4 Fall 1976 pp57-75.
1929 Benedict, J. F. Effect of a swimming pool on single-family home. Appraisal Journal, 49(3) July 1981 pp376-381.
1930 Berry, B. J. Ghetto expansion and single-family housing prices: Chicago 1968-1972. Journal of Urban Economics, 3 October 1976 pp397-423. (Bibliography pp420-423)
1931 Bible, Douglas S. Measuring dwelling unit and neighborhood attribute importance. Real Estate Appraiser and Analyst, 45 January 1979 pp32-34.
1932 Bible, Douglas S. and Crunkleton, J. R. The effects of financing on the sale of multi-family properties. Real Estate Appraiser and Analyst, 49 Summer 1983 pp33-37.
1933 Birks, K. Stuart. Money supply changes and movements in urban house property prices. New Zealand Valuer, 25(11) September 1984 pp657-659.
1934 Bisset, R. Quantification, decision-making and environmental impact assessment in the U. K. Journal of Environmental Management, 7 1978 pp43-58.
1935 Bissonet, W. L. Residential exchange: another tool to use. Real Estate Today, 14 May 1981 pp41-44.
1936 Bjornstad, David J. and Vogt, David P. Some comments relating to model specification on "Effects of nuclear power plants on residential property values". Journal of Regional Science, 24(1) 1984 pp135-136. (Answer to Gamble and Downing, no. 2027, followed by their response pp137-138)
1937 Blinder, C. L. Effect of overhead transmission lines on residential property values. Laurel, Md., Johns Hopkins University Press, 1983. (Report no PPSP/JHU/PPSE-T-19)
1938 Bloom, G. F. and Harrison, H. S. Appraising the single family residence. Chicago, American Institute of Real Estate Appraisers, 1978,

1980 and 1982.
1939 Boleat, Mark. Economic factors affecting house prices. Valuer(ISVA), 52(7) August/September 1983 pp194-195.
1940 Boren, Patricia. Codebook for the survey of residential buildings, Site 1, Wave 2. Housing assistance supply experiment. Santa Monica, Cal., Rand Corporation, 1979. (Data for market value)
1941 Bowcock, Philip. Capital values for dwelling houses. Rating and Valuation, June 1981 pp173-175.
1942 Boyce, D. E. and Allen, W. B. Impact of high speed rapid transit facility on residential property values. High Speed Ground Transportation Journal, 8(2) 1974 pp54-60.
1943 Boyle, C. An expert system for valuation of residential properties. Journal of Valuation, 2(3) 1984 pp271-286.
1944 Bradley, D. M. Appraising the brownstones of Manhattan. Appraisal Journal, 47 April 1979 pp176-184.
1945 Braitman, H. L. and Stine, J. B. Playing the odds: condo conversion profit vs. capital gains treatment. Real Estate Review, 11 Summer 1981 pp58-63.
1946 Brody, M. Critical appraisal. Barron's, 63(48) 28 November 1983 pp24-26.
1947 Bromley, D. W. Property rules, liability rules, and environmenal economics. Journal pf Environmental Issues, 12(1) March 1978 pp43-59.
1948 Brown, P. M. Financing our future houses. New Zealand Valuer, 24(5) March 1980 pp325-343.
1949 Buchanan, S. and Weber, W. A. Growth and residential property taxes: a model for estimating direct and indirect population impacts. Land Economics, 58 August 1982 pp324-337.
1950 Buck, G. H. Case for the planned unit residential development. Real Estate Review, 6 Summer 1976 pp104-107.
1951 Byrne, C. R. Housing prices: an urban model approach. Valuer(Australia), 26 July 1980 pp204-208.
1952 Byrne, C. R. Interest rate movements: how to forecast and evaluate. Valuer(Australia), 26 July 1981 pp556-562.
1953 Byron, R. The building society valuer: including the survey and valuation of houses and flats for owner occupation. London, Estates Gazette, 1979.
1954 Cahn, J. G. Small townhouse projects sell big in inner city. Housing, 53 February 1978 pp56-65.
1955 Cahn, J. G. What attached-home shoppers want. House and Home, 52 September 1977 pp78-81.
1956 Cahn, J. G. What single-family buyers are looking for. House and Home, 52 July 1977 pp77-79.
1957 Cahn, J. G. and Vollman, J. R. Single-family scene: it's time to home in on your markets. House and Home, 52 October 1977 pp58-75.
1958 Calvan, Rita A. Are property values and taxes affected by the home conversion phenomenon? Realtor, 61(11) 1984 pp17-19.
1959 Cantrell, W. F. Scenic easements: evaluation considerations. Real Estate Appraiser and Analyst, 49(2) 1983 pp61-67.
1960 Cantrell, W. F. and others. Noise, we have heard it before. Real Estate Appraiser and Analyst, 49 Fall 1983 pp51-56. (Highways)
1961 Cardew, R. V. House lot speculation is consumer-led. Royal Australian Planning Institute Journal, 15(3) 1977 pp85-86.
1962 Carmon, Edward C. and Smith, David A. Rental housing in the eighties: a demographic analysis and prognosis for the future. Real Estate Issues, 9(1) 1984 pp1-5.
1963 Carpenter, M. D. and others. Selecting the optimal method of depreciation for new residential rental property. Journal of Taxation,

55 August 1981 pp94-98.
1964 Cebula, R. J. Analysis of the impact of property taxation on human migration in the United States. Review of Business and Economic Research, 13 Winter 1977-78 pp85-94.
1965 Chais, Richard and Felder, Joseph. Procedures to estimate airport residential relocation costs. Silver Spring, Md., Ori Inc, 1981. (Sponsored by Environmental Protection Agency, Washington, D.C.)
1966 Changing American family and its effects on real estate. Real Estate Today, 14 November/December 1981 pp52-55.
1967 Cho, C. and Reighert, A. K. Application of multiple regression analysis for appraising single-family housing values. Business Economics, 15 January 1980 pp47-52.
1968 Chok, W. Y. An appraisal of the relative costs of renting versus owning a home. New Zealand Valuer, 24(12) December 1981 pp969-998. (Bibliography)
1969 Chrystal-Smith, G. House-building prices based on floor area. Building Trades Journal, 175(5241) 17 March 1978 pp26-28.
1970 Church, Albert M. Effects of local government expenditure and property taxes on investment. American Real Estate and Urban Economics Association Journal, 9 Summer 1981 pp165-180.
1971 Cirz, Raymond T. Valuation and condominium conversion. Appraisal Journal, 50(1) January 1982 pp43-56.
1972 Clark, A. V. and Heskin, A. D. The impact of rent control on tenure discounts and residential mobility. Land Economics, 58(1) 1982 pp109-117.
1973 Cochrane, Harold C., Revier, Charles and Nakagawa, Takayoshi. Impact of disasters on construction costs. Fort Collins, Colo., Colorado State University, Department of Economics, 1978. (Sponsored by National Science Foundation, Washington, D.C. Report NSF/RA-780480)
1974 Cohen, Arthur C. Appraising converted lofts. Real Estate Review, 12(1) 1982 pp83-87,
1975 Cohen Arthur C. Appraising cooperative residences. Real Estate Review, 9 Fall 1979 pp90-93.
1976 Coleman, D. and Noxon, C. Effects of accelerated cost recovery on condo investment. Real Estate Review, 12 Fall 1982 pp100-105.
1977 Colwell, Peter F. and Foley, K. W. Electric transmission lines and the selling price of residential property. Appraisal Journal, 47 October 1979 pp490-499.
1978 Combining forecasts to predict property values for single-family residences. Land Economics, 54 November 1978 pp524-430.
1979 Corgel, J. B. and Smith, H. C. The concept and estimation of economic life in the residential appraisal process. Chicago, Society of Real Estate Appraisers Foundation, 1981.
1980 Corgel, J. B. and others. Measuring energy efficiency for selection and adjustment of comparable sales. Appraisal Journal, 50(1) January 1982 pp71-78.
1981 Correll, M. R. and others. Effects of greenbelts on residential property values: some findings on the political economy of open space. Land Economics, 54 May 1978 pp207-217.
1982 Coyne, Thomas J. and others. Residential real estate versus financial assets. Journal of Portfolio Management, 7(1) 1980 pp20-24.
1983 Crockett, J. H. Price competition for residential brokerage. Real Estate Review, 13 Winter 1984 pp98-101.
1984 Cronin, F. J. Market structure and the price of housing services. Urban Studies, 20(3) 1983 pp365-376.
1985 Cullingworth, J. B. A bibliography of rent control. Toronto, Univ- of Toronto, Centre for Urban and Community Studies, 1982. (Not

intended to be comprehensive, additions to literature)

1986 Curcio, Richard J. and others. Bayesian regression procedures applied to the valuation of residential real estate. Real Estate Appraiser and Analyst, 47(4) 1981 pp46-48.

1987 Curley, A. J. and Guttentag, J. M. Value and yield risk on outstanding insured residential mortgages. Journal of Finance, 32 May 1977 pp403-312, 415.

1988 Dale-Johnson, David. Hedonic prices and price indexes in housing markets: the existing empirical evidence and proposed extensions. Berkeley, Cal., University of California, Institute of Business and Economic Research, 1979.

1989 Damm, D. Response of urban real estate values in anticipation of the Washington metro. Journal of Transport Economics and Policy, 14(3) 1980 pp315-336. (Bibliography)

1990 D'Arcy, B. E. Analysis of urban leasehold land sales. New Zealand Valuer, 24(3) September 1979 pp158-166, 133.

1991 De Lacy, P. B. Cash equivalency in residential appraising. Appraisal Journal, 51(1) 1983 pp81-88.

1992 DeLisle, James R. Residential appraisal: a behavioral approach to energy efficiency. Appraisal Journal, 52(1) January 1984 pp41-47.

1993 Derven, Ronald. Carrying the torch for distressed rehab. Buildings, 71 September 1977 pp56-59.

1994 Dewees, D. N. The effect of a subway on residential property values in Toronto. Journal of Urban Economics, 3(4) 1976 pp357-369. (Developed from a University of Toronto/University of York study of 1973)

1995 Diamond, D. B. Relationship between amenities and urban land prices. Land Economics, 56 February 1980 pp21-32.

1996 Diamond, D. B. and Tolley, G. S. The economics of urban amenities, New York, Academic Press, 1982.

1997 Doling, John. The identification of the determinants of house prices. Birmingham, University of Birmingham, Environmental Modelling and Survey Unit, 1978.

1998 Doling, John. The use of content analysis in identifying the determinants of house prices. Urban Studies, 15 1978 pp89-90.

1999 Dombal, R. W. Residential condominiums: a guide to analysis and appraisal. Chicago, American Institute of Real Estate Appraisers of the National Association of Realtors, 1976.

2000 Downs, Anthony. Investing in housing rehabilitation can be successful. Real Estate Review, 6(2) 1976 pp66-73.

2001 Duncan, G. J. and Morgan, J. N. Effects of inflation and taxes on the costs of home ownership. Journal of Consumer Affairs, 14 Winter 1980 pp383-393.

2002 Dusansky, R. and others. Impact of property taxation on housing value and rents. Journal of Urban Economics, 10 September 1981 pp241-255.

2003 Eckart, W. Land speculation and the rental price of housing. Journal of Urban Economics, 13 January 1983 pp1-21.

2004 Edwards, M. and Lovatt, D. Understanding urban land values: a review. London, Social Sciences Research Council, 1980. (Inner city in context 1)

2005 Effect of traffic on house values. Rating and Valuation Reporter, 16(3) March 1976 pp75-77.

2006 Ellson, Richard and Roberts, Blaine. Residential land development under uncertainty. Journal of Regional Science, 23(3) August 1983 pp309-323.

2007 Ellworth, D. G. and Dillingham, B. P. Condominium securities emerge as a financing and marketing form. Real Estate Review, 13 Spring

1983 pp60-67.
2008 Enns, D. Real estate, real assets and real wealth. AIM, 22(4) November 1978 pp8-10. (Also in Appraisal Journal, 48(4) October 1979 pp532-537.
2009 Evans, Alan W. The determination of the price of land. Urban Studies, 20(2) 1983 pp119-129.
2010 Falcke, C. O. Water quality and property prices: an econometric analysis of environmental benefits. Commentationes Scientorum Socialium 18 1982 pp1-189.
2011 Feagin, J. R. Urban real estate speculation in the United States: implications for social science and urban planning. International Journal of Urban and Regional Research, 6(1) 1982 pp35-60.
2012 Feinberg, I. ERTA: winning hand for rental housing. Mortgage Banker, 43 February 1983 pp44-49.
2013 Fenton, G. S. R. Single-unit to multi-unit residential use. New Zealand Valuer, 25(6) 1977 pp313-324.
2014 Fischel, W. A. Zoning and suburban housing costs: the effects of legal rights and government structure. Hanover, New Hampshire, Dartmouth College, Department of Economics, 1979. (Sponsored by United States, Department of Housing and Urban Development)
2015 Fletcher, D. R. Condominium sales and listings. Reston, Va., Reston, 1982.
2016 Foute, S. J. Appraising and underwriting the energy efficient home: the energy mortgage value method. Real Estate Appraiser and Analyst, 48 Spring 1982 pp5-9.
2017 Frederick, B. J. Effect of a swimming pool on single-family home value. Appraisal Journal, 49 July 1981 pp376-381.
2018 Freeman, M. Cooperative housing: an escalating market. Mortgage Banker, 43 October 1982 pp48-49.
2019 Fuerst, J. S. Valuing subsidized housing: the tax assessor's dilemma. Real Estate Review, 8 Fall 1978 pp90-93.
2020 Gabriel, Stuart A. and Wolch, Jennifer R. Local land-use regulation and urban housing values. Berkeley, Cal., University of California, Institute of Business and Economic Research, 1980. (Publication 80-18)
2021 Gaines, James. P. Residential rehabilitation appraisals: problems and prospects. Appraisal Journal, 48 April 1980 pp236-247.
2022 Galchus, K. E. Property values in an integrated neighborhood: some further evidence. Real Estate Appraiser and Analyst, 43 March 1977 pp17-21.
2023 Gallagher, D. D. Effect of financing terms on residential property values. Federal Home Loan and Bank Board Journal, 14 June 1981 pp20-21.
2024 Galloghy, F. D. A study of family decision-making regarding housing in a planned house development. New York, New York University Press, 1973.
2025 Gamble, H. B., Downing, Roger H. and Sauerlender, Owen H. Effects of nuclear power plants on residential property values: final-report. Washington, D. C., Nuclear Regulatory Commission, 1979. (NUREG/CR-0454)
2026 Gamble, H. B. and Downing, Roger H. Effects of the accident at Three Mile Island on residential property values and sales. University Park, Pa., Pennsylvania State University, Institute for Research on Land and Water Economics, 1981. (Sponsored by Nuclear Regulatory Commission, Washington, D. C.)
2027 Gamble, H. B. and Downing, Roger H. Effects of nuclear power plants on residential property values". Journal of Regional Science, 22

1982 pp457-458. (See no. 1936)
2028 Gamble, H. B. and others. Community growth around nuclear power plants American Real Estate and Urban Economics Association Journal, 8 Fall 1980 pp268-280.
2029 Gamble, H. B. and others. The influence of highway environmental effects on residential property values. University Park, Pa., Pennsylvania State University, 1974.
2030 Gamby, M. E. Marketing value and finance: urban property. New Zealand Valuer, 25(2) December 1984 pp692-699.
2031 Garrigan, R. T. Case for rising residential rents. Real Estate Review, 8 Fall 1978 pp36-41.
2032 Gau, George W. Taxonomic model for the risk-rating of residential mortgages. Journal of Business, 51 October 1978 pp687-706.
2033 Gerardi, N. How to spot a market upswing. Housing, 54 July 1978 pp72-77.
2034 Gerardi, N. and Vollman, J. R. Townhouses: targeting your markets. House and Home, 51 May 1977 pp60-73.
2035 Gibson, J. The interpretation of property price changes for a measure of the welfare benefits of pollution control: two simple models. Urban Studies, 13 1976 pp45-50.
2036 Glassman, S. A guide to residential management. Washington, D. C., National Association of Home Builders, 1978.
2037 Gold, S. D. Homeowner property taxes, inflation and property tax relief. National Tax Journal, 34 June 1981 pp167-184.
2038 Goldberg, M. A. and Ulinder, D. D. Residential developer behaviour 1975: additional empirical findings. Land Economics, 52 August 1976 pp563-570.
2039 Golub, K. L. Valuation of leased group homes. Appraisal Journal, 47 July 1979 pp325-331.
2040 Goodwin, G. E. Land for residential building sites. New Zealand Valuer, 24(7) September 1980 pp530-542.
2041 Gosney, J. Private means and public land shake hands on housing needs. Contract Journal(UK), 318(5446) 1 March 1984 pp16-17.
2042 Great Britain. Department of the Environment. The development brief: private residential development. London, H.M.S.O., 1976. (Development advice note 1)
2043 Great Britain. Department of the Environment. Residential density: in development briefs. London, H.M.S.O., 1976. (Development advice note 2)
2044 Great Britain. Law Commission. Who owns that house?: a question about titles and land. London, Law Commission, 1984.
2045 Greaves, M. The determinants of residential values: the hierarchical and statistical approaches. Journal of Valuation, 3(1) 1984 pp5-23.
2046 Grebler, L. and Mittelbach, F. M. The inflation of house prices, its extent, causes and consequences. Lexington, Ma., Lexington Books, 1979.
2047 Green, J. E. Real estate office desk book for appraising residential property. Englewood Clifs, N.J., Prentice-Hall, 1980.
2048 Guntermann, K. L. and Colwell, Peter F. Property values and accessibility to primary schools. Real Estate Appraiser and Analyst, 49 Spring 1983 pp62-68.
2049 Guy, R. The right to buy - in practice. Rating and Valuation, October 1982 pp269-274.
2050 Haase, R. O. Value of the house is inversely proportional to the size of the dog. Appraisal Journal, 47 July 1979 pp453-455.
2051 Hackett, D. W. and Darling, J. R. Comparison of consumer and realtor

attitudes regarding consumer issues affecting the housing industry. American Real Estate and Urban Economics Association Journal, 4 Fall 1976 pp91-99.

2052 Hale, C. G. Buying-down interest rates: new form of typical financing. Real Estate Appraiser and Analyst, 49(2) 1983 pp21-26.

2053 Hall, C. Turnaround opportunities in residential properties. Real Estate Review, 7 Winter 1978 pp66-67.

2054 Halstead, P. H. To be or not to be (a house): that is the question. Conveyancer and Property Lawyer, March/April 1984 pp121-129.

2055 Haney, R. L. Race and housing value: a review of their interrelationship. Appraisal Journal, 45 July 1977 pp356-364.

2056 Hanushek, J. A. and Quigley, J. M. Determinants of housing demand. in Henderson, J. Vernon. Research in Urban Economics, Vol.2 Greenwich, Conn., JAI Press, 1982. pp221-242.

2057 Hanushek, J. A. and Quigley, J. M. Dynamics of the housing market: a stock adjustment model of housing consumption. Journal of Urban Economics, 6 January 1979 pp90-111.

2058 Hanushek, J. A. and Quigley, J. M. What is the price elasticity of housing demand? Review of Economics and Statistics, 62(3) 1980 pp449-454.

2059 Harris, D. G. Real property depreciation and the homeowner. Taxes, 62 January 1984 pp54-64.

2060 Harris, J. P. and Sheehan, J. B. Land speculation. Valuer(Australia), 26 April 1980 pp126-128.

2061 Harrison, H. S. Residential appraiser. Real Estate Appraiser, 42 September 1976 pp55-56: November 1976 pp47-50: 43 January 1977 pp53-54.

2062 Haynes, K. E. A market-consumer model of residential property values: the airport noise-land-use problem. Environment and Planning A , 8 May 1976 pp271-287.

2063 Hemmer, Edgar H. Valuing the solar home. Real Estate Today, 11 October 1978 pp16-20.

2064 Hendershott, P. H. and Hu, S. Cheng. The allocation of capital between residential and nonresidential uses: taxes, inflation and capital market constraints. Journal of Finance, 38 June 1983 pp795-812.

2065 Hensler, Deborah and others. Codebook for the survey of residential buildings, Site II, Baseline. Housing assistance supply experiment. Santa Monica, Cal., Rand Corporation, 1977. (Working note)(see also Boren, Patricia)

2066 Hiban, A. W. and Derry. J. T. Ten biggest budgeting mistakes made by community associations. Journal of Property Management, 43 January 1978 pp33-35.

2067 Holsman, A. J. and Paparoulas, A. Impact of the eastern suburban railway on property prices in Edgecliff, New South Wales. Valuer (Australia), 27 July 1982 pp255-261.

2068 Hosp, M. M. Residential listing: an organized approach. Real Estate Today, 12 August 1979 pp53-56.

2069 Housel, John M. UFFI: a potential hazard in residential housing. Real Estate Appraiser and Analyst, 49(2) 1983 pp13-15. (urea-formaldehyde foam insulation)

2070 Housing demand index. House and Home, 52 November 1977 pp93-99; 53 January 1978 pp112-117; 53 April 1978 pp85-90.

2071 Hughes, M. Filtering process finds 'true' figures. Estates Times, 6 July 1984 p10.

2072 Ihlanfeldt, K. R. Property tax incidence on owner-occupied housing: evidence from the annual housing survey. National Tax Journal, 35 March 1982 pp89-97.

2073 International Association of Assessing Officers. Condominiums and cooperatives: appraisal and assessment. Chicago, International Association of Assessing Officers, 1981. (Bibliography series)
2074 Investors find a new home: small-town main streets. Business Week, 6 August 1984 pp71-72. (Renovation)
2075 Isaacson, A. L. and Segal, E. L. Rolling options for residential building lots. Real Estate Review, 9 Summer 1979 pp67-71.
2076 Jackson, F. S. Developer's guide to homeowner's associations. Real Estate Review, 7 Fall 1977 pp79-85.
2077 Jackson, J. R. and others. The measurement of land prices and the elasticity of substitution in housing production. Journal of Urban Economics, 16 July 1984 pp1-12.
2078 Jackson, R. D. Valuation of a life estate. Real Estate Appraiser and Analyst, 49 Summer 1983 pp47-49.
2079 Janssen, C. T. L. Regression analysis of homes. AIM, 22(2) April 1978 pp18-21.
2080 Janssen, C. T. L. and Talwar, P. P. Ridge estimates in house valuation models. Interfaces, 12 August 1982 pp120-127.
2081 Johnson, M. S. and Lea, M. J. Differential capitalization of local public service characteristics. Land Economics, 58(2) 1982 pp189-203.
2082 Jones, D. S. To sell the house first sell the school. Real Estate Today, 11 January 1978 pp34-36.
2083 Jud, G. Donald and Watts, James M. Schools and housing values. Land Economics, 57(3) August 1981 pp459-470.
2084 Kain, J. F. and Apgar, W. C. The modelling of housing change. Cambridge, Mass., Harvard University, Department of City and Regional Planning, 1977.
2085 Kamath, R. R. and Yantek, K. R. Linear and multiple regression analysis applied to valuation of single family homes. Real Estate Appraiser and Analyst, September/October 1979 pp36-41.
2086 Katz, Lawrence and Rosen, Kenneth. The effects of land-use controls on housing prices. Berkeley, Cal., University of California, Institute of Business and Economic Research, 1980.
2087 Katz, Lawrence and Rosen, Kenneth. The interjurisdictional effects of land-use controls on housing prices. Berkeley, Cal., University of California, Institute of Business and Economic Research, 1984.
2088 Kau, James B. and Sirmans, C. F. The demand for urban residential land. Journal of Regional Science, 21(4) November 1981 pp519-528.
2089 Kau, James B. and Sirmans, C. F. Urban land value functions and the price elasticity of demand for housing. Journal of Urban Economics, 6 January 1979 pp112-121.
2090 Kau, James B. and Sirmans, G. Stacey. Interest rates, inflation and specific bias in housing models. Berkeley, Cal., University of California, Institute of Business and Economic Research, 1984. (Publication 84-90)
2091 Kellough, W. R. Towards a methodology of valuation in urban renewal areas. Valuation, 25(3) November 1979 pp50-59.
2092 King, A. Thomas and MacRae, C. Duncan. Sectoral dynamics in urban housing: aa feasibility study. Washington, D.C., Urban Institute, 1978. (Sponsored by Department of Housing and Urban Development. Report HUD-0000775)
2093 Kirk, David S. and Smith, David A. Using the reversion/shelter approach to appraise subsidized housing. Appraisal Journal, 51(3) July 1983 pp326-345.
2094 Klepper, M. and others. Innovative financing for energy-efficient

improvements. Washington, D.C., Lane and Edson, 1982. (Sponsored by Departmentof Energy, Washington D.C., Report no. DOE/CS/22804-1)
2095 Koch, J. H. Profits from country property: how to select, buy, maintain and improve country property. New York, McGraw-Hill, 1981.
2096 Koch, J. H. Profits from small-town property. New York, Van Nostrand, 1984.
2097 Kohlepp, D. B. and Ingene, C. A. Effect of municipal services on local taxes on housing values. American Real Estate and Urban Economics Association Journal, 7 Fall 1979 pp318-343.
2098 Krantz, D. P. and others. Residential property tax capitalization: consistent estimates using micro-level data. Land Economics, 58 November 1982 pp488-496.
2099 Langley, C John. Adverse impacts of the Washington Beltway on residential property values. Land Economics, 52 February 1976 pp54-65.
2100 Laurenti, L. Property values and race. Westport, Conn., Greenwood, 1976.
2101 Levine, J. Houses and profits. Venture, 5 August 1983 pp30-33.
2102 Levine, M. B. Valuing a condominium conversion: the issue of tenant protection laws. Appraisal Journal, 51 July 1983 pp363-375.
2103 Lewis, Georgia. Marketing public housing. Journal of Property Management, 42(3) May/June 1977 pp121.
2104 Lewsley, C. Hereditaments with special facilities for disabled persons. Rating and Valuation Reporter, 19(1) January 1979 pp3-6; 19(2) February 1979 pp30-31; 19(3) March 1979 pp56-57; 19(4) April 1979 pp87-88.
2105 Linneman, P. Some empirical results on the nature of the hedonic price function for the urban housing market. Journal of Urban Economics, 8 July 1980 pp47-68.
2106 Lippman, W. J. Tax aspects of cooperative condominium conversion. Real Estate Review, 9 Winter 1980 pp39-45.
2107 Lipton, R. M. Handling the treatment of renting a former residence while awaiting its sale. Journal of Taxation, 58 March 1983 pp170-175.
2108 Little, D. M. Effect of the energy crisis on land value - city buildings. Valuer(Australia), 26 April 1981 pp458-461.
2109 Lockard, W. E. Historic zoning considerations in neighborhood and district analysis. Appraisal Journal, 51 October 1983 pp485-497.
2110 Longstreth, M. Conservation characteristics among determinants of residential property value. Journal of Consumer Research, 11 June 1984 pp564-571.
2111 Lucas, Andrew. Influence of Adelaide airport and associated jet aircraft noise on surrounding residential property values. Valuer(Australia), 27 July 1982 pp247-251.
2112 Lusht, Kenneth M. Inflation and real investment value. Real Estate Appraiser and Analyst, 45 November 1979 pp23-29.
2113 Lyons, P. J. Investing in residential real estate: a guide to increasing your income and profit. Reston, Va., Reston, 1981.
2114 McCraw, J. D. Factors affecting unstable land. New Zealand Valuer, 24(7) September 1980 pp524-529.
2115 McDougal,E. Appraising economically disadvantaged neighborhoods. Real Estate Appraiser and Analyst, 44 September 1978 p49.
2116 McFadyen, S. and Hobart, R. An alternative measurement of housing costs and the Consumer Price Index. AIM, 23(1) February 1979 pp14-17.
2117 McGrath, John C. Buy the home, lease the land. New England Business, 1(2) 1 February 1979 pp23-24.
2118 McGuire, C. C. Housing depreciation and optimal tax policy. National Tax Journal, 32 December 1979 pp371-379.

2119 McMillan, M. L., Bradford, G. R. and Gillem, D. W. Extension of the hedonic approach for estimating the value of quiet. Land Economics, 56(3) 1980 pp315-328.
2120 McPhee, K. Effect of the energy crisis on land values and real estate market. Valuer(Australia), 26 April 1981 pp471, 475.
2121 Manheim, U. Condohotels: promise versus performance. Real Estate Review, 7 Fall 1977 pp23-29.
2122 Marales, Dominic, Boyce, B. N. and Favretti, Rudy J. The contribution of trees to residential property value: Manchester, Connecticut. Valuation, 23(2) October/November 1976 pp26-343.
2123 Marcuse, P. The determinants of housing policy. New York, Columbia University, Graduate School of Architecture and Planning, 1980. (Papers in planning 22)
2124 Margo, A. Residential property - theory and practice. Valuer(ISVA), 50(2) 1981 pp42-43.
2125 Marks, D. The effect of rent controls on the price of rental housing. Land Economics, 60(1) 1984 pp81-94.
2126 Markusen, J. R. and Scheffman, D. The timing of residential land development: a general equilibrium approach. Journal of Urban Economics, 5 1978 pp411-424.
2127 Martin, J. K. Offering consulting services to self-managed community associations. Journal of Property Management, 48 1983 pp40-41.
2128 Mieskowski, P. and Saper, A. M. Estimate of the effects of airport noise on property values. Journal of Urban Economics, 5 October 1978 pp425-440.
2129 Miller, G. H. and Gilbeau, Kenneth W. Residential real estate appraisal: an introduction to real estate appraising. Englewood Cliffs, Prentice-Hall, 1980.
2130 Miller, J. A. Valuation of railroads - a decade of activity. Valuation 28(1) November 1982 pp14-25.
2131 Miller, K. An intertemporal cross-city comparison of single-family housing prices. Santa Barbara, Cal., University of California, Urban Ecnomics Program, 1977.
2132 Mills, David. Interdependencies and the urban land market. Journal of Urban Economics, 6 1979 pp1-11.
2133 Moreton, Peter. Insurance valuations. Valuer(ISVA), 53(9) November 1984 pp266-267.
2134 Moreton, R. Valuation of residential property for insurance purposes. Estates Gazette, 246(585) 3 June 1978 pp809-813.
2135 Mulligan, B. Suburban offices: how to cash in on a natural market for homebuilders. Housing, 56 Summer 1979 pp46-59.
2136 Mulligan, B. Survey: how buyers view key housing problems. House and Home, 52 October 1977 pp80-84.
2137 Nelson, J. P. Aircraft noise and the market for residential housing: empirical results for seven selected airports, University Park, Pa. Pennsylvania State University, 1978. (Sponsored by Department of Transportation, Washington, D.C., Report no. DOT/RSPA/DPB-50/78/24)
2138 Nelson, J. P. Residential choice, hedonic prices, and the demand for urban air quality. Journal of Urban Economics, 5 July 1978 pp357-369.
2139 Nelson, J. P. Three Mile Island and residential property values: empirical analysis and policy implications. Land Economics, 57 August 1981 pp363-372.
2140 Nicholls, D. C. and others. The risk business: developer's perceptions and prospects for house building in the inner city. Urban Studies, 19(4) November 1982 pp331-341.
2141 Nicholls, D. C. Valuation commentary. Rating and Valuation, January

1983 pp5-6.
2142 Noll, S. A. Residential solar home resale analysis. Los Alamos, N.M., Los Alamos Scientific Laboratory, 1980. (Report CONF-800604-15) (Sponsored by the United States, Department of Energy)
2143 Opelka, F. Gregory. Insulation exposes lenders, appraisers to legal challenges. Savings and Loan News, 104 March 1983 pp110-111.
2144 Opelka, F. Gregory. School closings open value problems. Savings and Loan News, 101 March 1980 pp96-97.
2145 Othick, F. A dwelling worth nothing? Local Government Chronicle, 21 July 1978 pp786-787.
2146 Oxley, Michael. Owner occupation in various European countries. in Chiddick, David and Millington, Alan. F. eds. Land management: new directions. London, Spon, 1984. pp144-151.
2147 Pennance, F. G. Residential building leases. AIM, 20(1) January 1976 pp16-18, 37-42.
2148 Pollakowski, H. O. Urban housing markets and residential location. Lexington, Mass., Lexington Books, and Aldershot, Gower, 1982.
2149 Pomerantz, W. How to tell if low-income housing rehabs make sense. Real Estate Review, 9 Winter 1980 pp87-90.
2150 Poon, L. C. L. Railway externalities and residential property prices. Land Economics, 54 May 1978 pp218-227.
2151 Quigley, J. M. Consumer choice of dwelling, neighborhood and public services. Berkeley, Cal., University of California, Institute of Business and Economic Research, 1984.
2152 Quigley, J. M. Residential energy standards and the housing market: a regional analysis. Berkeley, Cal., University of California, Institute of Business and Economic Research, 1984.
2153 Rabiega, William A., Lin, Ta-Win, and Robinson, Linda M. The property value impacts of public housing projects in low and moderate density residential neighbourhoods. Land Economics, 60(2) May 1984 pp174-179.
2154 Ragas, W. R. and Wyatt, J. M. Residential energy capitalization technique and single-family home underwriting. Real Estate Appraiser and Analyst, 44 March 1978 pp13-17.
2155 Ramsey, D. How to make $100,000 a year selling residential real estate. New York, Prentice-Hall, 1980.
2156 Rayner, Michael. Variables affecting house prices. in Chiddick, David and Millington, Alan. eds. Land management: new directions. London, Spon, 1984. pp108-117.
2157 Real Estate Research Corporation. Selling the solar home: some preliminary findings. Washington, D. C., U.S. Government Printing Office, 1978. (United States, Department of Housing and Urban Development, Solar Demonstration Program)
2158 Real Estate Research Corporation. Selling the solar home '80: market findings for the housing industry. Chicago, Real Estate Research Corporation, 1980.
2159 Reenstierna, E. T. Value spreads: the effects of occupancy, financing and buyer/seller motivations on most probable selling price. Real Estate Appraiser and Analyst, 49(2) 1983 pp39-43.
2160 Reiger, A. J. Appraising the sun: experience to date. Appraisal Journal, 48(2) April 1980 pp224-229.
2161 Residential investments: a guide through the maze. Property Letter, 282 January/February 1979 pp16-24.
2162 Resource allocation to housing investment: comments and further results. Economic Development and Cultural Change, 28 January 1980 pp389-399.
2163 Rhodes, C. A. The most desirable location in heaven? Real Estate and

Stock Journal, 47(1) March 1983 pp14, 16-17.
2164 Ricker, T. B. The solar economic ABCs. AIM, 26(2) May 1983 pp17-22. (Reprint from Real Estate Appraiser and Analyst, Winter 1982)
2165 Ritchie, W. B. Houses that move. Real Estate Today, 14 June 1981 pp9-11.
2166 Robins, P. K. and West, R. W. Measurement errors in the estimation of home value. American Statistical Association Journal, 72 June 1977 pp290-294.
2167 Robinson, Noel. Effect of the energy crisis on land values - housing design. Valuer(Australia), 26 April 1981 pp469-470, 482.
2168 Romney, K. B. and B. Condominium development guide: procedures, analysis, forms. Revised edition. Boston, Warren Gorham & Lamont, 1983.
2169 Rosen, Kenneth. A comparison of European housing finance systems. Berkeley, Cal., University of California, Institute of Business and Economic Research, 1981.
2170 Rosen, Kenneth. Creative financing and house prices a study of capitalization effects. Berkeley, Cal., University of California, Institute of Business and Economic Research, 1982.
2171 Rosen, Kenneth and Smith, Lawrence. The price-adjustment process for rental housing and the natural vacancy rate. American Economic Review, 73(4) 1983 pp779-786.
2172 Rosen, Kenneth and Smith, Lawrence. The price-adjustment process for rental housing and the natural vacancy rate. Berkeley, Ca.,University of California,Institute of Business and Economic Research,1982.
2173 Rowan, R. Condomania's first family. Fortune, 104(3) 10 August 1981 pp106-113.
2174 Royal Institution of Chartered Surveyors. Survey and valuation of residential properties: the RICS approach: One day conference, Birmingham, 16 June 1981. London, Surveyor's Technical Publications, 1981.
2175 Royal Institution of Chartered Surveyors. The valuation of residential property: conditions of engagement. London, Royal Institution of Chartered Surveyors, 1984.
2176 Roydon, T. House-builder's concern over problems of down-valuation. Building Societies Gazette, 116(1410) 1984 pp822-823, 827. (Reprinted in Estates Gazette, 271(6194) 21 July 1984 p255)
2177 Rudnitsky, H. and Lappen, A. A. Getting burned on the beach. Forbes, 127 16 March 1981 pp93-94.
2178 Rydin, Yvonne. Housing land: a question of supply and demand. Town and Country Planning, 52(6) June 1983 pp179-180.
2179 Salkin, M. S. and Durning, D. What is a house really worth? Mortgage Banker, 43(8) 1983 pp76-83.
2180 Sally, William D. Pricing residential property management fees - fairly and accurately. Journal of Property Management, 41(5) September/October 1976 pp233-238.
2181 Saltojanes, N. M. Inflation in housing costs. Appraisal Journal, 52 January 1984 pp113-126.
2182 Sands, Gary. Land-office business: land and housing prices in rapidly growing metropolitan areas. Lexington, Mass, Lexington Books, 1982. (Bibliography pp137-148)
2183 Schaeffer, Pierre. Private property: vehicle of the European housing industry. Appraisal Journal, 11(3) July 1981 pp409-412.
2184 Schussheim, Morton J. The impact of demographic change on housing and community development. Appraisal Journal, 52(3) July 1984 pp375-381.
2185 Schwab, R. M. Expected inflation and housing: tax and cash flow considerations. Southern Economic Journal, 49 April 1983 pp1162-1168.

2186 Schwartz, A. L. Influences of seller financing upon residential property sales prices. Real Estate Appraiser and Analyst, 48 Winter 1982 pp35-42.

2187 Schwartz, A. L. Seller-financing of homes: a consumer economic perspective. Journal of Consumer Affairs, 18 Summer 1984 pp131-146.

2188 Schwartz, Seymour I., Hansen, David E. and Green, Richard. Measuring house price effects of growth management: methodological issues and empirical results. Land Economics, 60(1) February 1984 pp110-114.

2189 Seek, N. H. Over capitalisation of owner occupied dwellings. Valuer (Australia), 27 October 1982 pp383-387.

2190 Seelig, S. A. and Freund, J. L. Homeowner's best investment. Real Estate Review, 11 Summer 1981 pp72-76.

2191 Seymour, C. F. Recycling United States real estate. Valuer(Australia), 27 January 1982 pp118-122, 127.

2192 Shaw, E. K. Tips on explaining residential financing. Real Estate Today, 11 March 1978 pp52-55.

2193 Sheehan, J. B. Residential site development. Valuer(Australia), 27 January 1983 pp418-421.

2194 Shenkel, W. M. and Gaines, James P. Effect of property tax variation on housing values. Review of Business and Economic Research, 13 Spring 1978 pp80-91.

2195 Shilton, L. Judging investment quality of section 8 housing. Real Estate Review, 12 Spring 1982 pp53-54.

2196 Siemion, R. and Ek, P. What consumers expect from housing in 1981. Professional Builder and Apartment Business, 45 December 1980 pp70-87.

2197 Skaburskis, A. Externalities and property prices: a test of the Schall hypothesis. Journal of Regional Science, 22(2) 1982 pp213-223.

2198 Skoyles, E. R. International price/cost comparisons. Chartered Surveyor Building and Quantity Surveying Quarterly, 4(1) 1976 pp1-6.

2199 Smal, C. The valuation of special residential land. South African Estate Agent, 5 September 1976 pp6-8.

2200 Smith, David A. The resyndication opportunity for subsidized housing partnerships. Real Estate Review, 13 Spring 1983 pp40-42.

2201 Smith, G. V. Portable home valuation guide. Englewood Cliffs, N.J., Executive Reports Corporation, 1981.

2202 Smith, K. The domestic hereditament and other problems. Estates Gazette, 272(6214) 8 December 1984 pp1139-1141.

2203 Smith, K. V. Residential location and environmental amenities: a review of the evidence. Regional Studies, 11(1) 1977 pp47-61.

2204 Smith, Lawrence and others. The demand for housing, household headship rates, and household formation: an international analysis. Urban Studies, 21 1984 pp407-414.

2205 Smith, Lawrence and others. The demand for housing, household headship rates, and household formation: an international analysis. Berkeley Cal., University of California, Institute of Business and Economic Research, 1982.

2206 Smyth, Hedley. Land banking, land availability and planning for private housebuilding. Bristol, University of Bristol, School for Advanced Urban Studies, 1982. (Working paper 23)

2207 Smyth, Hedley. Land supply, housebuilders and government policies. Bristol, University of Bristol, School for Advanced Urban Studies, 1984. (Working paper 43)

2208 Society of Real Estate Appraisers. Energy considerations in real estate appraising. Chicago, Society of Real Estate Appraisers, 1980.

2209 Spence, H. Residential investment for property institutions. Chartered Surveyor, 111(11) June 1979 p483.

2210 Stebbins, G. A guide to appraising residences. 3rd edition. Chicago, Society of Real Estate Appraisers, 1976.
2211 Stellmacher, R. A. and H. B. Appraisal by legislative fiat. Real Estate Appraiser and Analyst, 49 Fall 1983 pp49-50.
2212 Stewart, D. O. Effect of differential property tax rates on the sales prices of single-family residential property. Economics and Statistics, 60 February 1978 pp150-153.
2213 Stewart, J. M. A housing bibliography. Birmingham, University of Birmingham, Centre for Urban and Regional Studies, 1980. (Research memorandum 84)
2214 Stratton, Ian G. C. Building land and estates. 2nd edition. London, Oyez Longman, 1983.
2215 Sumka, H. J. Measuring the quality of housing: an econometric analysis of tax appraisal records. Land Economics, 53 August 1977 pp298-309.
2216 Talbot, E. A. Implied warranty of habitability - where will it go now? Appraisal Journal, 50 January 1982 pp135-140.
2217 Temple, D. M. Investing in residential income property. Dual edition. Washington, D.C., U.S. News and World Report Books, 1976. Further edition, Chicago, Contemporary Books, 1981.
2218 Thaler, R. Note on the value of crime control: evidence from the property market. Journal of Urban Economics, 5 January 1978 pp137-145.
2219 Thorns, D. C. The role of the family life-cycle in residential mobility. Birmingham, University of Birmingham, Centre for Urban and Regional Studies, 1980. (Working paper 69)
2220 Turner, B. M. Development of residential and rural retreat properties. Valuer(Australia), 26 October 1980 pp308-311, 354.
2221 Tutorow, N. E. Home sweet investment. Real Estate Today, 14 April 1981 pp4-8.
2222 University of Birmingham, Centre for Urban and Regional Studies. Building societies and the local housing market: a report by the housing monitoring team. Birmingham, University of Birmingham, Centre for Urban and Regional Studies, 1982. (Research memorandum 90)
2223 University of Birmingham, Centre for Urban and Regional Studies. The role of the Local Authority in land programming and the process of private residential development. Birmingham, University of Birmingham, Centre for Urban and Regional Studies, 1980. (Research memorandum 80)
2224 University of Reading, College of Estate Management, Centre for Advanced Land Use Studies. The market for small houses in the Reading area. Reading, University of Reading, College of Estate Management, Centre for Advanced Land Use Studies, 1977.
2225 University of Reading, College of Estate Management, Centre for Advanced Land Use Studies, Estate Agency Study Group. Subject to contract procedures in house purchase. Reading, University of Reading, College of Estate Management, Centre for Advanced Land Use Studies, 1984.
2226 University of Reading, College of Estate Management, Centre for Advanced Land Use Studies, Housing Research Study Group. Elderly persons and housing mobility. Reading, University of Reading, College of Estate Management, Centre for Advanced Land Use Studies, 1984.
2227 Urban Land Institute. Residential development handbook. Washington, D.C., Urban Land Institute, 1978.
2228 Urban Land Institute, Research Division. Effects of regulation on housing costs: two case studies: a report. Washington, D.C., Urban Land Institute, 1977.

2229 Urguidi, D. W., Leighton, D. and Hubbard, B. Speculation in redlined areas: investigation into relationship between redlining and housing speculation. Los Angeles, Cal., California State University, Department of Political Science, 1977.

2230 Valachi, Donald J. Refinancing a personal residence. Real Estate Review, 11(4) Winter 1982 pp73-76.

2231 Valuing new homes perks. Estates Gazette, 269(6176) 17 March 1984 p1053.

2232 Vance, M. Housing costs: a bibliography. Monticello, Ill., Vance Bibliographies, 1982. (Architecture series A-781)

2233 Vandell, K. D. and Harrison, B. Racial transition among neighborhoods: a simulation model incorporating institutional parameters. Journal of Urban Economics, 5 October 1978 pp441-470.

2234 Vidger, L. P. Borrowing and lending on residential property: fundamentals for home owners, investors and students. Lexington, Mass., Lexington Books, and Aldershot, Gower, 1982.

2235 Von Colditz, W. and Daniels, L. Reducing litigation in condominium development. Mortgage Banker, 43 October 1982 p23.

2236 Wade, J. R. Condominiums: the professional's complete manual and guide. Englewood Cliffs, N.J., Prentice Hall, 1983.

2237 Walters, A. A. Noise and prices. London, Clarendon Press, 1975.

2238 Watson, A. Single-family rentals: a gold mine or loss leader? Journal of Property Management, 43 January 1978 pp16-20.

2239 Weaver, R. C. Rental housing: an endangered species? Journal of Property Management, 44 September 1979 pp271-274.

2240 Webb, James R. and Emig, J. W. Housing prices and the CPI. Real Estate Appraiser and Analyst, 49(2) 1983 pp16-20.

2241 Webb, James R. Nuclear power plants: effects on property values. Appraisal Journal, 48(2) 1980 pp230-235.

2242 Weitz, Stevenson. Affordable housing: how local regulatory improvements can help. Washington, D.C., Department of Housing and Urban Development, 1982. (Report no. HUD/PDR-714: HUD-0002733)

2243 West, W. J. The appraisal of limited interests. AIM, 25(3) August 1981 pp35-36.

2244 White, Michelle. On the short-term effects of long-term change in cities: an efficient land markets model. Journal of Urban Economics, 5 1978 pp485-504.

2245 White, W. L. Price indexing for time adjustments. Appraisal Journal, 48(1) January 1980 pp15-23.

2246 Whitehead, C. M. R. House prices and public policy. Cambridge, University of Cambridge, Department of Land Economy, 1981. (Discussion paper 2)

2247 Wildasin, D. E. Local public goods, property values and local public choice. Journal of Urban Economics, 6 October 1979 pp521-534.

2248 Williams, R. J. Valuation aspects caused by environmental considerations on land development. Valuer(Australia), 25(8) October 1979 pp624-628, 636.

2249 Williamson, J. M. J. and Kirwan, M. R. Housing Associations: accounting and audit guide. London, Deloitte Haskins and Sells, 1984. (Jointly with Great Britain. Department of Health and Social Security and Housing Corporation)

2250 Willis, Cleve E., Foster, John H. and Sewall, Kenneth. Valuation of intangibles: the case of water quality, Amherst, Mass., Massachusetts University, Water Research and Technology Center, 1983.

2251 Wilson, D. J. The valuation of pre-paid residential building leases. Canadian Appraiser, 28(11) November 1984 pp28-33.

2252 Wilson, R. S. Investor's guide to investing in multiple dwellings.

Lexington, Mass., Heath, 1976.
2253 Witte, A. D. Examination of various elasticities for residential sites Land Economics, 53 November 1977 pp401-409.
2254 Wright, Arthur L. Characteristics of the duplex buyer: the Texas case. Appraisal Journal, 47 April 1979 pp287-292.
2255 Wurtzebach, Charles H. and Waller, Neil G. The feasibility, underwriting and valuation of residential energy components. Appraisal Journal, 51(1) January 1983 pp66-80.

Australia
2256 Archer, R. W. Urban consolidation for Sydney: the housing and land use planning approaches. Valuer(Australia), 26 April 1981 pp441-446, 450.
2257 Bardy. T. E. State and local government's role in causing high residential land prices in the Sydney Metropolitan Area. Valuer(Australia), 26 October 1980 pp301-307.
2258 Deans, David R. Future of the housing industry. Valuer(Australia), 27 January 1983 pp422-426.
2259 Kiefer, D. M. Equity of alternative policies for the Australian homeowner. Economic Record, 54 April 1978 pp127-139.
2260 Webb, D. J. and Harmer, J. A. Price behaviour and market trends in existing housing markets in Sydney 1968-78. Valuer(Australia), 26 July 1980 pp226-228.

Canada
2261 Genstar Homes. Observations on housing and land development. AIM, 22(4) November 1978 pp24-37.
2262 Hessian, R. V. How will a changing housing market affect the appraisal business and the CMHC program objectives. AIM, 24(3) August 1980 pp8-10. (Canada Mortgage and Housing Corporation)
2263 Lorimer, James. The sweetest game in the country. Canadian Business, 51(11) November 1978 pp71-75.
2264 Purves, S. G. An analysis of house price trends during the 1970s - Toronto. AIM, 25(3) 1981 pp20-23.
2265 Smith, Lawrence. The crisis in rental housing: a Canadian perspective. Berkeley, Cal., University of California, Institute of Business and Economic Research, 1982.
2266 Stiller, O. F. Construction costs of a single family dwelling, Vancouver - spring 1977. AIM, 21(3) July 1977 pp30-33.

Colombia
2267 Grimes, O. S. and Lim, G. C. Employment, land values and the residential choice of low-income households: the case of Bogota, Colombia. Land Economics, 52 August 1976 pp347-354.

France
2268 Ullmo, Pierre A. The demand for housing, household headship rates, and household formation in France. Berkeley, Cal., University of California, Institute of Business and Economic Research, 1983.

Great Britain
A number of Building Societies publish regular statistics on the residential markets: Abbey National, Anglia, Halifax, Nationwide. BSA Bulletin, from the Building Societies Association, publishes regular statistics ansd occasional analytical articles. Regular figures are also to be found in the Annual abstract of statistics, for the whole country, in local authority publications, the fullest of which is the Greater London Council's Annual

abstract of Greater London statistics. Fox & Sons (Southampton) produce a series jointly with the Department of Economics of Exeter University. Mann Countrywide's figures cover 250 towns throughout the country and are published in *Estates Gazette* and *Chartered Surveyor Weekly*. Most regional estate agents publish surveys covering their region. Auction prices are covered in the fortnightly *Under the hammer* (Birmingham, Rogers(Printers) Birmingham Ltd.).

2269 Ashmore, G. *The owner-occupied housing market*. Birmingham, University of Birmingham, Centre for Urban and Regional Studies, 1975. (Research memorandum 41)

2270 British Property Federation. *Review of the rent acts*. London, British Property Federation, 1977.

2271 Carmichael, K. Tax problems of owning a home. *Accountancy*, 87 December 1976 pp36-37.

2272 Crook, A. D. H. and Bryant, C. L. *Local authorities and private landlords*. Sheffield, Sheffield Centre for Environmental Research, 1982.

2273 Eadon Lockwood & Riddle. *Residential review 1979-*. Sheffield, Eadon Lockwood & Riddle, annual.

2274 Great Britain, Department of the Environment. *National dwelling and housing survey*. London, HMSO, 1980.

2275 Great Britain, Department of the Environment. A new index of average house prices. *Economic Trends*, 348 October 1982 pp134-138.

2276 Great Britain, Parliament. *The private rented sector, report by the House of Commons Select Committee on the Environment*. London, HMSO, 1982.

2277 Great Britain. Scottish Development Department. *Movement to and within the owner-occupied sector of the housing market*. Edinburgh, Scottish Development Department, 1984.

2278 Hamnett, C. Variations in regional house price inflation 1969-81. *Estates Gazette*, 268(6164) 10 December 1983 pp1090, 1092, 1094.

2279 House price explosion hits London. *Investor's Chronicle*, 20 July 1979 pp198-199.

2280 Incorporated Society of Valuers and Auctioneers. *Housing index*. London, The Society, quarterly.

2281 Inter-Company Comparisons Ltd. *House builders, estate and property developers: ICC financial survey and directory: turnover/profits/ assets/liabilities*. London, Inter-Company Comparisons, 1983.

2282 Johnston, B. Still doubt on housing land debate. *Planning*, 561 23 March 1984 pp8-9.

2283 Kemeney, J. and Karn, V. *House purchase in inner Birmingham 1975/9: second interim report of the Inner City Home ownership project*. Birmingham, University of Birmingham, Centre for Urban and Regional Studies, 1981. (Working paper 83)

2284 Kemeney, J. *Polarisation in the inner Birmingham market 1972-80: second interim report of the Inner City Home ownership project*. Birmingham, University of Birmingham, Centre for Urban and Regional Studies, 1981. (Working paper 81)

2285 Kenneth Ryden & Partners. *Scottish residential property review*. Edinburgh, Kenneth Ryden & Partners, 1979 - . (semi-annual: from 1983 incorporating the Ryden/Halifax House Price Index)

2286 Mann Countrywide and Association of Estate Agents. *Price Index*. London Mann & Co., quarterly.

2287 Merrett, S. with Gray, F. *Owner-occupation in Britain*. London and Boston, Routledge Kegan Paul, 1982.

2288 Neuberger, H. L. I. and Nichol, B. M. *The recent course of land and* property prices and the factors underlying it. London, Department of the Environment, 1976. (Research report 4)

2289 Paley, B. Attitudes to letting in 1976. London, Department of the Environment, 1978.

2290 Robinson, V. The dynamics of ethnic succession - a British case study. Oxford, University of Oxford, School of Geography, 1981. (Working paper 2) (Bibliography)

2291 University of Birmingham, Centre for Urban and Regional Studies. The housebuilding industry and changes in the market for housebuilding work: a review of the British experience in the 1970s. Birmingham, University of Birmingham, Centre for Urban and Regional Studies, 1981. (Research memorandum 81)

2292 University of Birmingham, Centre for Urban and Regional Studies. House price analysis: monitoring the private housing market. Birmingham, University of Birmingham, Centre for Urban and Regional Studies, 1980. (Research memorandum 83)

2293 University of Birmingham, Centre for Urban and Regional Studies. Survey of landlords in Cheltenham. Birmingham, University of Birmingham, Centre for Urban and Regional Studies, 1978.

2294 Walker, S. The 1980 Housing Act: implications for the housing market with special reference to local authority housing. London, Polytechnic of the South Bank, Department of Town Planning, 1981. (Occasional paper 6/81)

2295 Williams, P. R. The role of institutions in the inner London housing market: the case of Islington. Transactions of the Institute of British Geographers, ns1(1) 1976 pp72-82.

Israel

2296 Gabriel, Stuart and Maoz, Ilan. Cyclical fluctuations in the Israel housing market. Berkeley, Cal., University of California, Institute of Business and Economic Research, 1983.

New Zealand

2297 Babe, E. J. Future outlook for housing industry. New Zealand Valuer, 25(3) September 1982 pp144-146.

2298 Jefferies, R. L. Urban valuation in New Zealand. Wellington, New Zealand Institute of Valuers, 1978.

2299 White, R. M. Future outlook for housing industry. New Zealand Valuer, 25(3) September 1982 pp147-153.

Phillipines

2300 Struyk, R. J. and Lynn, R. Determinants of housing investment in slum areas: Tando and other locations in metro Manila. Land Economics, 59 November 1983 pp444-454.

Sweden

2301 Ratzka, A. D. Land banking in Stockholm: an evaluation of municipal residential leasehold as a public finance and housing subsidy. Journal of American Planning Association, 47(3) 1981 pp279-288.

United States

Studies of the residential market appear regularly in National Real Estate Investor, Real Estate Appraiser and Analyst, Real Estate Review and Real Estate Today as well as the many local journals some of which are listed in the appendix. The volume is too great to cover in any depth. Those given in the following selective listing are indicative of the general content. Most relating to specific geographic areas are indexed in Business Periodicals Index, in print or online.

2302 5 & 10 year outlook for housing, Real Estate Today, 13 August 1980 pp4-8.

2303 Agarwal, Vinod B. and Phillips, Richard A. The effect of mortgage rate buydowns on housing prices: recent evidence from FHA-VA Transactions. American Real Estate and Urban Economics Association Journal, 11(4) 1983 no pages given.

2304 Beach, Elmo E. and others. Annual housing survey: 1976. United States and Regions. Washington, D. C. Bureau of the Census, Housing Division, 1978. (Series of 25 reports sponsored by Department of Housing and Urban Development, Office of Policy Development and Research)

2305 Cerf, Alan R. Homeownership: tax incentives and national policy. Berkeley, Cal., University of California, Institute of Business and Economic Research, 1983.

2306 Cooperative financing review Milwaukee neighborhood. Professional Builder and Apartment Business, 48 December 1983 pp18-19.

2307 Dole, Charles E. Boston: vacancies rise, but rent levels are holding firm. National Real Estate Investor, 24 July 1982 pp38+ .

2308 Dowall, David E. and Landis, John. Land-use controls and housing costs an examination of San Francisco Bay Area Communities. Berkeley, Cal., University of California, Institute of Business and Economic Research, 1981.

2309 Engelsman, C. 1979 residential cost manual: new construction modelling and valuation. New York, Van Nostrand Reinhold, 1978.

2310 Engle, Robert F. De facto discrimination in residential assessments: Boston. National Tax Journal, 28 December 1975 pp445-451.

2311 Gerardi, N. and Gers, B. B. Phoenix. Housing, 54 October 1978 pp67-69.

2312 Gerardi, N. and Gers, B. B. San Diego. Housing, 54 October 1978 pp74-76.

2313 Gers, B. B. Fourth annual home-shopper survey: buyer preferences. Housing, 60 December 1981 pp49-64.

2314 Gordon, M. Hawaiian resort condos: strong dollar, scars from Iwa. Barrons, 63 7 November 1983 pp66-67.

2315 Harrison, R. T. A non-market income approach to value for HUD-subsidized Co-ops. Appraisal Journal, 45(2) 1977 pp180-192.

2316 Hoben, James E. Affordable housing: what states can do. Urban Land, 42(4) 1983 pp20-23.

2317 Jud, G. Donald. Real estate brokers and the market for residential housing. Journal of the American Real Estate and Urban Economics Association, 11 Spring 1983 pp69-82.

2318 Kent, J. Examining the Ventura housing market via linear regression techniques. Santa Barbara, University of California, Urban Economics Program, 1978.

2319 Landis, John D. California housing profiles: 1980. Berkeley, Cal., University of California, Institute of Business and Economic Research, 1982.

2320 Leigh, W. A. Estimates of economic depreciation rates for the efficiency-adjusted residential housing stock of the United States 1950-1970. Cambridge, Mass., Harvard University, Department of City and Regional Planning, 1979.

2321 Levy, Susan G. Consumer response to high housing prices: the case of Palo Alto, California. Berkeley, Cal., University of California, Institute of Business and Economic Research, 1980.

2322 Lewis, P. Condominiums in Florida: not always a sunny investment. Accountancy, 94 February 1983 pp77-78.

2323 Lucas, E. C. Effects of neighbourhood quality, income, and race on the value of single-family homes in New Orleans. Review of Black Policy and Economics, 7 Winter 1977 pp182-189.
2324 McDougall, G. S. Local public goods and residential property values: some insights and extensions. National Tax Journal, 29 December 1976 pp436-447.
2325 McMillan, Melville and Carlson, R. Effects of property taxes and local public services upon residential property values in small Wisconsin cities. American Journal of Agricultural Economics, 59 February 1977 pp81-87.
2326 Martin, R. C. Credit conditions and the postwar US residential investment cycle. Applied Economics, 10 September 1979 pp46-59.
2327 Meagher, J. P. Homebuilders surviving in Chicago. Barrons, 62 16 August 1982 pp14+ .
2328 Miller, G. H., Mercer, H. Glenn and Gilbeau, Kenneth W. California real estate appraisal: residential properties. 2nd ed. Englewood Cliffs, Prentice-Hall, 1977. (First edition 1972)
2329 Nelson, J. F. Special report: the outlook for housing. United States Banker, 95(7) July 1984 pp17-18,20.
2330 Paris, E. Darkness on the golden miles. Forbes, 133 16 January 1984 pp90-92.
2331 Quigley, J. M. Local residential mobility and local government policy. in, Clark, W. A. and Moore, Eric G. Residential mobility and public policy. Beverly Hills, Sage Publications, 1980.
2332 Quigley, J. M. Residential construction and public policy: a progress report. Berkeley, Cal., University of California, Institute of Business and Economic Research, 1981.
2333 Real Estate Research Council of Southern California. House price trends in Southern California: being a supplemental report providing detailed results from prices of existing single family houses. Sherman Oaks, Ca., Real Estate Research Council of Southern California, 1979.
2334 Robert A McNeil Corporation. The American housing market: a national view. San Mateo, Cal., Robert A McNeil Corporation, 1979.
2335 Rosen, Kenneth, The affordability of housing in 1980 and beyond. Berkeley, Cal., University of California, Institute of Business and Economic Research, 1980.
2336 Rosen, Kenneth, The affordability of housing in California. Berkeley, Cal., University of California, Institute of Business and Economic Research, 1981.
2337 Rosen, Kenneth. The demand for housing units in the 1980s. Berkeley, Cal., University of California, Institute of Business and Economic Research, 1980.
2338 Rosen, Kenneth. Housing policies for California in the 1980s. California Management Review, 26 1984 pp138-147.
2339 Rosen, Kenneth and Smith, Lawrence. The 'used house market'. Berkeley, Cal., University of California, Institute of Business and Economic Research, 1982.
2340 Shepherd, W. G. Building $1 million homes. Venture, 3(6) June 1981 pp36-43.
2341 Sternlieb, G. Multi-family housing demand, 1975-2000: a study prepared for the use of the Subcommittee on priorities and economy in Government of the Joint Economic Committee, Congress of the United States. Washington, D.C., U.S. Government Printing Office, 1978.
2342 Strazheim, M. R. An economic analysis of the urban housing market. New York, National Bureau of Economic Research, distributed by Columbia University Press, 1975.

2343 Tasker, Fred. Miami-Fort Lauderdale: area still struggling to rebound from condominium debacle. National Real Estate Investor, 18 November 1976 pp77-78.

2344 Tharpe, Gene. Atlanta: concessions are the rule as the vacancy rate rises. National Real Estate Investor, 24 July 1982 pp42+ .

2345 Tschappat, C. J. Atlanta: case study of a suburbanizing city. Real Estate Appraiser, 42 September 1976 pp5-8.

2346 United States. Department of Housing and Urban Development. Annual housing survey. Washington, D.C., Bureau of the Census, annual series of reports and papers.

2347 Warren, E., Aduddell, R. M. and Tatalovich, R. The impact of subsidized housing on property values: a two-pronged analysis of Chicago and Cook County suburbs. Chicago, Loyola University of Chicago, Center for Urban Policy, 1983.

2348 Weicher, John C. Disinflation and the housing market in the 1980s. Real Estate Issues, 992) 1984 pp6-14.

2349 What home buyers will want in 1982. Professional Building and Apartment Business, 46 December 1981 pp64-81.

2350 What 1983 buyers want in housing. Professional Building and Apartment Business, 47 December 1982 pp60-75. (Results of regular annual survey published in December)

2351 Wilmore, E. St Louis: condo conversions to increase: new projects limited. National Real Estate Investor, 21 February 1979 pp40+ .

2352 Wolfe, Marian F. Investment performance of existing rental housing in selected San Francisco Bay Area communities. Berkely, Ca.,University of California, Institute of Business and Economic Research,1983.

Apartments

2353 Amies, F. A. Disabled person's flat at full gross value. Rating and Valuation Reporter, 16 February 1976 pp38-41.

2354 Amies, F. A. Possible nil value for dilapidated flat. Rating and Valuation Reporter, 18 August 1978 pp191-194.

2355 Apartments, anyone? here's how - and why - three pros bucked the don't build trend. Housing, 57 March 1980 pp56-67.

2356 Arnison, C. Flats: theory and practice. Estates Gazette, 259(6047) 15 August 1981 pp547-548.

2357 Arnold, Alvin L. How to evaluate apartment building investments. Boston, Warren Gorham Lamont, 1978. (Real Estate review portfolios 18)

2358 Bible, Douglas S. and Crunkleton, J. R. The effects of financing on the sale of multi-family properties. Real Estate Appraiser and Analyst, 49(2) 1983 pp33-38.

2359 Brenner, Stephen W. Repositioning and marketing a transient lodging property. Journal of Property Management, 49(6) November/December 1984 pp16+ .

2360 Burchell, R. W. and Sternlieb, G. Multi-family housing demand. American Real Estate and Urban Economic Association Journal, 7 Spring 1979 pp1-38, 123-130.

2361 Crockett, Robert G. The special concerns of condominium management. Journal of Property Management, 43(4) July/August 1978 pp181-185.

2362 Cutsinger, S. Valuing apartments with the unit mix adjustment technique. Real Estate Appraiser and Analyst, 45(3) May/June 1979 pp16-19.

2363 Damm, W. E. A. R. P.s cannot be appraised. AIM, 22(1) January 1978 pp16-19.

2364 Davidson, Harold A. The impact of rent control on apartment investment. Appraisal Journal, 46(4) October 1978 pp570-580. (Also Journal of Property Management, 44(5) September/October 1979 pp241-246.
2365 Diamond, T. W. SREA market data center, APTWD: a more efficient way to analyze apartments. Real Estate Appraiser and Analyst, 44 January 1978 pp23-30.
2366 Eikmeyer, L. J. Appraising the apartment building. AIM, 28(1) February 1984 pp26-32.
2367 Farrell, Paul J. Apartment leasing: new ideas and techniques. Journal of Property Management, 41(3) May/June 1976 pp128-131.
2368 Garrigan, R. T. Multifamily properties: an attractive investment for the 1980s. Real Estate Review, 12 Summer 1982 pp103-111.
2369 Gipe, G. W. Mass appraisal of apartments with comparable sales, presented at Lincoln Institute of Land Policy, Colloquium on Computer Assisted Mass Appraisal, October 19-22, 1975. Cambridge, Mass., Lincoln Institute of Land Policy, 1977.
2370 Grant, M. E. Funds to finance apartment buildings. Real Estate Today, 13 April 1980 pp24-27.
2371 Haddow, D. F. How feasibility studies benefit apartment builders. Real Estate Review, 10(2) 1980 pp64-67.
2372 Halper, E. B. People and property: requiem for apartment houses. Real Estate Review, 6 Summer 1976 pp53-59.
2373 Halper, E. B. People and property: representation clauses in apartment house sales contracts. Real Estate Review, 7 Winter 1978 pp46-52.
2374 Hartley, J. RICS flat-buyer's report is completed. Chartered Surveyor Weekly, 4(5) 4 August 1983 p241.
2375 Hiban, A. W. Management - a key word in the condo concept. Journal of Property Management, 43(2) March/April 1978 pp97-100.
2376 Hirsch, Gerald. Marketing apartment space: opportunity for managers. Journal of Property Management, 48(1) January/February 1983 pp16+.
2377 Hollamby, John P. Caveat charleys. Chartered Surveyor Urban Quarterly, 3 1976 pp3-4.
2378 Institute of Real Estate Management. Income/expense analysis: apartments. Chicago, Institute of Real Estate Management, 1980.
2379 Jaffe, Austin J. Evaluating rules of thumb. Real Estate Today, 11 October 1978 pp22-25.
2380 Kelley, E. N. Cost, rent, and profit computer: rental apartments. New York, McGraw-Hill Housing Press, 1978.
2381 Kinnard, W. N. and Boyce, B. N. An introduction to appraising real property. Rev. ed. Chicago, Society of Real Estate Appraisers, 1978.
2382 Kinnard, W. N. and Everett, E. Roger. A guide to appraising apartments 5th edition. Chicago, Society of Real Estate Appraisers, 1979. (1st edition 1965)
2383 Langendoen, G. Grading apartments for maximum rents. Journal of Property Management, 42(6) November/December 1977 pp298-300.
2384 Levine, M. B. Valuing a condominium conversion: the issue of tenant protection laws. Appraisal Journal, 51(3) July 1983 pp363-375.
2385 Lovell, D. D. Condominium and subdivision discounting. Appraisal Journal, 51(4) October 1983 pp524-539.
2386 Miller, E. R. Apartment investing: climate for success. Mortgage Banking, 42 February 1982 pp52-54.
2387 O'Connell, D. J. Apartment building valuation, finance and investment analysis for real estate professionals and investors. New York and Chichester, Wiley, 1982.
2388 Pollard, B. Valuation of cooperative apartment buildings. Appraisal

Journal, 50(2) April 1982 pp243-252.

2389 Reduction of valuation for lost privacy and lost open view from multi-storey flats. Rating and Valuation Reporter, 17(5) May 1977 pp121-123.

2390 Reed, J. T. Apartment investment check lists. New York, Harcourt Brace Jovanitch Press, 1979.

2391 Rental rights in residential condominiums: a caveat to the investor. International Property Investment Journal, 2(2) 1984 pp329-344.

2392 Sally, William D. So you want to convert to condos .... Journal of Property Management. 41(3) May/June 1976 pp105-109.

2393 Stebbins, H. G. A guide to appraising residences. 3rd ed. Chicago, Society of Real Estate Appraisers, 1976.

2394 Stokes, P. W. Advising clients on buying a rental investment flat, property management, the agent's role, estimating outgoings and incomings. Real Estate and Stock Journal, 45(1) January-February 1981 pp8-12.

2395 Strauss, George and Lewman, Harry. Ratios and methodology in apartment house valuation. Chicago, American Institute of Real Estate Appraisers, 1975.

2396 Tootelian, D. H. An examination of the buying considerations and purchase feelings of middle and low income apartment dwellers and college seniors toward single family dwelling units. Sacramento, Cal., California State University, 1976.

2397 York, John C. Section 223 (f):a viable method of financing apartment buildings. Journal of Property Management, 45(1) January/February 1981 pp224+ .

United States

2398 Blazar, S. M. and Hilton, H. G. Investment opportunities in existing apartment buildings. Real Estate Review, 6 Summer 1976 pp47-52.

2399 Chaplin, M. C. Los Angeles: apartment office markets exhibit continued realty resurgence. National Real Estate Investor, 19 February pp41-42.

2400 Downs, Anthony. Landlord fears a factor in rental housing shortage. National Real Estate Investor, 18 September 1976 pp26 + .

2401 McDougall, G. S. Local public goods and residential property values: some insights and extensions. National Tax Journal, 29 December 1976 pp436-447.

Residential homes

2403 Entrekin, H. C. The appraisal of retirement centers. Real Estate Appraiser and Analyst, 45(5) 1979 pp11-15.

2404 Golub, K. L. Valuation of leased group homes. Appraisal Journal, 47(3) July 1979 pp325-331.

2405 Healy, R. J. Valuation of an 'institutional residence'. Valuer(Australia), 26 April 1980 pp143-145.

2406 Hogan, J. J. Valuation of nursing homes. Appraisal Journal, 48(2) April 1979 pp185-194.

2407 Lewsley, C. Valuing a private clinic. Rating and Valuation Reporter, 19(10) October 1979 pp245-246. (Nursing home)

2408 Lister, Robert I. Proficient nursing home evaluation. Valuer(Australia), 26 October 1981 pp610-623,625.

2409 Wildman, D. Rapid growth of private retirement developments is seen. Chartered Surveyor Weekly, 7(13) 28 June 1984 pp864.

Residential property

Mobile homes

2410 Amies, F. A. The rating (Caravan Sites) Bill. Rating and Valuation Reporter, 76 January 1976 pp4-6.
2411 Better way to appraise mobile homes. Banking, 70 October 1978 pp118+ .
2412 Bishop, David A. Caravan parks: a guide to value. Real Estate and Stock Journal, 44(10) November 1980 pp5-6, 30.
2413 Bishop, David A. Valuation of caravan parks. Valuer(Australia), 26(4) October 1980 pp330-332.
2414 Bishop, David A. Valuation of privately owned caravan parks. Valuer (Commonwealth Institute of Valuers), 25(1) January 1978 pp55-58.
2415 Caravan parks - a guide to value. Real Estate and Stock Journal, November 1980 pp5-6, 30.
2416 Darlow, Clive and Long, Peter. Tax and holiday property. Estates Gazette, 272(6206) 13 October 1984 pp138, 141.
2417 Harris, M. S. and D. G. Taxation of investments in manufactured housing. Taxes, 62 May 1984 pp337-347.
2418 International Association of Assessing Officers. Mobile homes and related issues: a bibliography. Chicago, International Association of Assessing Officers, 1977. (Bibliography series)
2419 Mack, J. M. Yesterday's wheel estate - today's real estate. Real Estate Today, 10 April 1977 pp16-22.
2420 Mobile home park values rise 12 percent. Professional Builder and Apartment Business, 49 March 1984 p114.
2421 Noble, Bruce. Country caravan parks. Valuer(Australia), 26 April 1980 pp146-149.
2422 Rating of holiday caravans. Rating and Valuation, January 1976 pp13-16.
2423 Rating of caravans. RICS Abstracts and Reviews, November 1975 R364.
2424 Roberts, D. F. Rating (Caravan Sites) Bill 1975. Rating and Valuation, February 1976 p46.
2425 West, W. T. Recent developments in caravan law. Solicitor's Journal, 120(21) 21 May 1976 pp344-346.

Holiday homes

2426 Avis, M. and Gibson, V. Valuing time-share interests. Journal of Valuation, 2(3) 1984 pp240-257.
2427 Baxter, Ross. Timesharing is fastest growing holiday industry. NZ Real Estate, 34(4) August 1983 pp14-15, 26.
2428 Bloch, S. M. and Ingersoll, W. B. Timesharing. Washington, D.C., Urban Land Institute, 1977.
2429 Bloch, S. M., Ingersoll, W. B. and Madsen, S. A. Timesharing II. Washington, D.C., Urban Land Institute, 1982.
2430 Christian, C. Timesharing. Management and Unit Holder, November 1981 pp1089-1091.
2431 Christian, C. Time-sharing: holiday homes or holiday heartaches. Law Societies Gazette, 79(32) 8 September 1982 pp1090-1091.
2432 Clatanoff, Robert M. Real property timeshares:an appraisal guide and bibliography. Chicago, International Association of Assessing Officers, 1982. (Bibliography series)
2433 Conroy, Kathleen. Assessing the fee timeshare property. New Zealand Valuer, 25(9) March 1984 pp503-512. (Originally published in Assessor's Journal, 16(2) 1981)
2434 Conroy, Kathleen and DiChiara, J. A. Timeshare property assessment and taxation. Washington, D.C., American Land Development Association, National Timesharing Council, 1983.

2435 Conroy, Kathleen. Valuing the timeshare property. Chicago, American Institute of Real Estate Appraisers, 1981.
2436 Cunnew, T. Time-share: impact and opportunities. Estates Gazette, 254(5988) 14 June 1980 pp977-979.
2437 Curtis, C. E. Endless vacation or endless headache? Forbes, 14 September 1981 pp114-116.
2438 David, G. I. and Goldman, L. Managing a time-share resort. Journal of Property Management, 45 1980 pp266-269.
2439 Edmonds, J. International timesharing. London, Services to Lawyers, 1984.
2440 Edmonds, J. Time-sharing in England and Wales. Law Society's Gazette 80(27) 13 July 1983 pp1776-1778.
2441 English Tourist Board. Holiday home development: timesharing. 2nd edition. London, English Tourist Board, 1983.
2442 Garnock, D. Timeshare in our time. Chartered Surveyor Weekly, 4(7) 18 August 1983 pp327-335.
2443 Green, D. Time-sharing: the licence solution. Law Society's Gazette, 80(37) 12 October 1983 pp2500-2502.
2444 Groom, M. Timeshare makes Court Barton bloom. Chartered Surveyor Weekly, 6(5) 2 February 1984 pp286-287.
2445 Hart, C. W. Method for valuing time-share intervals. Real Estate Review, 10 1980 pp107-113.
2446 Hart, C. W. and Pfrommer, S. Financing the timeshare project. Real Estate Review, 12(3) 1982 pp72-78.
2447 Hoare, John. Timesharing - a catalyst to future development in Queensland or a consumer nightmare? Valuer(Australia), 27 October 1983 pp721-724.
2448 Johnson, G. C. Timeshare financing: a lending opportunity. Mortgage Banker, 42 April 1982 pp6-8.
2449 Jones, G. L. Timesharing and the valuer. Valuer(Australia), 28(4) October 1984 pp308-310.
2450 Jones, G. L. Timesharing practice and operation. Valuer(Australia), 27(8) OCtober 1983 pp700-707. (Also in New Zealand Valuer, 25(9) March 1984 pp513-521.
2451 Lynge, R. J. and Trowbridge, K. W. Real estate broker's guide to resort timesharing. Chicago, Real Estate Education Company, 1984.
2452 Macleod, H. J. An introduction to timesharing. New Zealand Valuer, 25(9) March 1984 pp497-502.
2453 Nygaard, T. R. Vacation homes and TRA: a grab bag of surprises. Real Estate Review, 7 Winter 1978 pp78-82.
2454 Pegg, Jan. The timesharing of property. I. General observations about the timesharing of property. Washington Real Estate News, 30(2) 1984 pp3-5.
2455 Pegg, Jan. The timesharing of property. II. Purchaser protections. Washington Real Estate News, 30(3) 1984 pp5-6, 8.
2456 Pegg, Jan. The timesharing of property. III. General observations about the timesharing of property. Washington Real Estate News, 30(2) 1984 pp3-6.
2457 Resorts Condominiums International UK Ltd and Greene Belfield Smith & Co. Great Britain timesharing survey 1983. London, Greene Belfield Smith, 1983.
2458 Tanzer, M. Converter's guide to high profts from condominium and time sharing conversions. Englewood Cliffs, N.J., Institute for Business Planning, 1982.
2459 Tarlo, H. The march of time. The legal structure of real estate time sharing in Australia. Melbourne, Legal Books Pty Ltd., 1981.
2460 Timeshare. Chartered Surveyor Weekly, 4(7) 18 August 1983 pp327-335.

Residential property

2461 Timesharing. RICS Abstracts and Reviews, 20(7) July 1984 pp121-122 Review R507.
2462 Timesharing in Victoria. Guideline for the operation of the time sharing industry. Melbourne, Government Printer, 1982.
2463 Timesharing turns holiday tenants into proud owners. Real Estate and Stock Journal, 144(7) August 1980 pp12-13.
2464 Trahan, D. Time-sharing - the big shakeout. Investor's Chronicle, 67(844) 13 January 1984 pp8-10.
2465 Urban Land Institute. Timesharing. Washington, D.C., Urban Land Institute, 1977.
2466 Wates, B. L. The future of timesharing. Chartered Surveyor, 113(5) December 1980 pp356-357.
2467 Wildman, D. British timeshare takes off. Chartered Surveyor Weekly, 9(2) 11 October 1984 p120.
2468 Williams, G. Code of practice for time ownership. Chartered Surveyor, 112(11) June 1980 pp492-493.

Hotels, restaurants

2469 Amies, F. A. Valuing an uncompleted hotel in a halted redevelopment scheme. Rating and Valuation Reporter, 18(1) January 1978 pp2-7.
2470 Bernstein, J. Hotels and motels as tax shelters. CA Magazine, 116 October 1983 pp72-74.
2471 Brener, S. W. Appraisal of budget motels. Real Estate Appraiser, 40 (2) 1974 pp18-20.
2472 Brener, S. W. and Gamoran, A. C. How much value at the inn? Real Estate Appraiser, 42(2) March/April 1976 pp37-41.
2473 Brookes, P. J. Hotel properties - investment considerations for trust officers. Trusts and Estates, 121 January 1982 pp57-59.
2474 Brookes, P. J. Mid-sized hotels are an investment opportunity. Real Estate Review, 11 Summer 1981 pp89-92.
2475 Butterworth, Robert T. Motels in Victoria - a guide to value. Valuer (Australia), 26 October 1980 pp326-329, 332.
2476 Cade, H. R. Valuation: the problem of restaurant premises. Estates Gazette, 263 28 August 1982. pp709, 716.
2477 Callnin, W. J. Investing in the casino hotel: the Atlantic City scene. Cornell Hotel and Restaurant Administration Quarterly, 20 August 1979 pp10-14.
2478 Chakravarty, S. N. and McGrath, A. Room at the top? Forbes, 133(6) 12 March 1984 pp58, 60-61.
2479 Christy & Co. Business price movements. London, Christy & Co., 1984.
2480 Connelly, J. R. How to turnaround a distressed hotel. Journal of Property Management, 43 January 1978 pp21-23.
2481 Connelly, J. R. Suburban hotel property: ripe field for investors. Mortgage Banker, 42 Summer 1982 pp32-35.
2482 Coyle, J. P. Hotel appraisal: valuation of licensed premises. New Zealand Valuer, 24(3) September 1979 pp133-147.
2483 Cunningham, R. P. Sensitivity analysis and probability study. Real Estate Appraiser and Analyst, 49(2) 1983 pp68-77.
2484 Daniels, A. Hotel beds and balance sheets. Chartered Surveyor Weekly, 4(4) 28 July 1983 pp204-205.
2485 Egan, A. Hotel valuation. AIM, 26(3) August 1982 pp10-14.
2486 Eisen, A. Losing a hotel, gaining a home. Real Estate Today, 11 July 1978 pp10-14.
2487 Emeny, R. Public houses and the mixed hereditament. Rating and Valuation, April 1981 pp109-110.
2488 Gamoran, A. C. How hotels are financed. Hotel and Motel Management,

194 September 1979 pp28-30.
2489 Gamoran, A. C. How to provide a hotel in a development and benefit both. Boston, Warren Gorham and Lamont, 1979.
2490 Gamrecki, J. A portfolio of investment ideas. Hotel Motel Manager, 198 November 1983 pp14-18.
2491 Gillham, B. Assessing rental values of public houses. Chartered Surveyor, 112(6) January 1980 pp197-200.
2492 Gillham, B. Current trends in the valuation of hotels. Valuer(ISVA), 50(5) 1981 pp1040-1041.
2493 Gillham, B. Valuing the contents of licensed premises. Chartered Surveyor, 111(12) July 1979 pp524-525.
2494 Greene, Belfield-Smith & Co.The hotel tariff study of Great Britain. 1975-1980. London, Greene, Belfield-Smith & Co., 1981. (annual keeping 1975 as the base year)
2495 Greene, Belfield-Smith & Co., Trends in hotel sales and profits 1970-1977: a survey for international investors. London, Greene, Belfield-Smith & Co., 1978.
2496 Grenney, K. E. F. Tourist hotel development in New Zealand. New Zealand Valuer, 25(11) September 1984 pp639-641.
2497 Gunnar, P. M. and others. The commercial condominium hotel: considerations for developers. Cornell Hotel and Restaurant Administration Quarterly, 23 November 1982 pp50-57.
2498 Hallinan, R. E. Urban renewal calculations in localities that win or lose. New Zealand Valuer, 25(2) June 1982 pp95-99. (Also in Valuer(Australia), 27 January 1982 pp128-132)
2499 Hanson, M. Where George III took the waters. Country Life, 215(4269) 3 May 1979 p1402.
2500 Hattersley, W. M. and others. How to value existing and new hotels. Chartered Surveyor, 113(12) 1981 pp784-790.
2501 Hattersley, W. M. Valuation of hotels. London, Royal Institution of Chartered Surveyors, 1981. (lecture)
2502 Herbert, C. Hotel appraisal: a hotelier's point view. New Zealand Valuer, 24(3) September 1979 pp147-150.
2503 Hines, M. A. Overseas investment in Chinese hotel joint ventures. Real Estate Issues, 9(2) 1984 pp45-47.
2504 Hotel appraiser. New Zealand Valuer, 24(3) September 1979 pp134-150.
2505 Hotels and licensed premises. Chartered Surveyor Weekly, 8(5) 2 August 1984 pp307-315.
2506 Hotels as investments:condo or co-op?Barrons, 63 3 October 1983 p79.
2507 How to value existing and new hotels. Valuation of free public houses. The long goodbye. Chartered Surveyor, 113(12) July 1981 pp784-790.
2508 Kennedy, E. C. Financing a major hotel development. New Zealand Valuer, 25(11) September 1984 pp650-653.
2509 Lepard, N. A property and a business. Estates Gazette, 266(6128) 2 April 1983 pp21-22.
2510 Lugton, D. B. Motel valuations using value indicators derived from sales and turnovers. New Zealand Valuer, 23(1) March 1976 pp23,24,27.
2511 Mackenzie, J. D. H. Hotel and motel valuation. AIM, 25(4) November 1981 pp32-37.
2512 Management and mathematics: developing hotel investments. Cornell Hotel and Restaurant Administration Quarterly, 20 February 1980 pp82-85.
2513 Marjason, Len. Brewery leases - Tooth & Co. Ltd. - valuation approach. Valuer(Australia), 26 July 1980 pp192-193.
2514 Marjason, Len. Hotel leases - valuation approach. Valuer(Australia), 27 October 1982 pp369-371.

2515 Mellen, S. R. Simultaneous valuation: a new capitalisation technique for hotel and other income properties. Appraisal Journal, 51(2) 1983 pp165-189.
2516 Miller, A. A national view of the local. Chartered Surveyor Weekly, 4(4) 28 July 1983 pp200-201.
2517 Molinaro, C. J. Motel market: the real values. Mortgage Banking, 42 November 1981 pp56-57.
2518 Moneghetti, R. H. Valuation of a country hotel. Valuer,(Commonwealth Institute of Valuers), 25(1) January 1978 pp47-49.
2519 Nicholls, A. D. Valuation commentary. Rating and Valuation, May 1979 pp143-144.
2520 Photios, James. Value the hotel - a reply. Valuer(Australia), 27 October 1982 pp362-363, 366.
2521 Property special 1979. Caterer and Hotelkeeper, 17 May 1979 pp1-38.
2522 Riches in older hotels. Business Week, 22 November 1976 pp120 +.
2523 Royal Institution of Chartered Surveyors. The valuation of licensed premises for rating in England and Wales: discussion paper November 1984. London, Royal Institution of Chartered Surveyors, 1984.
2524 Rushmore, Stephen. Appraisal of food service facilities. Appraisal Journal, 48 July 1980 pp354-360.
2525 Rushmore, Stephen. Appraisal of lodging facilities. Cornell Hotel and Restaurant Administration Quarterly, 19 August 1978 pp17-25.
2526 Rushmore, Stephen. Hotels, motels, and restaurants: valuations and market studies. Rev. ed. Chicago, American Institute of Real Estate Appraisers, 1984.
2527 Rushmore, Stephen. Valuation of hotels and motels. Chicago, American Institute of Real Estate Appraisers, 1978.
2528 Rushmore, Stephen. What can be done about your hotel's real-estate taxes? Cornell Hotel and Restaurant Administration Quarterly, 18 May 1977 pp78-81.
2529 Rushmore, Stephen and Rubin, Karen E. The valuation of hotels and motels for assessment purposes. Appraisal Journal, 52(2) April 1984 pp270-287.
2530 Skynner, W. A. T. Valuation of public houses. London, Royal Institution of Chartered Surveyors, 1981. (Lecture)
2531 Synergy on the Atlantic: combined real-estate and resort projects. Cornell Hotel and Restaurant Administration Quarterly, 21 May 1980 pp41-48.
2532 Taylor, A. Developing a motor hotel. Hotel and Motel Management, 194 June 1979 pp30-32.
2533 Teale, M. Hospitality business back on the tracks. Property Business, May 1984 pp45, 47, 51.
2534 Technology: property management systems. Hotel Motel Management, 198 October 1983 pp36-37.
2535 Tharmalingam, V. Kumar. Resorts - Malaysia. Valuer(Australia), 27 January 1982 pp38-42.
2536 Two London hotel cases. Estates Gazette, 247(5891) 15 July 1978 pp205-107.
2537 Valuation. Part 1: Public houses and hotels. RICS Abstracts and Reviews, 17(2) February 1981 pp43-44. (Review R450)(Bibliography)
2538 Valuation of public houses for compulsory acquisition. Estates Gazette, 250(5938) 16 June 1979 pp1104-1105; 250(5940) 30 June 1979 p1312.
2539 Westbrook, R. Valuation of licensed premises. Revised edition. London, Estates Gazette, 1983. (First edition 1967)
2540 Wheeler, T. J. Public houses - validity of mixed hereditament status. Rating and Valuation, March 1981 pp73-74.

Rural leisure and other property

Non-urban property has been brought together. The range of information includes agricultural, rural and all other property not clearly included in another chapter. Land which is discussed in relation to no particular usage is also included here. Farming and other occupations based on the land are kept together where principles are concerned and only sub-divided geographically where there is specific, market-related discussion. The many articles in the farming press, particularly in Australia, which discuss value in relation to farm management have been excluded. Due to the paucity of literature in some topics subject groupings are limited and greater reliance is placed on indexing. The final section contains those special property types which would fit in no other category, or which are not represented in sufficient quantity to merit their own section.

2541 Abbema, J. The influence of managerial expertise on agricultural property value. AIM, 21(3) July 1977 pp18-20.

2542 Almey, E. V. Country kits: selling farm and ranch land. Real Estate Today, 11 January 1978 pp9-14.

2543 Alter, R. J. The erosion of private ownership of shorefront property. Real Estate Review, 12 Winter 1983 pp45-51.

2544 American Institute of Real Estate Appraisers. The appraisal of real property. Chicago, American Institute of Real Estate Appraisers, 1983.

2545 Anderson, R. C. and Dower, R. C. Land price impacts of the Adirondack Park land use and development plan. American Journal of Agricultural Economics, 62 August 1980 pp542-548.

2546 Armitage, L. A. Coastal Protection Act, 1979 New South Wales: a valuation perspective. Valuer(Australia), 26 January 1980 pp56-57, 80.

2547 Aspects of agricultural valuations. Estates Gazette, 240(5802) 16 October 1976 p232.

2548 Aston, Peter. Farm business and management and land ownership. no place, Echo Press, 1979.

2549 Barnard, J. R. Externalities from urban growth: the case of increased storm run-off and flooding. Land Economics, 54 August 1978 pp298-315.

2550 Barry, P. J. Capital asset pricing and farm real estate. American Journal of Agricultural Economics, 62 August 1980 pp549-553. (Discussion 63 August 1981 pp578-581)

2551 Bauer, L. Farm properties as a capital investment. AIM, 27(3) August 1983 pp16-28.

2552 Bentinck, B. L. Capitalized property taxes and the viability of rural enterprise subject to urban pressure. Land Economics, 56 November

1980 pp 451-456.

2553 Berry, H. Monopoly property - monopoly value. *Appraisal Journal*, 52(4) October 1984 pp528-538.

2554 Bertelson, M. K. and Shabman, L. Use of development value estimates for coastal wetland permit decisions. *Land Economics*, 55 May 1979 pp213-222.

2555 Boykin, James H. Developmental method of land appraisal. *Appraisal Journal*, 44 1976 pp181-192.

2556 Brown, G. M. and Pollakowski, H. O. Economic valuation of shoreline. *Review of Economics and Statistics*, 59 August 1977 pp272-278.

2557 Brown, G. T. Impact of energy on value. *Real Estate Appraiser and Analyst*, 46 December 1980 pp5-12.

2558 Brown, Ralph J. Study of the impact of the wetlands easement program on agricultural land values. *Land Economics*, 52 November 1976 pp509-517.

2559 Brown, Ralph J. and Schmitz, J. M. Appraising wetlands easements. *Appraisal Journal*, 46 April 1978 pp176-184.

2560 Brunoehler, R. How pros make farm appraisals. *Banking*, 69(3) March 1977 pp132, 134.

2561 Burns, G. A. Timber and timberland appraisal. *ASA Valuation*, 29(1) December 1983 pp74-82.

2562 Burris, L. M. Inspection problems of desert properties. *Appraisal Journal*, 52 January 1984 pp127-129.

2563 Butler, J. R. A new look at partial takings. *Appraisal Journal*, 50 October 1982 pp591-596. (Properties condemned for erecting power transmission lines)

2564 Cantrell, W. F. Scenic easements: evaluation considerations. *Real Estate Appraiser and Analyst*, 49 Summer 1983 pp61-67.

2565 Castle, E. N. and Hoch, I. Farm real estate price components, 1920-78. *American Journal of Agricultural Economics*, 64 February 1982 pp8-18

2566 Chicoine, D. L. Farmland values at the urban fringe: an analysis of sale prices. *Land Economics*, 57 August 1981 pp353-362.

2567 Clarke, C. H. H. Valuation of sub-division block land. *New Zealand Valuer*, 23(8) December 1977 pp416-419.

2568 Clatanoff, Robert M. *Valuation and property taxation of forests, orchards and trees*. Chicago, International Association of Assessing Officers, 1982. (Bibliography series)

2569 Clipperton, W. H. How a rural appraisal practice operates. *Canadian Appraiser*, 28(3) August 1984 pp42-44.

2570 Coleman, K. J. Good earth. *Real Estate Today*, 11 July 1978 pp48-53

2571 Constam, E. Methodology of industrial water lots evaluation. *AIM*, 20(3) July 1976 pp24-28, 48.

2572 Constam, E. Methodology of water lot evaluation. *Appraisal Journal*, 45 January 1977 pp70-79.

2573 Cordell, H Ken and Stanley-Saunders, Barbara. *The private sector role in rural outdoor recreation in the United States: an annotated bibliography*. Chicago, International Association of Assessing Officers, 1984. (Bibliography series)

2574 Coughlin, R. E., Berry, D. and Plant, T. *Differential assessment of real property as an incentive to open space preservation and farmland retention*. Philadelphia, Regional Science Research Institute, 1978.

2575 Coughlin, R. E. and others. Differential assessment of real property as an incentive to open space preservation and farmland retention. *National Tax Journal*, 31 June 1978 pp165-179.

2576 Currie, W. The tobacco industry. *Valuer*(Australia), 28(4) October 1984 pp321-322.

2577 Dempsey, W. E. DUPA techniques for electric transmission-line easement acquisitions. Appraisal Journal, 49 July 1981 pp382-390.

2578 Dixon, T. J. and others. Valuation of a perpetual easement over submerged offshore lands. Real Estate Appraiser and Analyst, 49 Fall 1983 pp57-66.

2579 Dolman, J. P. and Seymour, C. F. Valuation of transportation/communication corridors. Appraisal Journal, 46 October 1978 pp509-522.

2580 Dorsey, T. A. Appraisers as energy experts: an introduction and review Real Estate Appraiser and Analyst, 49 Winter 1983 pp70-72.

2581 Dugan, J. W. Marshland valuations for pipelines. Appraisal Journal, 48 pril 1980 pp206-214.

2582 Dunford, R. W. and Marousek, D. C. Sub-county property tax shifts attributable to use-value assessments on farmland. Land Economics, 57 May 1981 pp221-229.

2583 Economic valuation of shoreline. Review of Economics and Statistics, 61 November 1979 pp634-636.

2584 Epp, D. J. and Al-Ani, K. S. Effect of water quality on rural nonfarm residential property value. American Journal of Agricultural Economics, 61 August 1979 pp529-534.

2585 Everett, C. D. Estate tax special use valuation: preparing the farmland appraisal for the estate and IRS. Appraisal Journal, 52 April 1984 pp165-176.

2586 Everhart, M. E. Environmental conservation hazards to harvesting timber and forage from critical lands: a basis for highest and best use. Real Estate Appraiser and Analyst, 49(1) 1983 pp69-72.

2587 Everhart, M. E. Use of suitability clauses in the valuation of nonagricultural lands. Real Estate Appraiser, 43 January 1977 pp32-36.

2588 Fear, Albert B. Rural portfolio management. New Zealand Valuer, 25(5) March 1983 pp247-256.

2589 Ferguson, G. E. A. Effect of the energy crisis on land values - the rural community. Valuer(Australia), 26 April 1981 pp451-453.

2590 Field, K. E. Factors affecting the value of development lands. AIM, 20(2) April 1976 pp18-19.

2591 Floyd, C. F. Valuation of floodplain lands for stream valley park. Appraisal Journal, 51 April 1983 pp202-210.

2592 Ford, Robert W. As the city grows. Valuer(Australia), 27 January 1982 pp94-97.

2593 Foster, S. G. The appraisal process in the valuation of water lots. AIM, 27(4) November 1983 pp23-25.

2594 Gadd, J. L. The integration of machinery and equipment appraisals into the real estate valuation report. Real Estate Appraiser and Analyst, 50 Spring 1984 pp5-7.

2595 Golub, K. L. Appraising the wilderness. Appraisal Journal, 48 July 1980 pp361-365.

2596 Green, J. C. Water rights and the real estate appraiser. Real Estate Appraiser and Analyst, 49 Fall 1983 pp67-71.

2597 Green, R. Farms and agricultural properties. Valuer(ISVA), 50(1) 1981 p8.

2598 Grover, M. R. Submerged land. AIM, 24(3) August 1980 pp11-15.

2599 Haddaway, Samuel C. Diversification possibilities in agricultural land investments. Appraisal Journal, 46(4) October 1978 pp529-537.

2600 Hargreaves, R. V. Apportioning rural land values. New Zealand Valuer, 25(12) December 1984 pp687-688.

2601 Harrison, D. and Rubinfield, D. L. Air pollution and property value debate: some empirical evidence. Review of Economics and Statistics 60 November 1978 pp635-638.

2602 Hembd, J. and Infanger, J. L. Application of trend surface analysis to a rural-urban land market. Land Economics, 57 August 1981 pp303-322.
2603 Hyde, J. V. Future for right of way and right of way appraising. Real Estate Appraiser, 44 March 1978 pp19-21.
2604 Ibbotson, N. R. Vineyard appraisal and establishment costs. New Zealand Valuer, 25(3) September 1982 pp156-160, 162.
2605 John H Walter & Sons and Stanbridge Munby and Moore, Farm business review. Lincoln, Stanbridge Munby and Moore, 1984. (irreg. serial)
2606 Johnson, M. S. and Leas, M. J. Differential capitalization of local public service characteristics. Land Economics, 58 May 1982 pp189-203.
2607 Johnston, B. F. and Clark, W. C. Redesigning rural development: a strategic perspective. Baltimore, Md., Johns Hopkins, 1982.
2608 Jundt, D. W. Buying and selling farmland: a guide to profitable investment. St. Louis, Mo., Doane Agricultural Service, 1980.
2609 Kelly, J. D. Rural valuations in the 1980s. Valuer(Australia), 26 July 1980 pp184-187, 225.
2610 Klemperer, W. D. Economic analysis of the case against ad valorem property taxation in forestry. National Tax Journal, 30 December 1977 p469.
2611 Kline, John E. An alternative method of valuing nondevelopable waterfront land and beaches. Appraisal Journal, 52 January 1984 pp53-59.
2612 Kletke, D. D. and Plaxico, J. S. Farmland profitability and feasibility appraisals: new concepts and procedures. Journal of the Amererican Society of Farm Managers and Rural Appraisers, 42(2) October 1978 pp51-58.
2613 Land prices substantially underestimate the value of environmental quality. Review of Economics and Statistics, 62 February 1980 pp154-156.
2614 Leung, H. L. Redistribution of land values. Cambridge, University of Cambridge, Department of Land Economy, 1979. (Occasional paper 11)
2615 Long, H.A.R. The valuation of woodlands. Journal of Valuation. 2(2) 1984 pp161-166.
2616 McGoldrick, J. D. and Hodges, A. Risk rating real estate investments in earthquake prone areas. Mortgage Banker, 38 November 1977 pp54-60.
2617 McPhaden, J. H. Appraising the farm. AIM, 25(2) May 1981 pp8-12.
2618 Markson, Henry E. Derating doubtfully defined: a tale of two fish farms: or as you like it. Journal of Planning and Environment Law, August 1976 pp487-496.
2619 May, J. E. Timberland: making it produce. Trusts and Estates, 120 September 1981 pp8-10.
2620 Mayne, Leslie S. Trees and landscape valuation. Valuation, 24(1) December 1977 pp26-33.
2621 Miles, C. W. N. Estate finance and business management. 4th edition. London, Estates Gazette, 1981.
2622 Miles, C. W. N. Some valuation issues in the calculation of capital transfer tax. British Tax Review, 5 1975 pp269-274.
2623 Miles, C. W. N., Long, H. A. R. and Seabrooke, W. Walmsley's rural estate management. 6th edition. London, Estates Gazette, 1979. (First edition 1948 by R. C. Walmsley)
2624 Millar, D. D. and others. The effect of town and country planning on coastal lands. New Zealand Valuer, 23(2) July 1976 pp74-126.
2625 Miller, Stuart W. Agricultural land, taxation and preservation. Chicago, International Association of Assessing Officers, 1981. (Bibl-

iography series)
2626 Mills, W. L. and Hoover, W. L. Investment in forest land: aspects of risk and diversification. Land Economics, 58 February 1982 pp33-48.
2627 Moffat, D. M. Farm input costs. AIM, 26(3) August 1982 pp33-35.
2628 Murray, W. G. Farm appraisal and valuation. 6th edition. Ames, Iowa, Iowa State University Press, 1983. (5th edition 1969)
2629 Needham, B. A neo-classical supply-based approach to land prices. Urban Studies, 18(1) 1981 pp91-104.
2630 New Zealand. Ministry of Energy. The effects of petroleum pipeline easements on property values. New Zealand Valuer, 25(8) 1983 pp438-451.
2631 Newman, Timothy D. Appraisal of timber: a direct sales approach. Appraisal Journal, 52(1) January 1984 pp17-26.
2632 Niskanen, W. A. and Hanke, S. H. Land prices substantially underestimate the value of environmental quality. Review of Economics and Statistics, 59 August 1977 pp375-377.
2633 Norton-Taylor, Richard. Whose land is it anyway? Wellingborough, Northamptonshire, Turnstone Press, 1982.
2634 Oster, M. and Carlson, J. Farmland buying strategies. New York, Wiley, 1984.
2635 Palmquist, R. B. Measuring environmental effects on property values without hedonic regressions. Journal of Urban Economics, 11 May 1982 pp333-347.
2636 Panissidi, A. R. Techniques of waterland appraisal: log raft storage areas. New Zealand Real Estate, 34(4) August 1983 pp60-71.
2637 Partaker, J. E. Easement compensation for transmission line rights-of way. AIM, 25(3) August 1981 pp17-19.
2638 Patchin, P. J. Grain elevators: three approaches to value. Appraisal Journal, 51(3) July 1983 pp392-400.
2639 Peters, Lewis C. Timber appraisals. Athens, Georgia, University of Georgia, September 1980 (Practicing Foresters Institute 7. Association of Consulting Foresters)
2640 Plattner, R. H. and Campbell, T. J. Study of the effect of water view on site value. Appraisal Journal, 46 January 1978 pp20-25.
2641 Primeaux, W. J. and others. Fair value versus original cost rate base valuation during inflation. Energy Journal, 5 April 1984 pp93-108.
2642 Pye, I. D. Rural investment trends. Valuer(Australia), 26 October 1980 pp312-314.
2643 The Railroads. Business Facilities, 17(10) December 1984 pp23-27.
2644 Reenstierna, E. T. Appraisal of wetlands. Real Estate Appraiser and Analyst, 46 1980 pp4-8.
2645 Reeves, H. Taxing problems on the farm. Chartered Surveyor Weekly, 5(3) 1983 pp152-153.
2646 Reisman, D. Buying and selling country land. New York, S. J. Durst, 1980.
2647 Rice, H. H. The value of developed land considered vacant and unimproved. Real Estate Review, 12 Summer 1982 pp45-50.
2648 Rosner, M. H. and Barrows, R. L. School reform and rural land use policy incentives. Land Economics, 53 August 1977 pp288-297.
2649 Ross, W. R. A. Investment in forestry. Accountant, 184 9 April 1981 pp389-390.
2650 Roulac, Stephen E. Agricultural land investment: profit opportunity or new speculative bubble. Appraisal Journal, 46 January 1978 pp53-66.
2651 Rowe, Robert D. and Chestnut, Lauraine G. Valuing environmental commodities revisited. Land Economics, 59(4) November 1983 pp404-410.
2652 Royal Institution of Chartered Surveyors. Land resources: development

and ownership: Annual conference 1977. London, Royal Institution of Chartered Surveyors, 1977.
2653 Royal Institution of Chartered Surveyors, National Farmer's Union and Country Landowners Association. Management agreements in the countryside. Basingstoke, Surveyor's Publications, 1984.
2654 Sandy, C. Tax aspects of woodlands development. Accountant, 190(5682) 1 March 1984 pp15-17.
2655 Schachter, S. Partial takings of a tank farm: estimating damages to the remainder. Appraisal Journal, 48 January 1980 pp120-123.
2656 Shabman, L. and Bertelson, M. K. Use of development value estimates for coastal wetland permit decisions. Land Economics, 55 May 1979 pp213-222.
2657 Smith, D. An appraiser looks at multiple regression. Appraisal Journal 47(2) April 1979 pp248-252.
2658 Smith, D. G. Professional rural appraisal manual. 4th edition. Champaign, Ill., Stipes Publishing Co., 1975.
2659 Smith, D. V. Problems/controls in the appraisal of wildlands. Appraisal Journal, 48 April 1980 pp215-223.
2660 Smith, T. R. and Kooros, A. Application of the opportunity cost doctrine to right-of-way valuation. Real Estate Appraiser and Analyst, 50 Spring 1984 pp15-20.
2661 Sowiak-Rudej, C. Valuation of rural properties subject to licences and quotas. Valuer(Australia), 28(3) July 1984 pp170-176.
2662 Steel, Anthony. Financial institutions, their investment and agricultural land ownership. Reading, University of Reading, Department of Land Management and Development, 1983.
2663 Steeves, P. F. The valuation of small holdings. AIM, 21(1) January 1977 pp25-27, 37-40.
2664 Stroud, H. B. Land development cooperation: a system for selling rural real estate. American Real Estate and Urban Economics Association Journal, 6 Fall 1978 pp271-284.
2665 Suter, R. C. The sales comparison versus the market data approach to farm real estate values. Real Estate Appraiser and Analyst, 49 Fall 1983 pp22-30.
2666 Suter, R. C. and Scaletta, P. J. Installment land contract: as used in farm sales. Real Estate Appraiser, 43 March 1977 pp47-52.
2667 Sutherland, C. F. and Tedder, P. L. Impacts of federal estate taxation on investments in forestry. Land Economics, 55 November 1979 pp510-520. (Discussion 57 February 1981 pp123-127)
2668 Taylor, T. H. C. Hypothetical subdivision statement. New Zealand Valuer, 23(8) December 1978 pp409-415.
2669 Teague, Keith W. Introduction to valuation procedures. Valuer(Australia), 26(1) November 1980 pp44-51. (for Interstate Railroad Transportation Operating Properties)
2670 Teale, M. Motorways developing the middle of nowhere! Property Business, 3 1984 pp41, 43-45.
2671 Thomas, J. G. Influence of environmental legislation on the appraisal process. Appraisal Journal, 46 January 1948 pp26-31.
2672 Thompson, C. K. Analyzing the fish farm. Appraisal Journal, 162(2) April 1979 pp195-203.
2673 Tomlinson, I. C. Rural multiples. New Zealand Valuer, 23(3) September 1976 pp153-160.
2674 Undiscovered gold. Television and Radio Age, 30 23 May 1983 p16. (Land around TV and radio masts)
2675 United Nations. Food and Agriculture Organisation. Soil Resources, Development and Conservation Service. A framework for land evaluation Rome, Food and Agriculture Organisation, 1976.

2676 Walsh, Richard G., Loomis, John B. and Gillman, Richard S. Valuing option, existence and bequest demands for wilderness. Land Economics, 60(1) February 1984 pp14-29.
2677 Washburn, G. L. Developing a farm - the intelligent method. Real Estate Today, 12 June 1979 pp42-47.
2678 Weiers, C. J. Soil classification and land valuation. Town and Country Planning, 43(9) September 1975 pp390-393.
2679 White, F. C. and others. Comparison of property tax circuit-breakers applied to farmers and homeowners. Land Economics, 52 August 1976 pp355-362. (Discussion 54 August 1978 pp390-399)
2680 Williams, R. G. Agricultural valuations: a practical guide. London, Estates Gazette, 1984.
2681 Wise, J. O. Modifying the income approach to farm appraisal. Appraisal Journal, 45 October 1977 pp505-510.
2682 Wood, Leslie S. Principles and practice of farm valuation. London, Estates Gazette, 1969.
2683 Young, J. Buying right in country real estate. New York, New American Library, 1979.

Australia

2684 Andrews, R. L. D. Avocado notes. Valuer(Australia), 26 October 1980 pp315-317, 319.
2685 Beatty, Ian. Land values. Valuer(Australia), 27 July 1982 pp242-243, 246.
2686 Brorson, W. Milk quota system in New South Wales and its effects on land values. Valuer(Australia), 26 July 1981 pp528-539.
2687 Hardey, G. H. Rural trends in South-west land markets. Valuer(Australia), 27 January 1983 pp464-471.
2688 Manning, Harry J. Valuation, property taxation and other aspects of farmlet subdivisions adjacent to Canberra. Valuer(Australia), 26 January 1980 pp25-30, 35.
2689 Murphy, T. J. and Mashman, I. Effect of government policies on irrigated land values in South-west New South Wales. Valuer(Australia), 27 January 1983 pp431-439.
2690 Young, Harold. Effect of the development of natural resources in South Australia. Valuer(Australia), 26 April 1980 pp82-90,97.

Canada

2691 Ashmead, R. Influences on land values. AIM, 26(3) August 1982 pp30-32.
2692 Gilson, J. C. Going! going! last call! sold! (What is the price of farm land?) AIM, 25(4) November 1981 pp10-14.
2693 Hoffman, D. W. Problems of farmland value in the urban fringe. AIM, 22(3) 1978 pp14-19. (Mississauga)
2694 Hoover, D. L. Agriculture in Northern Canada - production and valuation. AIM, 21(3) July 1977 pp14-17.
2695 Toma, D. M. Farmland prices in Alberta and Ontario - What about the future? Canadian Appraiser, 28(3) August 1984 pp19-22.

Great Britain

2696 Agricultural land, its ownership, price and rent. Economic Trends, December 1979.
2697 Apsion, Gordon. Farm tax and finance. Bicester, Oxon, Gordon Apsion, 1983 - . (bi-weekly) (Leaflet giving advice and news)
2698 Bowers, J. K. and Black, C. J. Investment appraisal and the environment: the Soar Valley improvement scheme. Leeds, University of Leeds, School of Economic Studies, 1983. (Discussion paper 129)
2699 Central Association of Agricultural Valuers. Costings 1983: applic-

able to valuations made on and after 1 July 1983. London, Central Association of Agricultural Valuers, 1983. (Publication 159)
2700 Central Association of Agricultural Valuers, and Royal Institution of Chartered Surveyors, Land Agency and Agricultural Division. Agricultural rent valuations: guidance, June 1980. London, Royal Institution of Chartered Surveyors, 1980.
2701 Clayton, J. Uncertain prospects for land prices. Estates Gazette, 270(6191) 30 June 1984 pp1280-1281.
2702 Farmland and fishing rights in a Welsh valley. Rating and Valuation Reporter, 16 March 1976 pp77-78.
2703 The farmland market. Estates Gazette and Farmers Weekly, biannual.
2704 Gladstone, A. UK agricultural investment - a trend towards diversification. New Law Journal, 134(6157) 8 June 1984 pp531-532.
2705 Great Britain. Ministry of Agriculture Fisheries and Food. Agricultural land prices in England and Wales. London, Ministry of Agriculture Fisheries and Food, annual. (ADAS Technical Report no.20) (Also available earlier as Press Notices and semi-annually as Sales of agricultural land in England and Wales.)
2706 Great Britain. Ministry of Agriculture Fisheries and Food, Agricultural Development Advisory Service and the Economic and Statistics Group. Farm rents. London, HMSO, annual. (ADAS Technical report no. 19)
2707 Hanson, M. Forecasting farmland prices. Country Life, 174(4504) 15 December 1983 pp1802.
2708 Humberts. Agricultural commentary. London, Humberts, regular, no frequency given.
2709 John Clegg & Co. Review of the forest year. John Clegg & Co, Cheltenham, Gloucestershire, annual.
2710 Jones Lang Wootton. The agricultural land market in Britain: an in-depth study of its mechanism, for owners, investors and advisors. London, Jones Lang Wootton, 1983.
2711 Leigh-Pemberton, R. Why the funds are not buying farmland. Chartered Surveyor Weekly, 6(9) 1 March 1984 p596.
2712 Marshall, R. Incorporating straw in valuations. Big Farm Weekly, 8(8) 23 February 1984 p35.
2713 Miles, C. W. N. Agricultural estates survey 1981/2. Estates Gazette, 270(6179) 7 April 1984 p25.
2714 Munton, R. J. C. Financial institutions: their ownership of agricultural land in Great Britain. Area, 9(1) 1977 pp29-37.
2715 Nicholls, A. D. Valuation commentary. Rating and Valuation, April 1983 pp99-101.
2716 Royal Institution of Chartered Surveyors. Managing the nation's land resources: Annual conference University College of North Wales, Bangor 1976. London, Royal Institution of Chartered Surveyors, 1977
2717 Savills. Agricultural land market report.October 1981 - . London, Savills, 1981 - . (annual)
2718 Savills. Agricultural land prices 1950-1980: an assessment of performance. London, Savills, 1980.
2719 Savills. Farm management in the U.K.. London, Savills, 1979 - . (annual)
2720 Savills. Investment in forestry in the United Kingdom. London, Savills, 1982.
2721 Savills. Savills - RTP Agricultural performance analysis. London, Savills, 1984. (Occasional paper no.1)
2722 Savills. Savills - RTP Agricultural performance analysis. 1981 - . London, Savills, 1981 - . (annual)
2723 Seymour, L. M., Shearman, T. G. and Thomas, R. Statutory instrument

1983 no 1475: Agriculture (Calculations of value for Compensation) (Amendment) Regulations: an explanation and guide to valuers. London, Surveyor's Publications, 1984.

2724 Wainwright, Richard. Property in the eighties: a problem or a pleasure. Agricultural property. London, Strutt & Parker, 1980.

New Zealand

2725 Brabyn, P. A. Kiwi fruit developments. New Zealand Valuer, 24(5) March 1980 pp344-346, 306.

2726 Fear, Albert B. Rural portfolio management. Valuer(Australia), 27 June 1982 pp70-81.

2727 Laing, A. P. Analysis of rural leasehold sales. New Zealand Valuer, 24(3) September 1979 pp188-193.

2728 Tierney, P. E. Kiwifruit experience. New Zealand Valuer, 25(9) March 1984 pp491-496.

2729 Watt, G. R. and Fraser, T. Principles and practice of valuing forest and forest land in New Zealand. Rotorua, Forest Research Institute, 1978. (Report no 115)

2730 Watters, J. A. Analysis of rural leasehold sales. New Zealand Valuer, 24(3) September 1979 pp186-187.

South Africa

2731 Darragh, J. D. South Africa - rural valuation techniques. New Zealand Valuer, 24(6) June 1980 pp413-415.

United States

2732 7% retreat in average United States farm value. Appraiser, 40(7) September 1984 p6.

2733 Baker, Robert D. Timber use-value assessment in Texas. College Station, Texas, Texas A & M University, 1981.

2734 Boyd, James M. and Davison, Dale L. Farming and real estate investment after the TRA of 1976. Arizona Business, 24(4) April 1977 pp3-7.

2735 Burns, G. Timber values for Houston County Texas. Crockett, Texas, Houston County Appraisal District, 1982.

2736 Duncan, M. R. Farm real estate values: what's happening. Kansas City Mo., Federal Reserve Bank of Kansas City, Research Division, 1979.

2737 Ellison, Brian. Water oriented real estate in the United States. Valuer(Australia), 26 April 1980 pp140-142, 145.

2738 Everett, C. D. Estate Tax special use valuation: preparing the farm-land appraisal for the estate and IRS. Appraisal Journal, 52(2) April 1984 pp165-176.

2739 Fischel, W. A. The urbanization of agricultural land: a review of the National Agricultural Lands Study. Land Economics, 58(2) 1982 pp236-259. (Critique by P Raup, pp260-274)

2740 Gilligan, G. S. A price guide for buying and selling rural acreage. 2nd edition. New York, McGraw Hill, 1976.

2741 Healy, R. G. and Short, J. L. The market for rural land: trends, issues, policies. Washington, D.C., Conservation Foundation, 1981.

2742 Howell, Donald E. Exhibit D. Oregon Forest. in Rural appraisal manual 5th ed. Denver, Colorado, American Society of Farm Managers and Rural Appraisers, 1981. pp195-240.

2743 Savills. Investing in agricultural land in the United States of America. London, Savills, 1982.

2744 Sayre, William B. Agricultural real estate: cash coop for pension funds. Pension World, 18(9) September 1982 pp43-48.

2745 Scott, Mina C. Best returns with OTC Stock but less risk in farm property. Pensions and Investment, 7(24) 19 November 1979 pp20, 57.

Rural leisure and other property

2746 Tarver, Charles M. Valuation of Southeastern timberland. The Consultant(Association of Consulting Foresters), January 1982 pp16-19.

2747 Weiner, Alfred A. Appraising national forest timber values: a concept reexamined. Journal of Forestry(Society of American Foresters), June 1981 pp367-369, 376.

Minerals

2748 Clatanoff, Robert M. Valuation and property taxation of extractive resources: a bibliography. Chicago, International Association of Assessing Officers, 1982.

2749 Cleland, N. A. The valuation of mineral rights. AIM, 25(3) August 1981 pp31-32.

2750 Gentry. D. W. Valuation of mines and mineral-bearing lands. Valuation, 27(1) November 1981 pp28-38.

2751 Hellewell, E. G. The dual rate mineral valuation principle index-linked. Chartered Land Surveyor/Chartered Minerals Surveyor, 1(4) 1979 pp15-24.

2752 Hellewell, E. G. Mineral valuation: the dual rate principle modified for inflation. Quarry Management and Products, 3(5) May 1976 p120-122.

2753 Hellewell, E. G. Valuation of variable future incomes on the dual-rate basis. Chartered Land Surveyor/Chartered Minerals Surveyor, 2(2) 1980 pp45-51.

2754 Humphreys, D. The value of mineral resources. Resources Policy, 9(3) September 1983 pp169-176.

2755 Mellett, H. F. The sampling and valuation of an irregular shaped ore-body. Journal of the Institute of Mine Surveyors of South Africa, 19(5) March 1978 pp68-72.

2756 Richards, T. Mineral valuation. Chartered Land Surveyor/Chartered Minerals Surveyor, 2(2) 1980 pp52-60.

2757 Rinaldi, A. J. A review of Hoskold and the valuation of mineral property. Appraisal Journal, 49(4) October 1981 pp574-579.

2758 Sani, E. Mineral investment valuation and the cost of capital. Resources Policy, 2(4) December 1976 pp284-298.

2759 Sheard, M. The 'Golightly' case. Estates Gazette, 260(6065) 19 December 1981 pp1179-1182.

2760 Smith, T. Development of taxation and its effect on minerals valuation Synopsis of a paper to the Royal Institution of Chartered Surveyors Minerals Division and Sheffield Polytechnic Minerals Valuation Seminar 6 April 1976. (Available at RICS)

2761 Van Landingham, S. L. Economic valuation of mineral property. Stroudsberg, Pa., Hutchinson Ross;Wokingham, Van Nostrand Reinhold, 1983.

2762 Vincent, P. A. Minerals: some problems of valuation. Estates Gazette, 269(6170) 4 February 1984 pp389-390, 393.

2763 Waite, G. C. Minerals: valuing the hidden asset. Valuer(ISVA), 49(9) November/December 1980 pp281-283.

2764 Willson, R. Mineral valuation: principles and problems. Typescript, 1984.(Royal Institution of Chartered Surveyors,Ryde Memorial Prize)

2765 Willson, R. Problems associated with the valuation of spoil heaps. Land and Minerals Surveying, 2(3) 1984 pp125-131.

Leisure and sporting facilities

2766 Ames, R. Appraisal and feasibility analysis of bowling centres. Real Estate Appraiser, 44 March 1978 pp15-18.

2767 Catliff, T. The Thorpe Park experience. Chartered Surveyor Weekly, 4(10) 8 September 1983 pp489-491.

2768 Clatanoff, Robert M. Valuation of resort and recreational property: a bibliography, Chicago, International Association of Assessing Officers, 1984. (Bibliography series)

2769 Daubert, John T., Young, Robert A. and Gray, S. Lee. Economic benefits from instream flow in a Colorado mountain. Fort Collins, Col., Colorado Water Resources Research Institute, 1979.

2770 Farwell, T. The appraisal of ski areas. AIM, 26(3) August 1982 pp18-29. (Also Valuation, 23(2) 1976 pp2-17)

2771 Fereday, A. W. National parks and wilderness areas: the effect of increased leisure time on land values. AIM, 22(2) April 1978 pp29-30.

2772 Galbraith, G. Sporting rights - an assessment. Valuer(ISVA), 50(10) December 1981 p302.

2773 Galbraith, G. Valuation of sporting rights. Chartered Surveyor, 112 (12) July 1980 pp564-565.

2774 Gimmy, A. E. Resort analysis in Mexico - delights and dilemmas. Appraisal Journal 44 October 1976 pp485-499.

2775 Gimmy, A. E. Tennis clubs and racquet sport projects:a guide to appraisal market analysis, development and financing. Chicago, American Institute of Real Estate Appraisers, 1982.

2776 Gordon, M. Underwater assets: boat moorings are the hotest thing in California real estate. Barrons, 60 7 January 1980 pp9 +.

2777 Helber, L. E. and Kaiser, C. Tourism: planning and development, Boston CBI Publishing Co., 1978.

2778 Henshall, Brian D. Tourism - its impact on the community. New Zealand Valuer, 25(11) September 1984 pp642-645.

2779 Heuer, K. L. and McKay, C. Golf courses: a guide to analysis and valuation. Chicago, American Institute of Real Estate Appraisers, 1980.

2780 Hillary, W. R. Market 'bottoms out' as bargain values lure buyers. Estates Times, 721 11 November 1983 pp10-11.

2781 Hillary, W. R. Valuations - 1980s and the leisure industry. Lecture IV. London, Surveyor's Technical Services, 1981.

2782 Hughes, D. A. Recreational land and islands. AIM, 24(3) August 1980 pp17-20.

2783 Larby, M. The valuation of sporting estates. Property, 2 1984 p22.

2784 Lusteck, J. A. and Mann, J. K. Feasibility of recreational land development. Appraisal Journal, 46 January 198 pp7-19.

2785 McKay, C. R. Golf course appraisals. Valuation, 27(1) November 1981 pp100-107.

2786 McMillan, Melville. Measuring benefits generated by urban water parks. Land Economics, 51 November 1975 pp379-381.

2787 Meister, A. D. and Ward, A. B. Valuation, tourism and changing land value. New Zealand Valuer, 25(11) September 1984 pp642-645.

2788 Mendoza, L. The valuation of amenity land. Valuer(ISVA), 50(3) 1981 pp82-84; 50(4) 1981 pp110-111.

2789 Millbank, P. Being positive about leisure losses. Surveyor, 147(4371) 19 March 1976 pp14-16.

2790 Miller, R. Are Scots salmon played out? Chartered Surveyor Weekly, 6(5) 2 February 1984 p281.

2791 Moir, J. Promoting tourism site development. British Travel News, 73 1981 pp30-32.

2792 Nicholson, S. Newest game: racquetball draws investment dollars. National Real Estate Investor, 19 July 1977 pp16-17.

2793 Paris, E. What price skiing? Forbes, 1 March 1982 pp120+ .

2794 Piddington, H. R. Land management for shooting and fishing. Cambridge,

University of Cambridge, Department of Land Economy, 1981. (Occasional paper 13)

2795 Reid, D. J. S. Tourist recreational development in rural areas. New Zealand Valuer, 23(6) June 1977 pp324-333.

2796 Risk element in leisure plans. Planning, 508 4 March 1983 p6.

2797 Robson, A. J. and Schaffman, D. T. The crunch, the boom and the recreational land market. AIM, 23(2) 1979 pp33-40.

2798 Seay, Edwin. Golf courses sought as profitable investment. Journal of Property Management, 42(1) January/February 1977 pp14-18.

2799 Shedlock, R. E. Developing successful theme recreation centers. Real Estate Review, 12 Winter 1983 pp86-90.

2800 Special report: leisure. Chartered Surveyor Weekly, 8(9) 6 September 1984 pp565-569.

2801 Stephens, R. L. Professional management: recreational condos need it too! Journal of Property Management, 42 September 1977 pp244-245.

2802 Talbot-Ponsonby, N. The 1983 leisure market reviewed. Estates Gazette, 269(6178) 31 March 1984 pp1235-1236.

2803 Valuation. Part II: sports and leisure facilities. RICS Abstracts and Reviews, 17(5) May 1981 R450.

2804 Whelan, C. Britannia bids for leisure market. Chartered Surveyor Weekly, 5(10) 8 December 1983 p618.

2805 William Hillary & Co. Leisure comment: golf courses. Salisbury, William Hillary & Co., 1984. (Leisure comment no.1: to be semi-annual)

2806 Young, C. E. and Teti, F. A. Influence of water quality on the value of recreational properties adjacent to St. Albans Bay, Vermont. Washington, D.C., Economic Research Services, Natural Resources Economics Division, 1984. (Report no AGES-831116)

2807 Young, R. P. New Zealand - leisure land use and development. New Zealand Valuer, 25(10) June 1984 pp579-584.

2808 Zomerplaag, H. Financing of tourist activites and leisure residences. in FIABCI, Thirty First annual congress. Athens 1980.

Cinemas and theatres

2809 Buono, Thomas, J. Valuation in broadcasting. Appraisal Journal, 52(3) July 1984 pp382-388.

2810 Callaghan, J. H. The long goodbye. Chartered Surveyor, 113(12) July 1981 p788, 790.

2811 Callaghan,J.H. Valuations - 1980s and the leisure industry. Lecture III. London, Surveyor's Technical Services, 1981.

2812 Kinloch, Bruce. The curtain rises on Maybox group. Property Business, October 1984 pp40-41.

Historic buildings

2813 Adams, W. N. Historic buildings: an approach to valuation. Valuer (ISVA), 45(7) August/September 1976 p201.

2814 Aldous, T. Christopher Buxton's character building. Chartered Surveyor Weekly, 9(10) 6 December 1984 p704.

2815 Atwell, D. To the manor reborn. Building, 246(40) 1 October 1982 pp28-30.

2816 Barling, L. and others. Property refurbishment. Financial Times, 18 May 1981 p23.

2817 Boykin, James H. and Epley, D. R. Renovation feasibility analysis. AIM, 26(4) November 1982 pp16-19.

2818 Catt, R. The conversion, improvement and extension of buildings. Lon-

don, Estates Gazette, 1981.
2819 Cerf, Alan R. Incentives for commercial property rehabilitation in the 1981 Tax Act. Real Estate Review, 12(2) 1982 pp88-94. (Also as Univeristy of California, Institute of Business and Economic Research PR28)
2820 Chartsearch Ltd. Property renovation profits. London, Chartsearch Ltd., 1981.
2821 City-Wide Development Corporation. City-Wide Development Corporation Development Services Package. Dayton, Ohio, City-Wide Development Corp., 1979.(Sponsored by U.S. Economic Development Administration. EDA-79-029)
2822 Cloud, Jack. Appraisal of historic homes. Real Estate Appraiser, 42(5) 1976 pp44-47.
2823 Compton, R. N. Certified historic structures: the overlooked and underrated tax shelter. Practical Accountant, 17 May 1984 pp57-62.
2824 Cook, A. The costs of refurbishment: a survey of architects, quantity surveyors and engineers. Birmingham, University of Aston, Joint Unit for Research on the Urban Environment, 1979. (Research note 7)
2825 Davis, J. C. Rehabbing for profit. New York, McGraw-Hill, 1981.
2826 De Giovanni, Frank F. and others. Private market revitalisation: its characteristics and consequences. Research Triangle Park, N.C., Research Triangle Institute, 1981. (Sponsored by U.S. Department of Housing and Urban Development. HUD-0002420)
2827 Dodge, Robert I. Rental properties can be rehabilitated using private investment, subsidy techniques. Journal of Housing, 37(9) October 1980 pp497-503.
2828 Dunham, H. W. Conversion of an obsolete railroad station into a modern restaurant. Appraisal Journal, 44(4) October 1976 pp500-509.
2829 Falk, N. Recycling industrial relics. Town and Country Planning, 52(9) September 1983 pp225-227.
2830 Faulkner, A. J. Opportunities for changes of use or renewal of buildings. Property Management, 2(4) 1984 pp296-300.
2831 Finn, M. and others. Property appraisal, refurbishment, development and maintenance. Pensions World, 13(11) November 1984 pp713-724.
2832 Freedman, P. Obtaining possession for redevelopment. Estates Gazette, 264(6109) 6 November 1982 pp509-511; 264(6110) 13 November 1982 pp603-604.
2833 Furlong, G. Adapting old space to the needs of new industries. Estates Times, 672 19 November 1982 pp11-12.
2834 Furlong, G. How to set the mills humming again. Chartered Surveyor Weekly, 3(1) 7 April 1983 pp32-33.
2835 Gaines, J. P. Residential rehabilitation appraisals: problems and prospects. Appraisal Journal, 48(2) April 1980 pp236-247.
2836 Gamzon, Melvin A. Adaptive use: an alternative for the 1980s. National Real Estate Investor, 22(1) January 1980 pp30, 90, 92.
2837 Get you to the church on time. Property Letter, 276 July 1978 pp2-13.
2838 Golicz, L. J. Historical facade easements: the impact of future costs. Appraisal Journal, 52 January 1984 pp9-15.
2839 Green, H. and Foley, P. Making homes for small firms. Town and Country Planning, 52(1) January 1983 pp17-20.
2840 Green, M and D, and Kirkwood, J. Redevelopment and rehabilitation: the economic appraisal of alternative schemes. Housing Review, 25(4) 1976 pp90-93.
2841 D. HowardGreen and Associates. Conversion of industrial premises to multiple units. No place, D. Howard Green and Associates, 1982. (Available Royal Institution of Chartered Surveyors)
2842 Hayman, A. J. and S. P. Rehabbing and the people priority. Mortgage

Banking, 43(3) September 1983 pp52-54, 56.
2843 Howe, R. C. and Hatton, N. C. A new challenge for the appraiser: tax credit incentives on historic property investment. Real Estate Appraiser and Analyst, 49 1983 pp59-63.
2844 Kellough, W. R. Towards a methodology of valuation in urban renewal areas. AIM, 22(4) November 1978 pp11-15, 18.
2845 Long Beach Department of Community Development. Long Beach Boulevard Revitalization Study, Long Beach, California. Long Beach, Ca., Long Beach Department of Community Development, 1981. (Sponsored by U.S. Economic Development Administration. EDA-81-084)
2846 McLeister, D. Recycling, remodelling: on big projects, get cash flowing fast. Professional Builder and Apartment Business, May 1979 pp154-157.
2847 Mann, E. Scottish renewal expands. Building, 244(21) 27 May 1983 pp32-34.
2848 Marsh, Paul. The refurbishment of commercial and industrial buildings Lancaster, Construction Press, 1983.
2849 Maskell, I. W. Commercial redevelopment - a case study. New Zealand Valuer, 23(6) June 1977 pp300-313.
2850 Miners, T. W. The economics of building maintenance. Pretoria, South Africa, National Building Research Institute, 1978.
2851 Oldham, S. G. Historic properties: variable valuations. Appraisal Journal, 50(3) 1982 pp364-377.
2852 Penfold, D. Palumbo tower - where's the debate? Estates Gazette, 270(6187) 2 June 1984 p797.
2853 Period property register. Chobham, Surrey, Historic Buildings Council, 1984 onwards. (Summaries in Chartered Surveyor Weekly)
2854 Rehabilitation or new building? Chartered Surveyor, 113(3) October 1980 pp166-167.
2855 Relph-Knight, L. A boom for industrial refurbishment? Civil Engineering, May 1983 pp33-35.
2856 Reynolds, Judith. Historic properties: preservational and valuation process. Chicago, American Institute of Real Estate Appraisers, 1982.
2857 Roddewig, Richard J. 'Certified' rehabilitation of historic buildings. Real Estate Review, 12(3) 1982 pp67-71.
2858 Roddewig, Richard J. and Schlaes, Jared. Preservation easements reconsidered: an alternative approach to value. Appraisal Journal, 52 July 1984 pp325-347.
2859 Royal Institution of Chartered Surveyors. Rehabilitation and associated economic factors. London, Surveyor's Publications, 1981.
2860 Royle, D. Is it a fine art to value fine art? Valuer(ISVA), 50(8) October 1981 pp238-239.
2861 Selinger, Joseph J. The use of real estate rehabilitation credits by Limited Partnerships. Journal of Real Estate Taxation, 10(2) 1983 pp129-173.
2862 Shepherd, J. Refurb. RIBA Journal, 90(2) February 1982 pp45-54.
2863 Sidwell, A. C. Managing rehabilitation projects. Chartered Surveyor Weekly, 5(2) 13 October 1983 pp88-89.
2864 Simon, T. Funding refurbishment schemes. Chartered Surveyor Weekly, 1(7) 9 December 1982 pp495-497.
2865 Summers, R. M. Quality counts. Accountant, 183(5509) 11 September 1980 pp416-418.
2866 Sykes, S. Periodic refurbishment and rental value growth. Journal of Valuation, 3(1) 1984 pp32-41.
2867 Sykes, S. Refurbishment and future rental growth. Estates Gazette, 272(6215) 12 December 1984 pp1231-1234.

2868 Urbed Ltd. Recycling industrial buildings. Edinburgh, Capital Planning Information, 1981.
2869 Valuing historically significant properties. Appraisal Journal, 42(2) April 1974 pp200-209.
2870 Vane, R. Historic houses or modern ruins. Journal of Planning and Environment Law, March 1978 pp145-153.
2871 Westside Local Development Corporation. Commercial revitalization project for the Southwest Boulevard commercial area, Kansas City, Missouri. Kansas City, Mo., Westside Local Development Corp., 1981. (Sponsored by U.S. Economic Development Administration. EDA-81-025)
2872 Whelan, C. The Triton titan. Chartered Surveyor Weekly, 7(13) 28 June 1984 pp880-881.
2873 Whipp, N. Is it worth refurbishing older office buildings? Chartered Surveyor Weekly, 6(12) 22 March 1984 p795.
2874 Will, M. T. Taxation and valuation of historic buildings. Monticello, Ill., Vance Bibliographies, 1979. (No P383)
2875 Williams, Harry G. C. and Seymour, C. F. Building for the ages (1933): Building for the ages (1982). Appraisal Journal, 50(2) April 1982 pp168-181.

Others

2876 Albritton, H. D. Valuation of special-use property types. Appraisal Journal, 48(3) 1980 pp367-371.
2877 Aloni, J. Appraising the ports of Israel. Chartered Surveyor, 113(5) December 1980 pp368-369.
2878 American Institute of Real Estate Appraisers. Readings in the appraisal of special use properties. Chicago, American Institute of Real Estate Appraisers, 1981.
2879 Anstey, J. The valuation of rights to light. Reading, University of Reading, College of Estate Management, Centre for Advanced Land Use Studies, 1981.
2880 Armon-Jones, C. Informal tenders. Estates Gazette, 269(6177) 24 March 1984 pp1121.
2881 Baker, J. Valuations of garages and petrol filling stations. Valuer (ISVA), 50(7) August/September 1981 pp212-213.
2882 Cemetery valuation - one more time. Appraisal Journal, 48 January 1980 pp133-135.
2883 Clatanoff, Robert M. Ad valorem assessment of telecomms property. Chicago, International Association of Assessing Officers, 1981. (Research and Information series)
2884 Clatanoff, Robert M. Valuation of utility and transportation property a classified annotated bibliography. Chicago, International Association of Assessing Officers, 1983. (Bibliography series)
2885 Denyer-Green, Barry. Academic assessment of RV. Chartered Surveyor Weekly, 9(11) 13 December 1984 pp787-788.
2886 Denyer-Green, Barry. Assessing rates for a car park. Chartered Surveyor Weekly, 5(2) 13 October 1983 pp110-111.
2887 Donias, C. H. Appraisal of major machinery and equipment. Valuation, 27(1) November 1981 pp84-99.
2888 Floyd, C. F. Issues in the appraisal of outdoor advertising signs. Appraisal Journal, 51(3) July 1983 pp422-435.
2889 Green, J. E. Valuation of railroads and utilities for property taxation. Appraisal Journal, 46 July 1978 pp373-384.
2890 Hagman, D. G. and Misczynski, D. J. Windfalls for wipeouts: land value capture and compensation. Chicago, American Society of Planning Officials, 1978.

2891 Hallinan, R. E. Replacement insurance certificates for buildings in the 1980s. New Zealand Valuer, 24(7) December 1980 pp654-664,653.
2892 Hoagland, G. Alaskan pipeline: right of way appraisal technique. Appraisal Journal, 45 April 1977 pp284-289.
2893 International Association of Assessing Officers. Assessor's data exchange. Chicago, International Association of Assessing Officers, 1908 + . (Physical, financial and geographical data on internally marketed or rarely transferred properties, quarterly figures)
2894 International Association of Assessing Officers. Cemeteries, federally-subsidized housing, hotels and motels, sand and gravel operations and theaters. Chicago, International Association of Assessing Officers, 1978. (Bibliography series)
2895 Jackson, R. D. Valuation of a life estate. Real Estate Appraiser and Analyst, 49(2) 1983 pp47-48.
2896 Johnson, P. Valuation of fine art for tax, probate and insurance. New Law Journal, 9 November 1984 pp999-1000.
2897 Kanner, G. Use of the substitution method in valuing highly depreciated public improvements. Appraisal Journal, 46 April 1978 pp296-298.
2898 Kay, Thomas S. Plant and machinery appraisals the UK experience. Valuation, 26(1) November 1980 pp2-11.
2899 Kellough, W. R. Analysis and theoretical implications of partial takings. AIM, 20(3) July 1976 pp21-23.
2900 Klein, L. The valuation of oil terminals: recent observations. Real Estate Appraiser and Analyst, 47(2) 1981 pp44-47.
2901 Krueger, R. Appraising service station properies for the oil company in transition. Real Estate Appraiser, 40(2) 1974 pp13-17.
2902 Lewsley, C. Valuing an advertising site. Rating and Valuation Reporter, 23(2) February 1983 pp26-27.
2903 Lewsley, C. Valuing a private clinic. Rating and Valuation Reporter, 19(10) October 1979 pp245-246.
2904 Lowry, W. V. Appraisal of Indian reserve lands. AIM, 25(3) August 1981 pp28-30.
2905 MacGowan, R. A. Valuation for sale: garage in East-end Glasgow. Surveying Technician, 13(2) 1984/5 pp4-5.
2906 Miles, Leslie H. and Bealmear, Allen D. Auction values, machinery and equipment appraisals. Valuation, 24(1) December 1977 pp46-49.
2907 Nelson, Wayne N. Machinery - cost approach vs Market approach. Valuation, 27(1) November 1981 pp138-143.
2908 Othick, F. Valuing new buildings. Local Government Chronicle, 5826 8 December 1978 pp1342-1343.
2909 The Earl Peel. Values of the grouse moor. Country Life, 174(4486) 11 August 1983 pp358-359.
2910 Phillips, D. Problems with fixtures. Solicitor's Journal, 128(6) 10 February 1984 pp87-90.
2911 Pottery assessment reduced. Rating and Valuation Reporter, 24(9) September 1984 p169.
2912 Profit basis valuation of privately owned railway. Rating and Valuation Reporter, 24(6) January 1984 p125.
2913 Rasbash, D. L. The use of changes in property values in the evaluation of highway schemes. Highways and Transportation, 30(8-9) 1983 pp22-25.
2914 Revaluation commentary: contractor's test valuations. Rating and Valuation, November 1973 pp299-300.
2915 Rutherford, J. L. Estimation of sewer asessments. Real Estate Appraiser and Analyst, 45 January 1979 pp35-38.
2916 Samuels, Warren J. Regulation and valuation. Public Utilities Fortnightly, 96 17 July 1975 pp17-20.

2917 Sanderson, I. J. V. Pioneer properties - a case for the crystal ball? Valuer(Australia), 27(1) January 1982 pp34-37, 55.

2918 Sedgwick, J. R. Garages and petrol stations. Estates Gazette, 257 (6021) 14 February 1981 pp561-566.

2919 Thomas, H. O. Valuation of buildings erected for a specific use. Valuer(Australia), 27(7) July 1983 pp630-635.

2920 Thompson, C. K. Analysing the fish farm. Appraisal Journal, 47(2) April 1979 pp195-203.

2921 Townsend, P. S. Appraisal of petroleum storage and distribution centers. Appraisal Journal, 46 April 1978 pp165-175.

2922 Troxel, Jay C. Appraisal of churches. Real Estate Appraiser, 44 March 1978 pp8-13.

2923 Valuing a garage and petrol filling station. Rating and Valuation Reporter, July 1975 pp284-286; August 1975 pp328-329.

2924 Valuing multi-storey car parks. Rating and Valuation Reporter, 18(4) April 1978 pp94-95.

Property market

Market studies are numerous and often very specific both to area and property type. Studies relating to the latter have been cited in the appropriate sections. Many must be ommitted from such a list as being of little lasting value (unless to historians) although they may be indicative of the likely sources of more recent information, particularly where localities are reviewed on a cyclical basis. Although a few of the annual studies are listed it is well to remember that most of the news journals study the past year's market either in December or January issues, often looking forward at the same time in predictive articles published shortly before or thereafter. The following is highly selective, as it would otherwise be never-ending and disproportionately long.

International

2925 Annual investment file. no place, Urban Publishing, May 1983.
2926 Balchin, P. and Kieve, J. L. Urban land economics. London, Macmillan, 1977.
2927 Cunnew, T. and Ellis, Richard. Economic ills discourage new construction. National Real Estate Investor, 23(1) 1981 pp39-54.
2928 Cunnew, T. and White, John R. Money is chasing deals, deals are hard to find: developers, investors recovering from overbuilding. National Real Estate Investor, 22(1) 1980 pp33-46, 80-86.
2929 Hillier Parker May & Rowden. International property bulletin. London, Hillier Parker May & Rowden, 1983 - . (annual)
2930 International property markets: London 19 and 20 January 1983. London, Financial Times Conference Organisation, 1983. (Speaker's papers)
2931 Jones Lang Wootton. International property review. London, Jones Lang Wootton, 1980 - . (annual)
2932 Jones Lang Wootton. JLW Property index. London, Jones Lang Wootton, 1978 - . (quarterly)
2933 Jones Lang Wootton. Progress in property. London, Jones Lang Wootton, 1979.
2934 Richard Ellis. International property. London, Richard Ellis, 1980 - . (annual)
2935 Richard Ellis. Property market indicators. London, Richard Ellis, annual.
2936 Richard Ellis. World rentals. London, Richard Ellis, 1983.
2937 Royal Institution of Chartered Surveyors. International property, London, Royal Institution of Chartered Surveyors, 1981.
2938 Squirrell, Maurice D. Overseas trends. Valuer(Australia), 26 April 1981 pp472-475.

Americas

Canada

2939 A E LePage Ltd. Market quarterly. London, A E LePage Ltd., quarterly.

2940 How far downtown?: a review of the plans of four cities. Plan Canada, 22(2) December 1982 pp45-66.

United States

The National Association of Realtors, Real Estate Information Network, REINET, maintains a number of databases and programs with market information and data on specific properties. National Real Estate Investor runs regular 'City reviews' on all cities in the United States, many appearing on an annual basis: it would not be possible to list all. Several articles illustrate their series, see Schultz, Tharpe, Tschirhart and Willmann below. Many articles appear in the regional real estate press, none of which has been included here.

2941 Annual real estate review. National Real Estate Investor, November issues.

2942 Asabere, Paul K. and Colwell, Peter F. Zoning and the value of urban land. Real Estate Issues, 9(1) Spring/Summer 1984 pp22-27.

2943 Cardiff, G. E. and English, J. W. The coming real estate crash. Revised edition. New York, Warner Books, 1980. (First ed. Arlington House, 1979)

2944 Debenham Tewson & Chinnocks. The United States of America: report on the real estate market, January 1979. London, Debenham Tewson & Chinnocks, 1979.

2945 Dole, Charles E. and others. Developers see brighter days ahead. National Real Estate Investor, 25(2) February 1983 pp36-60, 101, 126-127.

2946 Feagin, J. R. Urban real estate speculation in the United States: implications for social science and urban planning. International Journal of Urban and Regional Research, 6(1) 1982 pp35-60.

2947 Focus on NE coast USA. Estates Gazette, 272(6213) 1 December 1984 pp1043-1067.

2948 Focus on New York. Estates Gazette, 268(6160) 12 November 1983 pp671-694.

2949 Hanford, Lloyd D. The real estate market - past, present and future. Journal of Property Management, 46(5) September/October 1982 pp12+.

2950 Hanford, Lloyd D., Downs, Anthony and Graaskamp, J. A. Real estate and the economy in 1984: what goes down must come up. Journal of Property Management, 49(1) January/February 1984 pp6+ .

2951 Huntley, J. Focus on New York. Property Busines, July 1984 pp37-57.

2952 The impact of market value real estate assessment on Long Island. Hemstead, NY., Hofstra University, School of Business, 1979.

2953 Ipsen, E. Famine to feast, but for how long? Euromoney, March 1984 pp96-97, 99-100.

2954 Jones Lang Wootton. An analysis of the city's economic and commercial investment opportunities. New York, Jones Lang Wootton, 1981

2955 Jones Lang Wootton. Houston: an analysis of the city's economy and commercial real estate investment opportunities. London, Jones Lang Wootton, 1980.

2956 Jones Lang Wootton. JLW Downtown property map. New York, Jones Lang Wootton, no date.

2957 Jones Lang Wootton. JLW Downtown report. New York, Jones Lang

Wootton, 1984.
2958 Jones Lang Wootton. JLW Midtown property map. New York, Jones Lang Wootton, no date.
2959 Jones Lang Wootton. JLW Midtown report. New York, Jones Lang Wootton, 1984.
2960 Jones Lang Wootton. Los Angeles: an analysis of the city's economic and commercial real estate investment opportunities. London, Jones Lang Wootton, 1981.
2961 Jones Lang Wootton. San Francisco property map. New York(?), Jones Lang Wootton, no date.
2962 Jones Lang Wootton. A report on the U S real estate market. London, and New York, 1978.
2963 Lockwood, C. Manhattan moves uptown. Boston, Mass., Houghton Mifflin, 1976.
2964 Quilter Goodison & Co. U S property market review. London, Quilter Goodison, no date.
2965 Real estate outlook in California. Proceedings of the conference on the Program in Real Estate and Urban Economy, University of California, Berkeley, May 1979. Berkeley, Cal., University of California Institute of Business and Economic Research, 1979.
2966 Redman, A. L. and Sirmans, C. F. Regional/local economic analysis: a discussion of data sources. Appraisal Journal, 45 April 1977 pp261-272. (Bibliography)
2967 Richard Ellis. United States property report. New York, Richard Ellis, annual. (Formerly Property report - United States(quarterly) and Real estate market report before 1980. Both published from London)
2968 Savills. Letter from America. London, Savills, 1983 - . (annual)
2969 Schultz, Gerald L. San Diego - all realty areas hotting up. National Real Estate Investor, 21(5) 1979 pp91-102.
2970 Special report - Texas. Chartered Surveyor Weekly, 8(12) 27 September 1984 pp799-815.
2971 Tharpe, Gene. Atlanta - major announcements herald resurgence of downtown market. National Real Estate Investor, 21(5) 1979 pp67-82.
2972 The new money target: profitable real estate. Business Week, 2494 1 August 1977 pp52-58.
2973 Tschirhart, Don. Detroit. National Real Estate Investor, 25(7) July 1983 pp67-75.
2974 U.S. property: shark infested waters for the unwary. Property Confidtial, 339 November 1983 pp9-15.
2975 Willmann, John B. Washington, D.C. - uneasiness reigns as formerly ebullient market quiets down. National Real Estate Investor, 22(6) June 1980 pp75-92.
2976 Wright, Arthur L. Real estate atlas of Texas. College Station, Texas, Texas A & M University, Texas Real Estate Research Center, 1979.

Asia

2977 Jones Lang Wootton. South East Asia property review. London, Jones Lang Wootton, 1981 - . (annual)
2978 Property in the Far East. RICS Abstracts and Reviews, 21(2) February 1985 pp28-30. (Review R514: bibliography)
2979 Richard Ellis. A report for South-East Asia:the property market 1981. London, Richard Ellis, 1981.

Hong Kong

2980 Hoare Govett Ltd. Hong Kong property. Hong Kong, Hoare Govett Ltd,

1982.

2981 Reader, S. Hong Kong property market and agency. The Valuer(Australia), 28(2) April 1984 pp108-109.

2982 Vickers da Costa Ltd. The Hong Kong property market May 1981. London, Vickers da Costa Ltd, 1981.

Malaysia

2983 International real estate Malaysia. National Real Estate Investor, 25(1) January 1983 pp100-101.

2984 Jones Lang Wootton. Malaysia: summary of property values. London, Jones Lang Wootton, 1983 - . (annual)

Singapore

2985 Hoare Govett Ltd. Singapore property. Singapore, Hoare Govett Ltd, 1982.

2986 Jones Lang Wootton. Property investment in Singapore. London, Jones Lang Wootton, 1984.

2987 Singapore: though growth rate slows construction moves up sharply. National Real Estate Investor, 26(1) January 1984 pp48,50.

Australasia

Australia

2988 Andrews, G. C. Valuer's view of Adelaide's first decade. Valuer(Australia), 27 July 1983 pp636-637,641.

2989 Archer, R. W. Land policy for Australian cities. Valuer(Australia), 27 April 1982 pp191-196,200.

2990 Callaghan, B. Foreign investment in Australian real estate. Valuer (Australia), 26 October 1981 pp632-634, 643.

2991 Cannon, M. The land boomers. Australia, Nelson & Son, 1976.

2992 Coombes, Paul. City property around Australia: guarded optimism is the name of the game. Real Estate and Stock Journal, 44(6) July 1980 pp5-7, 27.

2993 Daly, M. T. Sydney boom, Sydney bust. London, Allen & Unwin, 1982.

2994 Hillier Parker May & Rowden. The Australian market. London(?), Hillier Parker May & Rowden, quarterly.

2995 Jones Lang Wootton. Australian property review. Sydney, Jones Lang Wootton, annual.

2996 Jones Lang Wootton. City map, Adelaide. Sydney, Jones Lang Wootton, no date.

2997 Jones Lang Wootton. City map, Melbourne. Sydney, Jones Lang Wootton, no date.

2998 Jones Lang Wootton. Melbourne real estate bulletin. Sydney, Jones Lang Wootton, 1984.

2999 Jones Lang Wootton. Paramatta - identiplan map. Sydney, Jones Lang Wootton, no date.

3000 Jones Lang Wootton. Sydney - identiplan map. Sydney, Jones Lang Wootton, no date.

3001 Richard Ellis. Property report Melbourne Australia March 1981. London, Richard Ellis, 1981.

Europe

3002 Hillier Parker May & Rowden. Passport to Europe. London, Hillier Parker May & Rowden, 1983.

3003 Property in the EEC. RICS Abstracts and Reviews, 20(8) August 1984 pp137-140. (Review R508: bibliography)

Belgium

3004 Bernard Thorpe & Partners. Antwerp property market report 1979-80. London, Bernard Thorpe & Partners, 1980.

3005 Bernard Thorpe & Partners. Antwerp property market report 1980-1. London, Bernard Thorpe & Partners, 1981.

3006 Bernard Thorpe & Partners and Hugo Ceusters. Survey of the Brussels real estate markets: general review of 1983. London, Bernard Thorpe & Partners, 1981.

3007 Gerald Eve & Co. Property review, Belgium. London, Gerald Eve & Co., 1980.

3008 Healey & Baker. Report on Liege April 1981. London, Healey & Baker, 1981.

3009 Jones Lang Wootton. Antwerp office market. London, Jones Lang Wootton/Universite Catholique de Louvain, 1981 - . (annual, formerly JLW-UCL office survey: Antwerp)

3010 Jones Lang Wootton. Belgium property review. London, Jones Lang Wootton, 1983.

3011 Jones Lang Wootton. Brussels office market. London, Jones Lang Wootton/Universite Catholique de Louvain, 1981 - . (quarterly, formerly JLW-UCL office survey: Brussels)

3012 Jones Lang Wootton. The office market in Liege. London, Jones Lang Wootton/Universite Catholique de Louvain, 1981 - .

3013 King & Co. Industrial property review: Belgium 1979 - 1980. London, King & Co., 1979.

3014 Richard Ellis. Property report Belgium September 1981. London, Richard Ellis, 1981.

3015 Richard Ellis. Property report Belgium February 1982. Brussels, Richard Ellis, 1982.

3016 St Quintin. Belgium property-review. Brussels, St Quintin with Ketteridge & Partners N.V., 1983.

Eire

3017 Jennings, R. Land transactions and prices in the Dublin area 1974-78. Dublin, National Institute for Physical Planning and Construction Research, 1980.

3018 Jones Lang Wootton. Depreciating fixed assets land and buildings - the new rules. London, Jones Lang Wootton, 1978.

3019 Jones Lang Wootton. Irish property index. Dublin, Jones Lang Wootton, 1983 - . (semi-annual)

3020 Jones Lang Wootton. Report on Dublin office property December 1980. London(?), Jones Lang Wootton, 1980.

France

3021 Jones Lang Wootton. The property market in France. London,Jones Lang Wootton, regular. (frequency not known)

3022 Weatherall Green & Smith. French property report. London, Weatherall Green & Smith, 1982.

Germany

3023 Weatherall Green & Smith. German property report. London, Weatherall Green & Smith, 1978 - . (annual)

Great Britain

3024 Alderton, R. Implementing planning policies: development control and the property market in Camden; a summary of trends. London, London Borough of Camden, Department of Planning and Communications, 1984.

3025 Allsop & Co. The Allsop property checklist: 57 key questions designed to provide a profitable insight into the property market. London, Allsop, 1977.
3026 Anderson, G. A. Prospects for property. Estates Gazette, 243(5845) 20 August 1977 pp577,579,581.
3027 Barras, Richard. The development cycle in the City of London. London, Centre for Environmental Studies, 1979. (Research series 36)
3028 Barron, P. Creating a property market-place in print. Estates Gazette, 270(6184) 12 May 1984 pp484,486.
3029 Bernard Thorpe & Partners. Property market report 1978-9. London, Bernard Thorpe & Partners, 1979.
3030 Bernard Thorpe & Partners. Property market report Edinburgh and Glasgow. London, Bernard Thorpe & Partners, 1980.
3031 Bernard Thorpe & Partners. Property market report Scotland 1978-79. London, Bernard Thorpe & Partners, 1978.
3032 Bernard Thorpe & Partners. Property review 1984. London, Bernard Thorpe & Partners, April 1981 - . (formerly Property trends quarterly survey.)
3033 Caws, R. B. Property: the present and the future. Estates Gazette, 248(5911) 2 December 1976 pp763-767.
3034 Cullingworth, J. B. Environmental planning 1939-1969 vol.4. Land values, compensation and betterment. London, HMSO, 1980.
3035 Darlow, Clive and Morley, S. 125 years of property investment. Estates Gazette, 266(6132) 30 April 1983 pp407-414.
3036 Deal's digest. London, Morgan Grampian, quarterly. (Estates Times)
3037 Debenham Tewson & Chinnocks. A digest of property statistics. London, Debenham Tewson & Chinnocks, 1982.
3038 Debenham Tewson & Chinnocks. Money into property 1970-1979. London Debenham Tewson & Chinnocks, 1980.
3039 Dunn, A. T. and White, G. C. Trends in sales of land and buildings 1973-1977. Economic Trends, 305 March 1979 pp100-114.
3040 Economist Intelligence Unit. Michael Laurie Property performance index London, Economist Intelligence Unit, 1982.
3041 Edward Erdman. Annual property review. London, Edward Erdman, 1978 -. (annual with various titles)
3042 Elliott & Green. The property report 1981. Lymington, Elliott & Green, 1981.
3043 Estates Times. Review of the property market 1968-1978. RICS Abstracts and Reviews, 14(11) 1978 R417. (Review R417: bibliography)
3044 Great Britain. Inland Revenue. The Valuation Office (England and Wales) Report and property market summary to the 31st March 1983. London, Inland Revenue, 1984. (Now published annually by Surveyor's Publications as Valuation Office property market report)
3045 Groves, R. Economic and social change in the West Midlands. Birmingham, University of Birmingham, Centre for Urban and Regional Studies, 1983. (Occasional paper 9)
3046 Hoare Govett Ltd. U K Property. London, Hoare Govett Ltd, 1982.
3047 Kenneth Ryden & Partners. Prospects for Aberdeen. Edinburgh, Kenneth Ryden & Partners, 1980.
3048 Knight Frank & Rutley. Annual review 1984/5. London, Knight Frank & Rutley, 1984.
3049 Laing & Cruikshank. Property sector. London, Laing & Cruikshank, monthly.
3050 Laing & Cruikshank. Property sector research. London, Laing & Cruikshank, weekly. (notes)
3051 Langton, R. S. and others. Development in London, 1967-1980. London, Bernard Thorpe and Partners, 1981.

3052 Merseyside County Council and Catterall Sutcliffe Associates. Merseyside urban land markets study final reports. Liverpool, Merseyside County Council, 1978.
3053 Panmure Gordon & Co. Property sector monthly. London, Panmure Gordon & Co, 1984 - .
3054 Pearce, B. J., Curry, N. R. and Goodchild, R. N. Land, planning and the market. Cambridge, University of Cambridge, Department of Land Economy, 1978. (Occasional paper 9)
3055 Plender, John. Property revisited. Estates Gazette, 271(6196) 4 August 1984 pp433-434,440.
3056 Property Market Analysis and Property Agents International. PMA/PAI property survey. London, PMA and PAI, 1982 - . (semi-annual) (Published as a leaflet and also in Estates Gazette)
3057 Quilter Hilton Goodison & Co. Property 1979. London, Quilter Hilton Goodison & Co, 1979.
3058 Richard Ellis. Property market indicators. London, Richard Ellis,a series of six regular sheets giving tables relating to: Capital and rental value indices; Regional rental and capital growth rates; 1981/82 Capital and rent growth rates; Estimated components of capital growth; Prime and equated yields.
3059 Richard Ellis. UK property. London, Richard Ellis, annual.
3060 St Quintin. Property market overview. London, St Quintin with Laing and Cruikshank, 1983 - . (quarterly)
3061 St Quintin. Property market survey 1983. London, St Quintin, 1983. (annual)
3062 Salter, T. A review of the property market 1968-1978 to mark the tenth anniversary of Estates Times. London, Morgan Grampian, 1978.
3063 Savills. Property outlook 1985. London, Savills, 1984.
3064 Savills. Wimborne and Salisbury property outlook: supplement. 1983. London, Savills, 1983.
3065 Scarrett, D. Practice-based market research: a brief survey of published research prepared by professional firms and by stockbrokers specialising in the property market together with a note of current property indices. Second edition. Leicester, Leicester Polytechnic, School of Land and Building Studies, 1984. (First edition, 1983)
3066 Scarrett, D. Practice-based market research and property indices. in Chiddick, David and Millington, Alan F. Land management: new directions. London, Spon, 1984.
3067 Smart, G. Land values and planning in the inner areas: report of a working party at the Royal Town Planning Institute. London, Royal Town Planning Institute, 1978.
3068 Strutt & Parker. Review 1978-1979. London, Strutt & Parker, annual.
3069 J P Sturge & Sons. Property 1984. Bristol, J P Sturge & Sons, 1983.
3070 Thorns, D. C. Industrial restructuring and change in the labour and property markets in Britain. Environment and Planning A, 14(6) 1982 pp745-764.
3071 Vickers da Costa Ltd. Quarterly property review. London, Vickers da Costa Ltd, quarterly. (No. 10 in 1978)
3072 Walls, C. J. B. Property indices. London, W Greenwell & Co., 1978.
3073 Weatherall Green & Smith. Weatherall's property report. London, Weatherall Green & Smith, 1979 - . (annual)
3074 White, H. P. The continuing conurbation: change and development in Greater Manchester. London, Gower for the British Association for the Advancement of Science, 1980. (in the series on British regions)

Greece

3075 Patton, C. and Sophoulis, C. Great expectations: illegal land development in modern Greece. Ekistics, 50(301) 1983 pp259-264.

Netherlands

3076 Jones Lang Wootton. Businessman's guide to the Hague. London(?), Jones Lang Wootton, 1983.

Real estate practice

A bibliography relating to the valuation aspects of a professional practice should include some consideration of the office management and profession itself. Until now references have concentrated on making the appraisal or valuation. This chapter and the following one cover related aspects: the business and the investment, or financial background within which the valuation is made. Many general texts are included here rather than in the general chapter as they relate to more practical aspects. However the running of the business is inextricably linked with the investment and financial aspects of property valuation and sales for investment purposes. This chapter must therefore be read closely with the following one.

In this chapter there is a higher volume of light, advisory articles of one or two pages in length than in earlier sections. Many have been excluded. Those remaining, particularly the shorter ones, reflect the uniqueness of their contribution to knowledge or their greater weight. The many books reflect the strength of publishing in this field in the United States. All yearbooks and lists of members which might have been included here or in the General section have been excluded since almost all membership associations publish some type of listing. An attempt has been made to include all aspects of practice work, including estate agency, in one sequence since it is not possible to create meaningful subdivisions.

3077 Aldridge, Trevor M. Guide to national conditions of sale. London, Oyez, 1981.

3078 Allen, J. B. Selling income property successfully. Revised edition. Los Angeles, Ca., California Association of Realtors, 1976. (First edition 1970)

3079 American Society of Real Estate Counselors. Real estate counseling. Chicago, American Society of Real Estate Counselors, 1984.

3080 American Society of Real Estate Counselors. Real estate counseling: a professional approach to problem-solving. Chicago, American Society of Real Estate Counselors of the National Association of Realtors, 1976.

3081 Anderson, E. Innocents abroad: selling to first-time buyers. Real Estate Today, 11 August 1978 pp48-51.

3082 Andrews, R. A. Reality: a simplified guide to the Estate Agents Act 1979. Warwick, National Association of Estate Agents, 1980.

3083 Armon-Jones, C. Revealing the art of estate agency. Estates Times, 20 March 1984 pp12-13.

3084 Arnold, A. L., Wurtzebach, Charles H. and Miles, M. E. Modern real estate. Boston, Warren, Gorham and Lamont, 1980.

3085 Art of negotiating. Real Estate Today, 12 March 1979 pp24-28.
3086 Baker, R. Getting rich in real estate partnerships. New York, Warner Books, 1982.
3087 Barnsley, D. G. Conveyances and declarations of beneficial ownership. Solicitor's Journal, 127(34) 26 August 1983 pp554-556.
3088 Barr, A. M. Master guide to high-income real estate selling. Englewood Cliffs, NJ, Executive Reports Corp., 1977.
3089 Bartlett, J. F. Getting started in Alabama real estate. Dubuque, Ia., Kendall/Hunt Publishing, 1978.
3090 Baxter, D. Property rights, economics and government. AIM, 20(4) October 1976 pp20-22, 36-41.
3091 Beaton, W. R. and Bond, R. J. Real estate. Santa Monica, Ca., Goodyear Publishing, 1976.
3092 Beaton, W. R., Bond, R. J. and Ferguson, J. T. Real estate. Glenview Il., Scott, Foresman, 1982. (Second edition of no. 3091 above)
3093 Bell, C. H. Texas real estate. 3rd edition. Houston, Gulf, 1977.
3094 Bernd, E. I. Business opportunities brokerage: strategies and techniques for real estate professionals. Englewood Cliffs, NJ, Prentice-Hall, 1983.
3095 Berston, H. M. California real estate principles. 4th edition. Homewood, Il., R. D. Irwin, 1983.
3096 Berston, H. M. California real estate practice. 4th edition. Homewood, Il., R. D. Irwin, 1983.
3097 Bond, R. J. Getting started in California real estate. 2nd edition. Dubuque, Ia., Kendall/Hunt Publishing, 1977.
3098 Bond, R. J. and Bowman, A. G. California real estate practice. 2nd edition. Santa Monica, Ca., Goodyear Publishing, 1981.
3099 Bond, R. J. and Bowman, A. G. California real estate principles. 3rd edition. Glenview, Il., Scott Foresman, 1982.
3100 Borello, R. A. How to be successful selling yourslef in real estate. Englewood Cliffs, NJ., Prentice-Hall, 1981.
3101 Bourne, E. O. Handbook of conveyancing searches. London, Sweet & Maxwell, 1984.
3102 Bove, R. X. Franchised real estate brokerage. Real Estate Review, 9(2) Summer 1979 pp46-52.
3103 Bowman, A. G. and Milligan, N. D. Real estate law in California. 5th edition. Englewood Cliffs, NJ., Prentice-Hall, 1978.
3104 But why should I list with you? Real Estate and Stock Journal, 44(9) October 1980 pp12-14, 30.
3105 Can a residential salesperson sell commercial property? Real Estate Today, 12 July 1979 pp55-60.
3106 Carlon, P. and others. Illinois supplement for Real Estate principles. Columbus, Ohio, Merrill, 1976.
3107 Carney, M. Costs and prices of home brokerage services. American Real Estate and Urban Economics Association Journal, 10 1982 pp331-354.
3108 Carr, E. J. Working with computers on the sales team. Real Estate Today, 10 January 1977 pp20-21.
3109 Case, Fred E. California real estate brokerage - 2000. California Management Review, 18 Spring 1976 pp68-75.
3110 Case, Fred E. Real estate brokerage: a systems approach. 2nd ed. Englewood Cliffs, Prentice Hall, 1982.
3111 Casey, W. J. Real estate desk book. 5th edition. Englewood Cliffs, Institute for Business Planning, 1977. (Previous edition 1971)
3112 Cochrane, W. Property research today. Property Business, May 1984 pp7, 10, 12. (Introduction to whole issue which lists research)
3113 Cohen, M. J. Don't call them, they'll call you. Real Estate Today, 11 September 1978 pp20-23.

3114 Conser, E. P. Real estate European style. New York, Exposition Press, 1976.
3115 Conser, E. P. Real estate practices in Europe. Real Estate Today, 10 July 1977 pp34-38.
3116 Considine, C. R. The philosophy of real estate. New York, Vantage Press, 1977.
3117 Consolidated Capital's real estate ideas digest. Oakland, Ca., Consolidated Capital, 1977.
3118 Couch, J. D. Reporting to owners of smaller properties. Journal of Property Management, 42 January 1977 pp19-21.
3119 Cracknell, D. G. Basic property acts and cases. London, Barry Rose, 1983/4.
3120 Crockett, J. H. Competition and efficiency in transacting the case of residential real estate. American Real Estate and Urban Economics Association Journal, 10 Summer 1982 pp209-227.
3121 CSW League of estate agents. Chartered Surveyor Weekly, 6(6) 9 February 1984 p345.
3122 Dallianis, H. T. Price-value pyramid: a way to master the listing process. Real Estate Today, 15 April 1982 pp30-32.
3123 Dallianis, H. T. Reorganization: the metamorphosis of a real estate company. Real Estate Today, 10 July 1977 pp4-13.
3124 Dasso, J. and Ring, A. A. Fundamentals of real estate. Englewood Cliffs, Prentice-Hall, 1977.
3125 Dasso, J. and Ring, A. A. Real estate principles and practice. 9th ed. Englewood Cliffs, NJ., Prentice-Hall, 1981.
3126 Davey, Homer C. and Driscoll, Donald C. The practice of real estate in California. Englewood Cliffs, Prentice-Hall, 1981.
3127 Davey, Homer C. and Mercer, H. Glenn. Real estate principles and practice in California. 4th ed. Englewood Cliffs, Prentice-Hall, 1981.
3128 Davies, K. Law of property in land. London, Estates Gazette, 1979.
3129 Davis, R. E. and Brown, K. B. Real estate. New York, McGraw Hill,1979.
3130 DeBenedictis, D. J. The complete real estate adviser. Revised edition New York, Simon & Schuster, 1978.
3131 Dilmore, G. Quantitative techniques in real-estate counseling. Lexington, Mass., Lexington Books; Aldershot, Gower, 1982.
3132 Doht, D. W. Establishing the regional real estate marketing facility. Real Estate Today, 11 November 1978 pp34-39.
3133 Donath, E. J. Implications of population changes on real estate business. Real estate and Stock Journal, 45(6) 1981 pp11-12.
3134 Donnell, J. Art of showing. Real Estate Today, 12 December 1979 pp33-36.
3135 Dowling, R. B. and Hines, M. A. Here comes the real estate franchise. Real Estate Review, 7 Summer 1977 pp48-52.
3136 Driscoll, E. J. Minnesota supplement for Modern real estate practice. 2nd edition. Chicago, Real Estate Education Council, 1979.
3137 Education. New Zealand Real Estate, centre of every monthly issue. (ways to improve real estate practice)
3138 Ellberger, S. Listing gets results. Real Estate Today, 13 March 1980 pp32-35.
3139 Ellis, J. T. and Horwood, B. Real estate practicum. Reston, Va., Reston, 1978.
3140 Epley, D. R. and Rabianski, J. Principles of real estate decisions. Reading, Mass., Addison-Wesley, 1981.
3141 Ervin, T. Real estate revolution: who will survive? Chicago, Real Estate Education Council, 1979.
3142 Estate agency today. Valuer(ISVA), 52(19) November 1983 pp270-271.

3143 FIABCI. Economic and political real estate survey. Paris, FIABCI,1982. (Fiabci Reporter, 33(1) 1982)
3144 FIABCI. Thirtieth annual congress. Tokyo. 1979. Paris, Fiabci, 1979.
3145 FIABCI. Thirty-first World Congress. Athens. 1980. Paris, Fiabci,1980.
3146 FIABCI. Thirty-second Congress. Stockholm. 1981: The future of the real estate industry until the end of the century. Paris, Fiabci, 1981. (Annual congress although not all details available)
3147 Ficek, E. F. and others. Real estate principles and practices. Columbus, Ohio, Merrill, 1976.
3148 Fisher, C. H. Rational management in the service sector: applications in the managing of a residential appraisal firm. Real Estate Appraiser and Analyst, 49 1983 pp18-25.
3149 Floyd, C. F. with Shedd, P. J. Real estate principles, New York, Random House, 1981.
3150 Forrest, H. Trusts for sale and co-ownership: a case for reform. Conveyancer and Property Lawyer, May-June 1978 pp194-208.
3151 Foster, R. Real estate ideas from Ray Foster. Reston, Va., Reston, 1981.
3152 Foster, R. Sensible real estate selling skills. Reston, Va., Reston, 1981.
3153 Foster, W. D., Lukes, R. E. and Harwood, B. Minnesota real estate. Reston, Va., Reston, 1980.
3154 Friedman, J. P. and Lindeman, B. Cash equivalent analysis. Appraisal Journal, 47 January 1979 pp35-43.
3155 Gaddy, W. E. and Hart, R. E. Real estate fundamentals. 2nd edition Chicago, Real Estate Education Council, 1984.
3156 Galaty, F. W., Allaway, W. J. and Kyle, R. O. Modern real estate practice. 9th edition. Chicago, Real Estate Education Council, 1982.
3157 Gale, J. L. Commercial - investment brokerage: an introduction with case studies. Chicago, National Association of Realtors, 1979.
3158 Gale, J. L. Listing real estate successfully. Revised edition. Reston, Va. Reston, 1983.
3159 Gettel, R. Real estate guidelines and rules of thumb. New York, McGraw Hill, 1976.
3160 Glubetich, D. Double your money in real estate every two years. Pleasant Hill, Ca., Impact Publishing, 1980.
3161 Glubetich, D. The monopoly game. 4th edition. Pleasant Hill, Ca., Impact Publishing, 1979.(3rd edition Nashville, Tenn.,Benson, 1978)
3162 Gobble, W. and Harwood, B. North Carolina real estate. 2nd edition. Reston, Va., Reston, 1984. (1st edition, 1980)
3163 Godi, A. L. Obtaining the buyer's commitment. Real Estate Today, 11 October 1978 pp14-16.
3164 Goodkin, S. R. The Goodkin guide to winning in real estate. New York, D McKay & Co., 1977.
3165 Great Britain. Law Commission. The transfer of land: the law of positive and restrictive covenants. London, H. M. S. O., 1984. (Report no 127)
3166 Great Britain. Price Commission. Charges, costs and margins of estate agents. London, H. M. S. O., 1979. (Cmnd 7647)
3167 Green, G. D. Anatomy of a sale. Real Estate Review, 12 1982 pp22-28.
3168 Greenberg, H. M. and J. Psychology of the successful commercial broker. Real Estate Today, 14 January 1981 pp21-25.
3169 Gross, J. S. Concise desk guide to real estate practice and procedure Englewood Cliffs, NJ., Prentice Hall, 1976.
3170 Haddow, D. F. The perils of real estate counseling. Real Estate Issues 9(2) 1984 pp30-32.
3171 Hanrahan, M. J. Dr Pond and the state of the literature in real est-

ate. California Management Review, 18 Spring 1976 pp103-109.
3172 Hansotte, L. B. Legal aspects of California real estate. New York & London, Wiley, 1982.
3173 Harwood, B. Real estate. Reston, Va., Reston, 1978.
3174 Harwood, B. Real estate principles. 3rd edition. Reston, Va., Reston, 1983. (previous edition 1977)
3175 Harwood, B. Real estate principles resource book. Reston, Va., Reston 1977.
3176 Harwood, B. and Jacobus, C. J. Texas real estate: an introduction to the profession. Reston, Va., Reston, 1978.
3177 Harwood, B. and New York State Association of Realtors. New York real estate. Reston, Va., Reston, 1980.
3178 Hascall, W. T. and Levi, D. R. Kansas real estate principles. Wichita, Ka., Woodlawn Publications, 1983.
3179 Healy, J. E. How to build quick value in real land. Englewood Cliffs, NJ., Executive Reports Corp., 1976.
3180 Henry, Rene A. How to profitably buy and sell land. New York, Wiley, 1977.
3181 Henszey, B. N. Broker's liability: cause for concern. Real Estate Review, 8 Fall 1978 pp57-60.
3182 Herring Son & Daw. The principles of professional estate agency in commercial property. London, Herring Son & Daw, no date.
3183 Hines, M. A. Principles and practice of real estate. Homewood, Il., Irwin, 1976.
3184 Hines, M. A. Real estate principles. New York, Harcourt Brace Jovanovitch, 1978.
3185 Hogue, Jack T. Decision support systems and the evaluation of real estate sales. Real Estate Issues, 9(1) 1984 pp34-36.
3186 Holtje, H. F. and Christman, D. Successful real estate negotiation strategy. New York and Chichester, Wiley, 1982.
3187 Houston, M. J. and Sudman, S. Real estate agents as a source of information for home buyers. Journal of Consumer Affairs, 11 Summer 1977 pp110-121.
3188 Huber, W. California real estate principles. 3rd edition. Covina, Ca., California Real Estate Publications, 1979.(First edition 1979)
3189 Hubin, V. J. New Jersey supplement for Real estate principles and practices. Columbus, Ohio, Merrill, 1976.
3190 Huff, R. L. The art of persuasion in selling real estate. Chicago, National Association of Realtors, 1979.
3191 James, J. Evolution of real estate practice in the United Kingdom under the Royal Institution of Chartered Surveyors including unification. Valuer(Australia), 26 January 1981 pp382-384.
3192 Johnson, Irwin E. Selling real estate by mortgage equity analysis: tools and techniques for marketing investment properties. Lexington Mass., Lexington Books, 1976.
3193 Jones, Peter and Robinson, Susan C. Expansion of estate agency branches. Chartered Surveyor, July 1980 pp576-578.
3194 Kaplan, J. M. Transaction tips: putting together a successful real estate package. Real Estate Today, 12 March 1979 pp15-17.
3195 Kearsley, J. E. Complete real estate exchange and acquisition handbook Englewood Cliffs, NJ, Prentice Hall, 1982.
3196 Kemp's property industry yearbook. Birmingham, Kemps Group, annual.
3197 Kent, D. L. Massachusetts supplement for Modern real estate practice. 2nd edition. Chicago, Real Estate Education Council, 1979.
3198 Kovats, F. W. Principles and practices of New Jersey real estate. Paramus, NJ., Kovco Publishers, 1978.
3199 Kristt, C. Complete real estate office desk book. Englewood Cliffs,

NJ, Prentice Hall, 1981.
3200 Lawson, D. Agent's chance to grab the Abbey habit. Property Business, 2/1984 p65.
3201 Lee, S. J. How to make money in real estate. New York, Boardroom Books, 1981.
3202 Levine, M. L. Real estate exchanges. Chicago, National Association of Realtors, 1981.
3203 Levine, M. L. Real estate fundamentals. New York, West, 1976.
3204 Lewis, S. E. Changing brokerage profession: growth of nationwide organizations will continue, creating new challenges for local independants. National Real Estate Investor, 21 December 1979 pp29-32.
3205 Lieberman, D. M. Your introduction to real estate. New York, Van Nostrand Reinhold, 1979.
3206 Lifton, R. K. Practical real estate: legal, tax and business strategies. 2nd edition. New York, Law and Business Inc., 1982. (First edition 1979)
3207 Lightman, S. International property transactions. no place, Institute for International Research, 1980.
3208 Lindeman, B. Real estate brokerage management. Reston, Va., Reston, 1981.
3209 Lipsett, D. C. Psychology of the sign. Real Estate Today, 11 March 1978 pp42-44.
3210 Listing presentation manual: front and center. Real Estate Today, 11 January 1978 pp37-50.
3211 Listings: reaping what you sow. Real Estate Today, 11 September 1978 pp4-11.
3212 Litka, M. P. and Skiliff, K. A. Contemporary real estate incidents. Columbus, Ohio, Grid, 1980.
3213 Lumley, J. E. A. How to sell real estate by using direct mail. 2nd edition. New York & Chichester, Wiley, 1982.
3214 Lumley, J. E. A. Real estate psychology: the dynamics of successful selling. New York & Chichester, Wiley, 1981.(Bibliography pp205-11)
3215 Lynn, T. S. and Goldberg, H. F. Real estate limited partnerships. 2nd edition. New York & Chichester, Wiley, 1983. (First edition, 1977)
3216 McCracken, V. R. Market research and the small company. Real Estate Today, 13 October 1980 pp52-55.
3217 McKenna, J. S. Uncover information solve problems with market research Real Estate Today, 13 October 1980 pp47-51.
3218 McKenzie, Dennis J. and Betts, Richard M. The essentials of real estate economics. 2nd edition. New York & Chichester, Wiley, 1980. (First edition, 1978)
3219 McKenzie, Dennis J. and others. California real estate principles. 3rd ed. New York & London, Wiley, 1983.
3220 McMahon, J. Future of the real estate industry. Real Estate Review, 7 Summer 1977 pp91-96.
3221 McMahon, J. Real estate industry reshapes itself. Real Estate Review, 6 Fall 1976 pp84-90.
3222 McMullen, C. W. Selling real estate investments on land contract. New York, Wiley, 1982.
3223 Malabre, A. L. Understanding the economy: and buying land, your last great chance, by A. M. Watkins. U. S. News & World Report, 1976.
3224 Maloney, R. T. Real estate quick and easy. Santa Monica, Ca., Deplhi Information Sciences Corp., 1980.
3225 Marcus, B. W. Marketing real estate - a new perspective. Real Estate Today, 14 April 1981 pp60-63.
3226 Mayer, A. P. Building the case for listing. Real Estate Today, 10 July 1977 pp24-27.

3227 Measuring the effectiveness of real estate advertising. _Real Estate and Stock Journal_, 44(1) 1980 pp14-15.
3228 Mepham, J. _Your own estate agency_. 2nd edition. London, Malcolm Stewart Books, 1982.
3229 Miller, N. G. Changing structure of residential brokerage. _Real Estate Review_, 8 Fall 1978 pp46-50.
3230 Mills, A. C. Counselling opportunities for the appraiser. _Appraisal Journal_, 51 October 1983 pp584-591.
3231 Mlynaryk, P. M. Franchising up-date. _Real Estate Today_, 10 January 1977 pp40-48.
3232 Morgan, R. A. Check list for listing. _Real Estate Today_, 14 January 1981 pp50-53.
3233 Morse, Milton A. _Modern real estate in Texas_. 3rd edition. Chicago, Real Estate Education Council, 1978.
3234 Murdoch, J. R. _The Estate Agents Act 1979_. 2nd edition. London, Estates Gazette, 1982. (First edition 1979)
3235 Murdoch, J. R. _The law of estate agency and auctions_. 2nd edition. London, Estates Gazette, 1984. (First edition 1975)
3236 Nathan, E. D. _Starting right in real estate_. Reading, Mass., Addison Wesley, 1980.
3237 Nessen, R. L. _The real estate book: a complete guide to acquiring, financing, and investing in a home or commercial property_. Boston, Little Brown, 1981.
3238 Norton, W. L. _Real property arrangements_. Norcross, Ga., Harrison, 1977.
3239 O'Donnell, P. T. and Maleady, E. L. _The practice of real estate_. Philadelphia, Pa., Saunders, 1978.
3240 O'Donnell, P. T. and Maleady, E. L. _The principles of real estate_. Philadelphia, Pa., Saunders, 1976.
3241 O'Donnell, P. T. and Maleady, E. L. _Real estate fundamentals_. Philadelphia, Pa., Saunders, 1976.(Published in the UK in 1976 as _Prin- iples of real estate_)
3242 O'Neill, J. T. Preparation is the key to survival. _Buildings_, 71 May 1977 pp74-76.
3243 _Ontario real estate law guide_. Don Mills, Ontario, CCH Canadian, loose-leaf continuously up-dated.
3244 Parker, F. J. and Schoenfeld, M. P. _Modern real estate_. Lexington, Mass., Lexington Books; Aldershot, Heath, 1979.
3245 Parks, J. _Real estate profit power: managing your own real estate office_. Reston, Va., Reston, 1981.
3246 Pearce, H. Agent's ponder institution's role. _Estates Gazette_, 269(6168) 21 January 1984 p178.
3247 Pearson, K. G. and Litka, M. P. _Real estate: principles and practices_. 3rd edition. Colombus, Ohio, Grid, 1980. (Previous edition 1977)
3248 Pembroke, J. J. _Your key to successful real estate sales_. Minneapolis, Burgess, 1977.
3249 Perelmuter, J. Accounting for the real estate broker. _CA Magazine_, 111 November 1978 pp60-63.
3250 Perkins, R. D. and J. R. Effective real estate negotiating. _Real Estate Today_, 14 May 1981 pp45-49.
3251 Plattner, R. H. _Real estate principles_. San Diego, Harcourt Brace Jovanovitch, 1984.
3252 Presentingthelisting manual. _Real Estate Today_, 10 April1977 pp4-12.
3253 _Private real estate limited partnerships_. New York, Practising Law Institute, 1979.
3254 _Professional real estate brokerage_. Homewood, Ill., Dow Jones Irwin,

1978.

3255 Property marketing. Valuer(ISVA), 53(1) 1984 pp2-3.

3256 Rambo, C. H. Arizona real estate. 2nd edition. Dubuque, Ia., Kendall Hunt, 1982.

3257 Rams, Edwin M. Real estate consultants handbook. Reston, Va., Reston, 1978.

3258 Real Estate and Stock Institute of Victoria. Real estate sales manual. Melbourne, Real Estate and Stock Institute of Victoria, 1981?.

3259 Real estate buying/selling guide for British Columbia. 3rd edition. Vancouver, BC., International Self-Counsel Press, 1978.

3260 Real estate consultants and counselors. National Real Estate Investor, annual usually June (26 15 June 1984 pp187-202)

3261 Real Estate Education Council. Illinois supplement for Modern real estate practice. 4th edition. Chicago, Real Estate Education Council, 1975.

3262 Real Estate Education Council, with Grubb & Ellis Commercial Brokerage Co. Successful industrial real estate brokerage. 3rd edition. Chicago, Real Estate Education Council, 1984. (Second edition, 1980)

3263 Real estate handbook. Homewood, Il., Dow Jones - Irwin, 1980.

3264 Real Estate Institute of Australia. Real estate practice in Australia. 6th edition. Canberra, Real Estate Institute of Australia, 1975.

3265 Real Estate Institute of Queensland. Listings that sell. Victorian Real Estate Journal, 48(1) March 1984 pp6-8, 10.

3266 Real estate practice. Richmond, Virginia State Bar and Virginia Bar Association, 1980. (Sponsored by the State Committee on Continuing Education of the Virginia State Bar Association and Real Estate Section, Virginia State Bar in cooperation with Roanoke Bar Association)

3267 Real Estate Research Corporation. Emerging trends in real estate. no place, Real Estate Research Corporation, 1984.

3268 Real Estate Review with Katz, Neil J. and Priore, Robert A. Real estate exchanges and how to make them. Boston, Warren, Gorham & Lamont 1977. (Real Estate Review Portfolios 15)

3269 Real estate today: ten years of the best. Chicago, Realtors National Marketing Institute of the National Association of Realtors, 1978.

3270 Realtors National Marketing Institute. Real estate sales handbook. 8th edition. Chicago, National Association of Realtors and Realtors National Marketing Institute, 1979.

3271 Regan, J. P. Massachusetts real estate principles and practices. Cambridge, Mass., Winthrop Publications, 1978.

3272 Reynolds, J. Working with the real estate appraiser. Journal of Property Management, 47 1982 pp6-8.

3273 Ring, A. A. and Dasso, J. Questions and problems, real estate principles and practices. 8th edition. Englewood Cliffs, NJ, Prentice Hall, 1977.

3274 Ring, A. A. and Dasso, J. Real estate principles and practices. 8th edition. Englewood Cliffs, NJ, Prentice Hall, 1977.

3275 Rose, S. Real estate buying/selling guide for Ontario. 3rd edition. Vancouver, BC., International Self-Counsel Press, 1977.

3276 Rossetti, M. D. Listing the business opportunity. Real Estate Today, 11 January 1978 pp16-20.

3277 Rossetti, M. D. Marketing the business opportunity. Real Estate Today, 11 May 1978 pp44-52.

3278 Royal Institution of Chartered Surveyors. Member's accounts regulations and Accountant's reports regulations. Revised edition. London, Royal Institution of Chartered Surveyor's, 1979.

3279 Royal Institution of Chartered Surveyors. Member's accounts regulations and notes for the guidance of members. London, Royal Institution of Chartered Surveyor's, 1977.

3280 Royal Institution of Chartered Surveyors. Notes for guidance for Chartered Surveying Practices considering appointments for services outside the U.K. London, Surveyor's Publications, no date.

3281 Royal Institution of Chartered Surveyors. Regulations for estate agency - changes 30 April 1984. Chartered Surveyor Weekly, 7(7) 17 May 1984 p470.

3282 Royal Institution of Chartered Surveyors. The RICS directory of international practices. 2nd edition. London, Surveyor's Publications, 1981.

3283 Royal Institution of Chartered Surveyors. The rules of conduct, disciplinary powers and procedures. Revised edition. London, Royal Institution of Chartered Surveyors, 1978.

3284 Royal Institution of Chartered Surveyors, General Practice Division. Practice notes for estate agents. 2nd edition. London, Surveyor's Publications, 1984.

3285 Royal Town Planning Institute. The structure and development of the property industry: a memorandum to the Property Advisory Group. London, Royal Town Planning Institute, 1979.

3286 Sale of Land Act. Real Estate and Stock Journal, 45(5) June 1981 pp13-16.

3287 Salespeople speak up. Real Estate Today, 11 November 1978 pp42-51.

3288 Sandifar, L. L. Real estate sales manager's desk book. Englewood Cliffs, NJ, Prentice Hall, 1981.

3289 Saylor, J. Real estate exchange desk book. Englewood Cliffs, NJ, Institute for Business Planning, 1978.

3290 Scammel, E. H. Butterworth's property law handbook. Sevenoaks, Kent, Butterworth, 1984.

3291 Schlaes, Jared. Real estate counseling practice. Appraisal Journal, 45 January 1977 pp110-119.

3292 Schomaeker, J. B. Beyond the listing presentation. Real Estate Today, 11 April 1978 pp24-27.

3293 Sedgwick, J. R. Conveyancing conveyed elsewhere? Estates Gazette, 270(6182) 28 April 1984 pp299, 302.

3294 Self-motivation: the power behind the sale. Real Estate Today, May 1978 pp4-10.

3295 Selling property like cornflakes. Property Confidential, 348 August 1984 pp10-12.

3296 Seminar on real property practice. 1977. Proceedings. Lexington, Ky., University of Kentucky, Office of Continuing Legal Education, College of Law, 1978.

3297 Shafer, T. W. Real estate and economics. Reston, Va., Reston, 1975.

3298 Shenkel, W. M. Closing the sale: theory and techniques. Real Estate Today, 11 November 1978 pp66-73.

3299 Shenkel, W. M. Marketing real estate. Englewood Cliffs, NJ, Prentice Hall, 1980.

3300 Shenkel, W. M. Modern real estate principles. Revised edition. Dallas, Business Publications, 1980. (First edition, 1977)

3301 Shenkel, W. M. The real estate professional. Revised edition. Homewood Il., Dow Jones Irwin, 1978.

3302 Sherman, H. and P. J. Profit from property you can't sell. Los Angeles, Ca., The authors, 1976. (1822 Hyperion Ave, LA 90027)

3303 Sherman, H. and P. J. Winning the real estate game. Los Angeles, Ca., The authors, 1977. (4011 Golden Ave., LA 90039)

3304 Short, P. and Thomas, J. The Estate Agent's Act 1979: the practitioner's companion. London, Surveyor's Publications, 1982. (Includes

text of the Act)
3305 Sklar, S. P. Liability of brokers for misrepresentation. Real Estate Today, 13 September 1980 pp33-41.
3306 Smith, J. B., Marlin, H. L. and Abercrombie, R. K. Real estate in California. 11th edition. San Francisco, General Educational Publications, 1980.
3307 Snader, J. R. Consultative selling for real estate. Real Estate Today, 15 February 1982 pp5-9.
3308 Spicer, J. S. and Grigg, A. R. An analysis of the usage of a property information system. Newcastle, Tyne and Wear Joint Information System, 1980.
3309 Stanberry, K. and Meyer, C. Texas real estate: a supplement to Real estate principles and practices by Unger/Karvel. Cincinnati, South Western Publishing Co., 1982.
3310 Stapleton, Tim. Estate management practice. London, Estates Gazette, 1981.
3311 Steele, R. M. and Berven, J. Creative real estate. Newport, Or., Newport Book Co, 1975.
3312 Stellmacher, H. B. Cases in real estate practice. New York, Macmillan, 1980.
3313 Stephens, N. The practice of estate agency. London, Estates Gazette, 1981.
3314 Stephens, N. The thinking man's agent. Chartered Surveyor Weekly, 7(4) 26 April 1984 p227.
3315 Stewart-Hunter, D. Property marketing: the impending revolution. Estates Gazette, 268(6161) 19 November 1983 pp764, 766, 768, 770.
3316 Synek, E. and Harwood, B. Ohio real estate. Reston, Va., Reston, 1980.
3317 Talbot, E. A. Mental anguish of real estate. Appraisal Journal, 48 October 1980 pp612-615.
3318 Talbot, E. A. Put it in writing! always? Appraisal Journal, 51 April 1983 pp299-304.
3319 Tanzer, M. Commercial real estate desk book. Englewood Cliffs, NJ, Institute for Business Planning, 1981.
3320 Tappan, W. T. Real estate exchange and acquisition techniques. Englewood Cliffs, NJ, Prentice Hall, 1978.
3321 Tappan, W. T. The real estate acquisition handbook: money making techniques for the serious investor. Englewood Cliffs, NJ, Prentice Hall, 1979.
3322 Techniques for developing a strong sales staff. Professional Builder and Apartment Business, 43 November 1978 pp112-132.
3323 Thau, W. A. Negotiating the purchase and sale of real estate. Boston, Warren, Gorham and Lamont, 1975. (Real Estate Review Portfolios 8)
3324 Third party business: how to get it - and keep it. Real Estate Today, 11 October 1978 pp56-61. (relocation services firms)
3325 Thompson, M. and others. Florida real estate resource book. Reston, Va., Reston, 1978.
3326 Todd, J. J. Selling in turbulent times: a strategic and tactical approach. Real Estate Today, 15 January 1982 pp57-61.
3327 Totman, E. Act defines agent controls. Property Business, 2 1984 p63.
3328 Tsagris, B. E. Modern real estate principles in California. Chicago, Real Estate Education Council, 1978.
3329 Turner, C. E. New role for the rural broker. Real Estate Today, 11 January 1978 pp4-8.
3330 Unger, M. A. and Karvel, G. R. Real estate, principles and practices. 7th edition. Cincinatti, Oh., South-Western Publishing, 1983.
3331 Unit for Retail Planning Information. Estate agency branches: develment and planning issues. Reading, Unit for Retail PLanning Infor-

mation, 1980. (Information brief 80/2)
3332 University of Reading, College of Estate Management, Centre for Advanced Land Use Studies. Discussion paper on Subject-to-contract procedures in house purchase. Reading, University of Reading, College of Estate Management, Centre for Advanced Land Use Studies, 1984.
3333 University of Reading, College of Estate Management, Centre for Advanced Land Use Studies. The role of computers in general practice estate agency. Reading, University of Reading, College of Estate Management, Centre for Advanced Land Use Studies, 1984.
3334 University of Reading, College of Estate Management, Centre for Advanced Land Use Studies, Estate Agency Study Group. Sole and multiple practices in residential estate agency. Reading, University of Reading, College of Estate Management, Centre for Advanced Land Use Studies, 1975.
3336 Walters, D. W. Real estate exchanges. New York and Chichester, Wiley, 1982.
3337 Webster, J. A. and Ketrick, P. K. North Carolina real estate for brokers and salesmen. 2nd edition. Englewood Cliffs, NJ, Prentice Hall, 1983.
3338 Weimar, A. M. and others. Real estate. 7th edition. New York, Wiley, 1978. (First edition 1939)
3339 Werth, M. A. Controlling costs through modern internal auditing. Journal of Property Management, 42 March 1977 pp72-75.
3340 What it takes to be a professional real estate counselor. Real Estate Today, 13 July 1980 pp29-32.
3341 Whittington, J. M. and Colleran, M. C. Basic accounting methods. Real Estate Today, 13 March 1980 pp43-48.
3342 Wigginton, F. P. The complete guide to profitable real estate listings Homewood, Il, Dow Jones Irwin, 1977.
3343 Wigginton, F. P. Residential real estate practice. Indianapolis, Bobbs Merrill, 1978.
3344 Wilkinson, H. W. The standard conditions of sale of land: a commentary on the Law Society and National General Conditions of Sale of Land. 3rd edition. London, Oyez Longman, 1982.
3345 Wofford, Larry E. Real estate. New York and Chichester, Wiley, 1983.
3346 Woodward, L. N. Cause of brokerage failure. Real Estate Today, 11 May 1978 pp12-15.
3347 Yinger, J. Search model of real estate brokerage behavior. American Economic Review, 71 September 1981 pp591-605.

Finance and investment

Valuations of landed property are made for a variety of purposes. Increasingly their purpose has been for sales and purchases of land and buildings for investment purposes. The literature of finance and investment is vast. However that which is included here is a highly selective sampling relating to real property. Valuation of the investment is essential in order to assess the rate of return. Rate of return discussions which do not relate to property have been excluded thus omitting, for example, the main texts on this aspect of investment management. The same principle has been followed for all topics within the scope of this chapter. Many of the references have been selected for their general applicability and for the weight of their contribution to the literature. Development of land is also seen in the light of its investment return and is therefore included selectively. No subdivisions have been attempted since many references are too general for meaningful analysis. Only the company studies have been separately placed at the end of the chapter.

3348 Abelson, P. W. Study of property valuations in relation to market prices and the characteristics. Economic Review, 55 December 1979 pp328-338.

3349 Achour, D. and Brown, R. L. The performance of real estate related investments. Real Estate Appraiser and Analyst, 49(4) 1983 pp64-69.

3350 Adams, J. E. and Lindeman, B. Speculation in underdeveloped land. Appraisal Journal, 47 April 1979 pp218-26.

3351 Akerson, Charles B. Capitalization theory and techniques: study guide. Revised edition. Chicago, American Institute of Real Estate Appraisers, 1984.

3352 Akerson, Charles B. The internal rate of return in real estate investments. Chicago, American Society of Real Estate Counselors and American Institute of Real Estate Appraisers, 1976.

3353 Aldrich, Peter C. and Upton, King. Real estate investment for pension funds. Harvard Business Review, 55 May 1977 pp14+ .

3354 Allen, T. F. REIT provisions substantially changed by TRA: greater complexity, more workable. Journal of Taxation, 46 February 1977 pp114-120.

3355 Alster, Henri. Forms of property investments: a comparative discussion Pension World, 16(5) May 1980 pp26-29.

3356 American Institute of Real Estate Appraisers. Readings in real estate investment analysis. Cambridge, Mass., Ballinger, 1977.

3357 Analysing and valuing high-yielding property investments. Estates Gazette, 272(6210) 10 November 1984 pp679-680.

3358 Apgar, Mahlon. Committment planning: an approach to reducing real

estate risks. *Appraisal Journal*, 44 July 1976 pp412-427.
3359 Apgar, Mahlon. Controlling the risks in real estate. *Business Horizons*, 19(2) April 1976 pp57-66.
3360 Archer, W. R. Towards a model of real estate project demand under uncertainty: an exploratory example of market simulation. *American Real Estate and Urban Economics Association Journal*, 4 Winter 1976 pp19-47.
3361 Arnett, G. *Real estate as an investment*. New York, Vantage, 1978.
3362 Arnold, L. E. *Commercial-investment real estate*. Chicago, Realtors National Marketing Institute of the National Association of Realtors, 1983.
3363 Atteberry, W. *Modern real estate finance*. 3rd edition. Columbus,Ohio, Grid, 1980. (2nd edition 1976)
3364 Babcock, G. C. and others. FMRR and duration: implications for real estate investment analysis. *American Real Estate and Urban Economics Association Journal*, 4 Winter 1976 pp49-67.
3365 Bagby, J. R. *Real estate financing desk guide*. Englewood Cliffs, NJ, Institute for Business Planning, 1981.
3366 Baker, C. J. *The institutional investor's viewpoint*. Reading, University of Reading, College of Estate Management, Centre for Advanced Land Use Studies, 1977.
3367 Ballard, C. M. and Strum, B. J. Pension funds in real estate: new challenges and opportunities for professionals. *Appraisal Journal*, 46 October 1978 pp551-569.
3368 Barak, R. S. *Foreign investment in United States real estate*. New York, Law and Business Press, 1981.
3369 Barasch, Clarence S. New York real estate brokerage law for the foreign investor. *International Property Investment Journal*, 1(1) 1982 pp95-120.
3370 Barham, Ronald. Ever had that sinking (fund) feeling. *Estates Gazette*, 261 23 January 1982 p219.
3371 Barksdale, Edgar W. Keys of real estate investing. *Pensions and Investments*, 8(14) 7 July 1980 p32.
3372 Barron, C. Pension funds, land and farmers. *Management Today*, April 1977 pp143+ .
3373 Barron, C. Property after the deluge. *Management Today*, September 1977 pp98,100,103,105-106,108,110,113,116.
3374 Beaton, W. R. *Real estate finance*. 2nd ed. Englewood Cliffs, Prentice-Hall, 1982.
3375 Beaton, W. R. and Robertson, Terry D. *Real estate investment*. 2nd ed. Englewood Cliffs, Prentice-Hall, 1977.(First edition 1971)
3376 Benke, William. *All about land investment*. New York, McGraw-Hill,1976.
3377 Berg, R. Developer's dilemma - to capitalise or not to capitalise. *Accountancy*, 89 October 1978 pp85-86.
3378 Bernard Thorpe & Partners. *Development in London 1967-1980: a special study*. London, Bernard Thorpe & Partners, 1981.
3379 Bible, Douglas S. and Celec, Stephen E. Real estate investment analysis: new developments in traditional leverage concepts. *American Real Estate and Urban Economics Association Journal*, 8(2) 1980 pp198-206.
3380 Bockl, G. *George Bockl on real estate investing*. Englewood Cliffs, NJ, Prentice Hall, 1977.
3381 Bond, R., Gavello, Alfred and McKenzie, Dennis J. *California real estate finance*. 3rd ed. London & New York, Wiley, 1984.
3382 Bowman, J. H. and Mikesell, J. L. Uniform assessment of property: returns from institutional remedies. *National Tax Journal*, 31 June 1978 pp137-152.

3383 Boykin, James H. Financing real estate. Lexington, Heath, 1979.
3384 Boyko, W. N. Guidebook for the smart investor: how to analyze real estate investment returns. San Diego, Cal., Rand Editions, 1981.
3385 Bozeat, N. and Williams, H. Property investment decisions by manufacturing and distributive industry. Birmingham, University of Aston, Joint Unit for Research and Urban Economics, 1979.(Working paper 23)
3386 Brannon, G. M. and Sunley, E. M. Recapture of excess tax depreciation on the sale of real estate. National Tax Journal, 29 December 1976 pp413-421.
3387 Brealey, R. A. and Pyle, C. R. A bibliography of finance and investment. London, Elek, 1973.
3388 Brown, G. Assessing an all-risks yield. Estates Gazette, 269(6173) 25 February 1984 pp700, 702, 704, 706.
3389 Brown, G. Making property investment decisions via capital market theory. Journal of Valuation, 2(2) 1984 pp142-160.
3390 Brown, G. Property - a falling idol? a reply. Estates Gazette, 266 (6129) 9 April 1983 pp105-106.
3391 Brown, R. K. Corporate real estate: executive strategies for profit making. Homewood, Il., Dow Jones - Irwin, 1979.
3392 Bruss, R. The smart investor's guide to real estate: big profits from small investments. New York, Crown, 1981.
3393 Burgess, K. Long-term mortgages are back in favour. Chartered Surveyor Weekly, 1(7) 1982 pp490-492.
3394 Byrne, P. and Cadman, David. Risk, uncertainty and decision making in property development. London, Spon, 1984.
3395 Cadman, David. He who pays the piper. Architect's Journal, 18 May 1983 pp53-55.
3396 Cadman, David. Property finance in the UK in the post-war period. Land Development Studies, 1 1984 pp61-82.
3397 Cadman, David and Austin-Crowe, Leslie. Property development. Second edition. London, Spon, 1983. (First edition 1978)
3398 Cairns, W. H. Effect of inflation on capitalisation rates. New Zealand Valuer, 25(5) March 1983 pp257-262, 266. (Commentary by Rod Jefferies)
3399 Capozza, D. R. The efficiency of speculation in urban land. Environment and Planning A, 8 1976 pp411-422.
3400 Carr, J. and Smith, Lawrence. Public land banking and the price of land. Land Economics, 51 November 1975 pp316-330. Discussion 52 November 1976 pp559-566.
3401 Case, F. E. Investing in real estate. Englewood Cliffs, NJ, Prentice Hall, 1978.
3402 Case, F. E. Professional real estate investing: how to evaluate complex alternatives. Englewood Cliffs, NJ, Prentice Hall, 1983.
3403 Case, F. E. and Clapp, J. M. Real estate financing. New York, Wiley, 1978.
3404 Caulkin, S. Where institutions will invest. Management Today, March 1977 pp146+ . (Interview with P. Sim)
3405 Chapman, J. Pension funds and insurance companies. Estates Gazette, 265(6117) 15 January 1983 pp106-111.
3406 Chiddick, David. Planning policies and the house-building industry. in Chiddick, David and Millington, Alan F. Land management: new directions. London, Spon, 1984. pp232-240.
3407 Chudleigh, W. H. and Brown, L. E. Real estate investment yield as correlation to the rate shown in money and capital markets. Real Estate Appraiser and Analyst, 44 November 1978 pp47-50.
3408 Clutton, R. Valuations for investment in the United Kingdom. Appraisal Journal, 37(1) 1969 p100.

3409 Coates, A. W. Property investments. Valuer(Australia), 26 January 1981 pp391-392,

3410 Cockhill, R. Institutional investment in property. Accountant, 183(5518) 13 November 1980 pp792-794.

3411 Construction shares: an investment gamble that could pay off. Contract Journal, 5 January 1984 p15.

3412 Cooper, James R. Real estate investment analysis. Lexington, Ma., Lexington Books; Aldershot, Heath, 1974.

3413 Coopman, R. Personal investment. Estates Gazette, 260(6054) 3 October 1981 pp23-27.

3414 Corgel, J. B. On improving interpretations of simulated investment values. Real Estate Appraiser and Analyst, 46(6) 1980 pp16-22.

3415 Coulter, W. R. Current and objective equity yield rate. Appraisal Journal, 45 January 1977 pp16-24.

3416 Cowen, S. S. and Phillips, L. C. New accounting burden for the REITs. Real Estate Review, 7 Spring 1977 pp72-77.

3417 Crean, M. J. Monetary and fiscal policies - their impact on real estate. Journal of Property Management, 41(2) March/April 1976 pp64-65.

3418 Creedy, J. and Wall, N. F. Real estate investment by objectives. New York, McGraw-Hill, 1979.

3419 Cullen, Thomas F. and Blake, Brian. How does real estate as an investment compare with stocks and bonds? Trusts and Estates, 119(7) July 1980 pp18-22.

3420 Cummings, J. Complete guide to real estate financing. Englewood Cliffs, NJ, Prentice Hall, 1978.

3421 Cunnane, M. J. The property sector 1976-1977: a survey of the sector and sixteen leading companies. London, Panmure Gordon & Co, 1976.

3422 Curcio, Richard J. and Gaines, James P. Real estate portfolio revision American Real Estate and Urban Economics Association Journal, 5(4) 1977 pp399-410.

3423 Darlow, Clive and Morley, S. 125 years of property investment. Estates Gazette, 266 30 April 1983 pp407-408. 411, 414.

3424 Darlow, Clive and Morley, S. Investment appraisal. Estates Gazette, 268(6154) 1 October 1983 pp21-25.

3425 Dasso, J. and Kuhn, Gerald W. Real estate finance, Englewood Cliffs, Prentice-Hall, 1983.

3426 Davey, Homer C. and Sharman, A. Financing real estate in California. San Francisco, Canfield Press, 1976.

3427 Davidson, A. W. and Leonard, J. E. The property development process. Reading, University of Reading, College of Estate Management, 1976. (Property Studies in the UK and Overseas 7)

3428 Davidson, Harold A. and Palmer, Jeffrey E. A comparison of the investment performance of common stocks, home building firms, and equity REITs. Real Estate Appraiser and Analyst, 44(4) 1978 pp35-39.

3429 Dean, R. The real estate manual for successful investing. Eugene, Or. Dean and Associates, 1979.

3430 Debenham Tewson & Chinnocks. Money into property: involvement in property by the financial institutions and banks 1970-1975. London, Debenham Tewson & Chinnocks, 1976. (Annual, extending the range from 1970-)

3431 Dellagrotta, S. G. Investment advice: orchestrating the elements. Mortgage Banking, 43(7) April 1983 pp64-74.

3432 Directory of developers, investors and financiers. London, Building Economics Bureau, annual.

3433 Dobbins, R. and Pike, R. The capital investment process. Managerial Finance, 6(2) 1980 pp13-24.

3434 Doeble, W. A. Land readjustment: a different approach to financing urbanisation. Lexington, Ma., Lexington, 1982.
3435 Dolby, C. A. Partners in exchange. Real Estate Today, 9 July 1976 pp10-12.
3436 Donaldson, B. Real estate: liquid or illiquid? National Tax Shelter Digest, 5(3) March 1983 pp33-36.
3437 Donaldson, R. M. Inflationary/recessionary economy - its effect on real estate development. Valuer(Australia), 28(3) July 1984 pp208-210.
3438 Drivers Jonas. The sale of land and buildings with development potential. London, Drivers Jonas, 1984.
3439 Drob, J. Will fortune smile again on real estate investment trusts? Appraisal Journal, 44 July 1976 pp450-451.
3440 Dungey, Denise M. Pension fund investment in the '80s: unprecedented potential for property managers. Journal of Property Management, 46(2) March/April 1982 pp20+ .
3441 Dunham, H. W. Real estate appraising from the viewpoint of the small investor. Real Estate Appraiser and Analyst, March/April 1979 pp31-36.
3442 Dygert, J. H. Land investment: guide to a second income fortune. Englewood Cliffs, NJ, Prentice Hall, 1976.
3443 Dyson, B. E. How to reap a fortune from real estate. Arizona, Mogan and Shaw, 1979.
3444 Economics of investing in property. Business owner, 7(12) December 1983 pp8-11.
3445 Edgar, Eion J. Factors that affect commercial decision on real estate. New Zealand Valuer, 25(7) September 1983 pp381-383.
3446 Edward Erdman. Property investment review. London, Edward Erdman, 1977 - . (monthly)
3447 Edwards, C. E. and Gaines, James P. Reversion value estimates and real estate investment returns. Real Estate Appraiser and Analyst, 48 1982 pp40-50.
3448 Eldred, G. W. and Zerbst, R. H. Critique of real estate market and investment analyses. Appraisal Journal, 46 July 1978 pp443-452.
3449 Enever, Nigel. The valuation of property investments. Third edition London, Estates Gazette, 1984. (Earlier editions, 1981, 1977)
3450 Englebrecht, T. D. Tax breaks for REITs under the Tax reform act. Real Estate Review, 7 Spring 1977 pp33-39.
3451 Epley, D. R. and Millar, J. A. Basic real estate finance and investments. Second edition. New York, Wiley, 1984. (First edition, 1980)
3452 Epstein, Charles. Real estate comes of age. Pensions and Investments, 8(14) 7 July 1980 pp13, 52.
3453 Epstein, Charles. Real estate offers diversification. Pensions and Investments, 8(13) 23 June 1980 pp23, 36.
3454 Etter, W. Leverage and the real estate investor. Real Estate Review, Fall 1977 pp86-90.
3455 Fairer-Smith, J. Safeguarding future investments. Estates Gazette, 256(6009) 8 November 1980 pp589-590
3456 Farragher, Edward J. Investment decision-making practices of equity investors in real estate. Real Estate Appraiser and Analyst, 48(2) 1982 pp36-41.
3457 Farrell, L. M. Speculation in real estate markets: is it socially undesirable? Real Estate Issues, 9(1) 1984 pp13-21.
3458 Fasano, Michael. Commingled real estate funds capture investor's interest. Pensions and investments, 7(7) 26 March 1979 pp22,27.
3459 Ferguson, J. Fundamentals of real estate investing. Glenview, Ill., Scott Foresman, 1984.

3460 Ferguson, J. and Berry, S. G. The professional real estate investment guidebook. Reading, Mass., Addison Wesley, 1982.
3461 Financial analysis of real estate investment. Boston, Warren, Gorham and Lamont, 1975. (Real Estate Review Portfolios 7)
3462 Financial Times - Actuaries property share index. regularly published in the Financial Times.
3463 Financing income-producing real estate. New York, McGraw Hill, 1977.
3464 Financing real estate during the inflationary 80s. Chicago, American Bar Association, Section of Real Property, Probate and Trust Law, 1981.
3465 Findlay, M. Chapman and Messner, Stephen D. Real estate investment analysis: IRR versus FMRR. Real Estate Appraiser, July-August 1975 pp5-20.
3466 Findlay, M. Chapman, Messner, Stephen D. and Tarantello, R. A. Real estate portfolio analysis. Lexington, Mass., Lexington, 1983.
3467 Findlay, M. Chapman and others. Optimal real estate portfolios. American Real Estate and Urban Economics Association Journal, 7(3) 1979 pp298-317.
3468 Flint, David. Legal regulation of foreign investment in Australian real estate. International Property Investment Journal, 1(4) 1983 pp615-652.
3469 Fogel, D. and Howe, R. Real estate is now: investment analysis and exchange. Dubuque, Ia., Kendall/Hunt Publishing, 1980.
3470 Franklin, P. J. Insurance into property. Banker, 126 October 1976 pp1127-1129.
3471 Fraser, W. D. Principles of property investment and pricing. Basingstoke, Hants., Macmillan, 1984.
3472 Fraser, W. D. Property - a falling idol? Estates Gazette, 264(6114) 11 December 1982 pp986-988.
3473 Fritts, C. J. The forward committment. Real Estate Review, 9(3) 1979 pp69-74.
3474 Galvin, P. Property investment. Chartered Surveyor, 111(10) 1979 pp429-431.
3475 Garrigan, R. T. and Young, Michael S. The role of real estate in a pension fund's mixed asset portfolio. Journal of Pension Planning and Compliance, 9(4) 1983 pp291-302.
3476 Gau, George W. Real estate investment returns: implications for management. Journal of Property Management, 46(4) July/August 1982 pp10+ .
3477 Gau, George W. and Kohlhepp, D. B. Estimation of equity yield rates based on capital market return. Real Estate Appraiser and Analyst, 44 November 1978 pp33-39.
3478 Gau, George W. and Kohlhepp, D. B. Reinvestment rates and the sensitivity of rates of return in real estate investments. American Real Estate and Urban Economics Journal, 4 Winter 1976 pp69-83.
3479 Gaumnitz, J. E. Conversion interest values based on less than market rates. Appraisal Journal, 45(2) April 1977 pp223-228.
3480 Gibbons, James E. Equity yield. Appraisal Journal, 48 January 1980 pp31-55. (Response October 1980 pp591-594)
3481 Gilbert, B. and Richardson, P. Investment appraisal. Chartered Quantity Surveyor, 7(1) 1984 pp17-18.
3482 Gillig, H. Real estate investment for high yield profit. Englewood Cliffs, NJ, Institute for Business Planning, 1978.
3483 Glascock, M. E. The real estate investing profit guide. Englewood Cliffs, NJ, Prentice Hall, 1982.
3484 Glover, T. Investing in property. Accountant, 191(5721) 29 November 1984 pp6-7.

3485 Golden, E. The art and science of real estate investment analysis. Los Angeles, Advanced Professional Seminars, 1980.
3486 Golemon, H. Financing real estate development. New Jersey, Aloray Publishing, 1974.
3487 Great Britain. Department of the Environment, Property Advisory Group. Structure and activity of the development industry. London, H.M. S.O., 1980.
3488 Greater Portland Landmarks Inc. Investing in old building. Portland, Me., Greater Portland Landmarks, 1980.
3489 Green, S. J Work-out solutions on real estate. Bankers Magazine, 159 Summer 1976 pp108-111.
3490 Greenberg, C. L. Profit opportunites in real estate investment. Englewood Cliffs, NJ, Prentice Hall, 1976.
3491 W Greenwell & Co. Monetary bulletin. London, W Greenwell, monthly. (Reveiwed Chartered Surveyor Weekly, 3 May 1984 p280)
3492 W Greenwell & Co. Prime property yields (1929-1984). London, W Greenwell, 1984. (Research paper)
3493 W Greenwell & Co. Property share review for 1976. London, W Greenwell, 1976.
3494 Greer, G. E. The real estate investment decision. Lexington, Ma., Lexington Books; Aldershot, Heath, 1979.
3495 Grenfell & Colegrave. The property sector. London, Grenfell & Colegrave, 1984.
3496 Greynolds, Elbert B. and Aronfsky, Julius S. Practical real estate financial analysis: using the HP-12C calculator. Chicago, Real Estate Education Council, 1983.
3497 Griffiths, B. E. Subdivision development costs. Valuer(Australia), 28(3) July 1984 pp205-207.
3498 Grooms, Albert. Vacating buildings for redevelopment. Journal of Property Management, 46(6) November/December 1982 pp45+ .
3499 Hall, C. The real estate turnaround: Craig Hall's investment formula that makes millions. Englewood Cliffs, NJ, Prentice Hall, 1978.
3500 Hall, P. Development: appraisal techniques. Estates Gazette, 263(6096) 7 August 1982 pp499-502.
3501 Hall, P. and Hargitay, S. Property portfolio - a selected approach. Property Management, 2(3) 1984 pp218-229.
3502 Hall, R. W. Real estate investment analysis. Englewood Cliffs, NJ, Institute for Business Planning, 1982.
3503 Halper, E. B. Buying land for development in the United States. International Property Investment Journal, 1(4) 1983 pp653-672.
3504 Hanford, Lloyd D. Capitalization process revisited. Appraisal Journal, 44 July 1976 pp393-404.
3506 Harney, K. R. Beating inflation with real estate. Revised edition. New York, Random House, 1981. (First edition 1979)
3507 Haroldsen, M. O. How to wake up the financial genius inside you. Second edition. Salt Lake City, Mark O Haroldsen Inc, 1977. (First edition 1976)
3508 Harps, W. S. The pitfalls of direct capitalisation. Appraiser, 40(6) June 1984 pp2, 4-5.
3509 Harris, R. Lee. The property manager and the development team. Journal of Property Management, 45(6) November/December 1980 pp338-340.
3510 Hatfield, W. P. The weekend real estate invester. New York, McGraw Hill, 1978.
3511 Hatten, K. J. and others. Matchmaking for investment. Real Estate Today, 9 October 1976 pp4-17: November/December 1976 pp16-18.
3512 Hawes, Jon and d'Amico, Michael. Developing a planned retirement community. Journal of Property Management, 46(6) November/December-

ber 1982 pp14+ .

3513 Henderson, G. V. and Walker, W. H. Analysis of installment sales. Appraisal Journal, 47 October 1979 pp485-489.

3514 Hickey, A. Financial institutions takeouts of real estate. Valuer (Australia), 27 January 1983 pp453-460.

3515 Hicks, T. G. How to borrow your way to real estate riches. Englewood Cliffs, NJ, Prentice Hall, 1981.

3516 Hicks, T. G. How to make one million dollars in real estate in three years starting with no cash. Englewood Cliffs, NJ, Prentice Hall, 1976.

3517 Hillier Parker May & Rowden. Development: cost & delays: study day report and findings of the investigating panel. London, Hillier Parker May & Rowden, 1977. (Based on Industrial development: a case study in factory building. Slough Estates Ltd.)

3518 Hinds, D. S. and Ordway,N. International real estate investment. Chicago, Real Estate Education Council, 1982.

3519 Hines, M. A. Income-property development, financing and investment. Lexington, Ma., Lexington Books, 1983.

3520 Hines, M. A. Real estate finance. Englewood Cliffs, Prentice-Hall, 1978.

3521 Hines, M. A. Real estate investment. New York, Harcourt Brace, 1981 reprint of 1978 edition.

3522 Hines, M. S. Integrated real estate development seen as wave of the future. Mortgage Banker, 37 November 1976 pp43-47.

3523 Hoagland, H. E. and Brueggeman, W. B. Real estate finance. 7th edition Homewood, Ill., Irwin, 1981. (First edition Hoagland 1954)

3524 Hornby, David. Equated yields in Sidney's CBD. in Chiddick, David and Millington, Alan F. Land management: new directions. London, Spon, 1984. pp99-107.

3525 Hoven, Vernon, and Holen, Harold H. Dramatic tax savings through real estate investments. Englewood Cliffs, Prentice-Hall, 1982.

3526 How density affects your development costs. House and Home, 51 April 1977 pp90-97.

3527 How to syndicate real estate. Boston, Warren Gorham and Lamont, 1977. (Real Estate Review Portfolios 11)

3528 Hubbard, E. W. Real estate ownership and management by large businesses. Real Estate Review, 6 Summer 1976 pp112-14.

3529 Huntley, A. Towards an occupier-led market. Chartered Surveyor Weekly, 6(1) 5 January 1984 p14.

3530 Hushak, L. J. and Sadr, K. Spatial model of land market behavior. American Journal of Agricultural Economics, 61 November 1979 pp697-702.

3531 Hussander, M. Real estate syndicator's manual and guide. Second edition. Englewood Cliffs, NJ, Prentice Hall, 1979.(First edition 1969)

3532 Institute for Business Planning. Real estate investment planning. Englewood Cliffs, NJ, Insitute for Business Planning, 1979.

3533 Institute for Continuing Legal Education. Financing real estate transactions. Illinois, Institute for Continuing Legal Education, 1976.

3534 International Association of Assessing Officers. Adjusting for terms of financing: a bibliography. Chicago, International Association of Assessing Officers, 1982.

3535 Investment in property. Property Business, 4 1984 pp33, 35-52. (Series of articles)

3536 Irwin, R. How to buy and sell real estate for financial security. New York, McGraw Hill, 1976.

3537 Jackson, H. F. Relating investment analysis to appraising and model building. Appraisal Journal, 48 January 1980 pp114-117.

3538 Jackson, James. Is real estate still a good investment? Industry Week, 211(1) 5 October 1981 pp77-78, 81.

3539 Jaffe, Austin J. and Sirmans, C. F. Improving real estate investment analysis. Appraisal Journal, 49(1) January 1981 pp85-94.

3540 Jaffe, Austin J. and Sirmans, C. F. Real estate investment decision making. Englewood Cliffs, Prentice-Hall, 1982.

3541 Jaffe, Austin J. and Wooldridge, J. Randall. Expanding the products and services of financial institutions: the case of third party real estate brokerages. Real Estate Issues, 9(2) 1984 pp19-24.

3542 Jannson, Solveig. The hot new opportunities in real estate. Institutional Investor, 14(6) June 1980 pp79-90.

3543 Johnson, K. B. A profile of real estate financing by large commercial banks in Connecticut. Revised edition. Storrs, Conn., University of Connecticut, School of Business Administration, Center for Real Estate and Urban Economic Studies, 1979. (Real estate report 28)

3544 Jones, R. D. & Finn, M. The property factor in company acquisitions. London, Drivers Jonas, 1982.

3545 Jones Lang Wootton. Index linked gilts and property investment. London, Jones Lang Wootton, 1982.

3546 Jones Lang Wootton. Property investment performance over 20 years. London, Jones Lang Wootton, 1982.

3547 Joseph Sebag & Co. Property share guide 1979. London, Joseph Sebag, 1979.

3548 Kahn, Sanders A. Internal rate of return and regressive analysis. Real Estate Review, 9(1) 1979 pp21-22.

3549 Kapplin, S. D. Financial theory and the valuation of real estate under conditions of risk. Real Estate Appraiser, 42(5) 1976 pp28-37.

3550 Kaster, Lewis R. Evaluation real estate syndicates. Journal of Real Estate Taxation, 5(4) 1978 pp337-342.

3551 Kelleher, D. G. How real estate stacks up to the S & P 500. Real Estate Review, 6 Summer 1976 pp60-65.

3552 Kelly, F. J. Real estate finance, commercial sector. Valuer(Australia) 28(2) April 1984 pp128-130.

3553 Kelting, H. Real estate investment. Columbus, Ohio, Grid, 1980.

3554 Kennedy, C. Funding is at the crossroads. Chartered Surveyor Weekly, 6(10) 8 March 1984 p643.

3555 Kerr, D. No property bourse for London. Management Today, March 1977 pp145+ .

3556 Kessling, A. D. A fortune at your feet. New York, Harcourt Brace Jovanovitch, 1981.

3557 Kimmel, K. Real estate investment: how to double your money every two to three years. New York, Cornerstone Library, 1980.

3558 Klepper, M. and Moyer, Dennis K. Structuring a joint venture with a foreign investor. Real Estate Review, 12(2) 1982 pp30-37.

3559 Knight Frank & Rutley. Institutional property investment. London, Knight Frank & Rutley, 1983 - . (quarterly)

3560 Koch, Donald L. and Steinhauser, Dolores W. Will second-mortgage financing be the REITs of today? Economic Review(Federal Reserve Bank of Atlanta), 66(7) 1981 pp4-12.

3561 Koch, Donald L. and others. The risks of creative financing. Economic Review(Federal Reserve Bank of Atlanta), 67(12) 1982 pp4-13.

3562 Koch, J. H. Profits from small-town property. New York and London, Van Nostrand Reinhold, 1984.

3563 Koelsch, J. P. Discounting projected cash flows. Appraisal Journal, 49 October 1981 pp522-533.

3564 Koskinen, J. A. Managing large portfolios of troubled real estate. Real Estate Review, 6 Summer 1976 pp95-99.

3565 Kudla, R .J. Some pitfalls in using certainty-equivalents: a note. Journal of Business Finance and Accounting, 7(2) 1980 pp239-243.
3566 Lang, Chris. How to prosper from property investment. Real Estate and Stock Journal, 44(8) 1980 pp19-21, 23.
3567 Lewis, S. E. Levy: office development offers great opportunity. National Real Estate Investor, 23(6) 1981 pp58-64.
3568 Lex, R. A. Charting the future of real estate prices: pick a theory. Real Estate Review, 11 1981 pp116-118.
3569 Liberman, Adam and Sternberg, Edward. Some legal aspects of real estate investment in Australia. International Property Investment Journal, 2(1) 1984 pp27-54.
3570 Lipscomb, J. B. Refinancing real estate investment: a strategy for maximising NPV. Appraisal Journal, 51(2) 1983 pp255-269.
3571 Lofland, Tandy O. and Eimer, Jack. Real estate development: a commercial tenant's option. Journal of Property Management, 46(1) January/February 1982 p45+ .
3572 Long, Mark H. The law and methods of real estate group investing. San Diego, Ca., Tofna Press, 1980. (10457-F Roselle, CA 92121)
3573 Loring, Carlos. Foreign real property investment in Spain: a legal primer. International Property Investment Journal, 2(2) 1984 pp163-184.
3574 Lovejoy, G. M. Funding commercial development. Valuer(Australia), 28(3) July 1984 pp211-216.
3575 Lowry, A. J. How you can become financially independant by investing in real estate. New York, Simon and Schuster, 1977.
3576 Lumley, J. E. A. Real estate investment guide. Amherst, Ma., REALUEST, 1977.
3577 Luscombe, Wendy. The analysis of property company accounts. Estates Gazette, 248(5910) 25 November 1978 pp674-676; 248(5911) 2 December 1978 pp771-775.
3578 Lusht, Kenneth M. Inflation and real estate investment value. Real Estate Appraiser and Analyst, 45(6) 1979 pp11-16.
3579 Lusht, Kenneth M. Measuring rate of return: two rules of thumb v. the internal rate. Appraisal Journal, 46 April 1978 pp245-256.
3580 Lyon, V. Need for a universal language. Estates Gazette, 251(5941) 7 July 1979 pp40-41.
3581 Lyon, V. A universal language for investment real estate analysis. in FIABCI. Thirtieth Annual Congress, Tokyo, 1979.
3582 McBirney, James J. Real estate financing in an inflationary economy. Appraisal Journal, 49(4) 1981 pp494-508.
3583 McCabe, A. and McMiles, T. Australian investment alternatives. Sydney, McCabe and McMiles Pty Ltd., 1977.
3584 McGoldrick, J. D. and Hodges, A. Risk rating real estate investments in earthquake prone areas. Mortgage Banker, 38(2) 1977 pp54-60.
3585 McIntosh, A. P. J. A guide to institutional property investment. London, Macmillan, 1984.
3586 McMahan, J. Measuring real estate returns. Real Estate Issues, 9(2) 1984 pp33-44.
3587 McMahan, J. Postwar development boom: real estate rides high. Real Estate Review, 6 Summer 1976 pp89-94.
3588 McMullen, C. W. Real estate investment: a step-by-step guide. New York and Chichester, Wiley, 1981.
3589 McNeil, Robert A. Advantages of investing in leveraged real estate. Pension World, 18(4) 1982 pp31-32.
3590 Mader, C. with Bortz, J. The Dow Jones-Irwin guide to real estate investing. Revised edition. Homewood, Ill., Dow Jones-Irwin, 1983. (Previous edition 1975)

3591 Magee, L. Market analysis aids objective evaluation of potential developments. Mortgage Banker, 36 July 1976 pp46-49.

3592 Maisel, S. J. and Roulac, Stephen E. Real estate investment and finance. New York and London, McGraw-Hill, 1977.

3593 Malzo, J. Union pension funds can add new dimension in real estate investment. Mortgage Banker, 37 November 1976 pp19-20+ .

3594 Manis, Michael S. Real estate investment analysis: a practical guide. London & New York, Wiley, 1983.

3595 Markland, Robert E. A simulation approach to real estate investment analysis. Computers and Operations Research(UK), 6(3) 1979 pp121-128.

3596 Martin, R. S. and Noble, L. S. Capitalization rates - the future. Appraisal Journal, 49(3) 1981 pp335-352.

3597 Martin, Vincent F. Real estate investing. Employee Benefits Journal, 6(4) 1981 pp21-24.

3598 Martin, W. B. A risk analysis rate-of-return model for evaluating income-producing real estate investments. Appraisal Journal, 46(3) 1978 pp424-442.

3599 Mason, L. R. Performance measurement. Estates Gazette, 256 13 December 1980 pp1091-1093, 1095.

3600 Mellor, R. M. Valuation and viability criteria of proposed projects. Valuer(Australia), 26(1) 1980 pp12-17.

3601 Messner, Stephen D., Schreiber, I. and Lyon, V. Marketing investment real estate: finance, taxation, techniques. Chicago, Realtors National Marketing Institute of the National Association of Realtors, 1975. (Reprint 1979)

3602 Michael Laurie & Partners. The MLP-CIG property performance index: the FRC property index 1978-1983. Michael Laurie & Partners and The Corporate Intelligence Group, 1984. (annual report formerly Economist Intelligence Unit and Michael Laurie & Partners)

3603 Miles, M. Real estate investor's complete handbook. Englewood Cliffs, NJ, Prentice Hall, 1982.

3604 Miles, M. and Esty, Arthur S. Relevant required rate of return. Appraisal Journal, 47(4) 1979 pp511-522.

3605 Miles, M. and McCue, T. Diversification in the real estate portfolio. Journal of Financial Research, 7(1) 1984 pp57-68.

3606 Miles, M. and Rice, Michael. Toward a more complete investigation of the correlation of real estate investment yield to the rate evidenced in the money and capital markets: the individual investor's perspective. Real Estate Appraiser and Analyst, 44(6) 1978 pp8-19.

3607 Miles, M. and Wurtzebach, Charles H. Risk analysis in the real property development process: a conceptual framework and a computer simulation model. Journal of Business Research, 5(4) 1977 pp325-327.

3608 Miller, D. A. How to invest in real estate syndicates. Homewood, Ill. Dow Jones-Irwin, 1978.

3609 Miller, Stanley F. Correlation of real estate investment yield to the rate evidenced in the money and capital market. Real Estate Appraiser and Analyst, 44(6) November 1978 pp20-31.

3610 Montgomery, Thomas. Real estate investment risk - basic concepts. Appraisal Journal, 44(1) 1976 pp9-22.

3611 Montgomery, Thomas and Raper, Charles F. Equity yields and the reinvestment issue. Appraisal Journal, 49(4) 1981 pp509-521.

3612 Moores, J. H. and Friedman, J. P. A mixed bag of blessings: corporate real estate. Financial Executive, 46 10 October 1978 pp56-58, 60, 62, 64, 66-67.

3613 Morgan, M. The appraiser's role in portfolio management. Canadian

Appraiser, 28(3) 1984 pp29-31.
3614 Morgan, M. Portfolio management in real estate. AIM, 25(1) 1982 pp31-37.
3615 Morris, Ronald A. and Pisem, E. Real estate investment under the accelerated cost recovery system. National Real Estate Investor, 24 15 November 1982 pp4-36. (Special series of articles)
3616 Mullinax, James P. Management strategies for real estate trusts. Journal of Property Management, 48(3) May/June 1983 p14+ .
3617 Myers, J. Investment in property abroad. New Law Journal, 133(6123) 30 September 1983 pp875-876.
3618 National Real Estate Investor directory. National Real Estate Investor. annual. (1978-79 in 20 15 June 1978 pp1-183)
3619 Nelson, G. S. and Whitman, D. A. Cases and materials on real estate finance and development. St. Paul, Minn., West, 1976.
3620 Nicholson, N. Banks trying to drop construction local risks: long-term lenders will take them for a price. National Real Estate Investor, 19 March 1977 pp29-32.
3621 Nicholson, S. Developer equity, variable rates are on lender's minds. National Real Estate Investor, 19 April 1977 p22.
3622 North, L. W. Real estate investment analysis and valuation. Winnipeg, Saults and Pollard, 1976.
3623 Opelka, F. Gregory. Hidden costs complicate inner-city rehab. Savings and Loan News, 97 October 1976 pp130-131.
3624 Opelka, F. Gregory. Inner-city rehab poses unique value problems. Savings and Loan News, 97 September 1976 pp90-91.
3625 Orchard-Lisle, P. Property investment: a working philosophy. Accoutant, 189(5662) 6 October 1983 pp414-415.
3626 Page, Daniel E. Criteria for investment decision making: an empirical study. Appraisal Journal, 51(4) October 1983 pp498-508.
3627 Parry, M. J. Capital investment appraisal and the inflation factor. Accountancy, 94(1073) 1983 pp78, 80, 82.
3628 Patrick, James E. The property manager's impact on the development process. Journal of Property Management, 44(4) July/August 1979 pp198-200.
3629 Patrick, M. J. What use is property performance analysis? Journal of Valuation, 2(2) 1984 pp137-141.
3630 Patterson, J. An overview of US real estate yields. Estates Gazette, 267(6150) 3 September 1983 pp818-826.
3631 Peiser, Richard B. Risk analysis in land development. American Real Estate and Urban Economics Association Journal, 12 1984 pp12-29.
3632 Penny, Peter E. Modern investment theory and real estate analysis. Appraisal Journal, 50(1) 1982 pp79-99.
3633 Phillips & Drew. Pension fund investment. London, Phillips & Drew, 1984. (Includes index of 12 pooled property funds)
3634 Phillips & Drew. The property share market. London, Phillips & Drew, monthly. (One of a number of similar reports on share performance)
3635 Pivar, W. H. Get rich on other people's money. New York, Arco, 1981.
3636 Plender, John. The dangerous decade: property investment. Estates Gazette, 264 23 October 1982 pp323-324, 326-327.
3637 Plender, John. Money into property. London, Andre Deutsch, 1982.
3638 Price, O. R. High leverage real estate investments: inside secrets using OPM. Englewood Cliffs, NJ, Prentice Hall, 1978.
3639 Price, O. R. Prentice Hall master guide to real estate investing. Englewood Cliffs, NJ, Prentice Hall, 1982.
3640 Profit from property. Accountant, 175 22 July 1976 pp95-99.
3641 Property investment. Chartered Surveyor Weekly, 2(10) 10 March 1983 pp539-551. (Series of articles)

3642 Pugh, J. W. and Hippaka, William H. California real estate finance. 4th ed. Englewood Cliffs, Prentice-Hall, 1984.

3643 Pyhrr, Stephen A. A computer simulation model to measure the risk in real estate investment. American Real Estate and Urban Economics Association Journal, 11 1973 pp48-78.

3644 Pyhrr, Stephen A. and Cooper, James R. Real estate investment: strategy, analysis, decisions. Boston, Mass., Warren, Gorham and Lamont, 1982.

3645 Rabinowitz, A. The real estate gamble: lessons from 50 years of boom and bust. New York, AMACOM, 1980.

3646 Rams, Edwin M. Markets, risk, feasibility and real estate ventures. Real Estate Appraiser, 40(3) 1974 pp29-32.

3647 Rams, Edwin M. Simulating land development as a measure of just compensation. Valuation, 25(1) 1978 pp2-23.

3648 Raper, Charles F. Internal rate of return - handle with care. Appraisal Journal, 44 July 1976 pp405-411.

3649 Ratcliffe, J. A new development ethic. in Chiddick, David and Millington, Alan F. Land management: new directions. London, Spon, 1984. pp211-231.

3650 Ratcliffe, J. The valuation of development properties. Journal of Valuation, 1(1) 1983 pp24-31: 1(2) 1983 pp142-152:1(3) 1983 pp268-274.

3651 Readings in real estate investment analysis Vol. 1. Cambridge, Ma., Ballinger, 1977.

3652 Real estate financing, today and tomorrow. Chicago, Probate and Trust Law sponsored by American Bar Association, Section of Real Property 1978.

3653 Real estate investment planning. Englewood Cliffs, NJ, Institute for Business Planning, 1975.

3654 Real estate tax shelters: a checklist approach. Practical Accountant, 9 July 1976 pp57-70.

3655 Real property investment in Canada: the Foreign Investment Review Act. International Property Investment Journal, 1(4) 1983 pp723-758.

3656 Rehabilitation: the prescription for success. Real Estate Today, 9 November/December 1976 pp19-33.

3657 Reyes, Juan C. Foreign investment in real estate in the Philippines. International Property Investment Journal, 2(2) 1984 pp185-216.

3658 Richard Ellis. Property investment report 1980. London, Richard Ellis, 1980. (annual)

3659 Richards, T. D. The guide to foreign investment in the United States. New York, Van Nostrand Reinhold, 1984.

3660 Rifenbark, R. K. and Johnson, D. How to beat the salary trap. New York, McGraw Hill, 1978.

3661 Rill, Douglas, J. Starting a real estate investment program. Financial Planning Today, 5(2) 1981 pp45-46.

3662 Roberts, J. A. C. and MacDonald, A. Investment in property. Chartered Surveyor Urban Quarterly, 3(4) 1976 pp8-10.

3663 Role of real estate in investment planning. Nations Business, 64 September 1976 pp76-80. (Interview with A. Downs)

3664 Rolo, Charles J. Investing in real estate - how to dig for profits in land. Money, 6(12) 1977 pp60-68.

3665 Rosenberg, M. An adjusted rate of return on real estate investments. Real Estate Review, 14(2) 1984 pp67-72.

3666 Roulac, Stephen E. Advanced real estate financial analysis. California Certified Public Accountants Foundation for Education and Research, 1977.

3667 Roulac, Stephen E. Can real estate returns outperform common stock.

Journal of Portfolio Management, 2 1976 pp26-43.
3668 Roulac, Stephen E. Changing economics imply new real property investment relationships. California Management Review, 18(3) 1976 pp57-66.
3669 Roulac, Stephen E. Modern real estate investment. San Francisco, Property Press, 1976.
3670 Roulac, Stephen E. Real estate investment analysis. California Certified Public Accountants Foundation for Education and Research,1977
3671 Roulac, Stephen E. Real estate investment economics. California Certified Public Accountants Foundation for Education and Research,1977
3672 Roulac, Stephen E. Real estate investment management: syndications against joint ventures. California Certified Public Accountants Foundation for Education and Research, 1977.
3673 Roulac, Stephen E. and King, D. A. Institutional strategies for real estate investment. Appraisal Journal, 46(2) 1976 pp257-270.
3674 Roulac, Stephen E. and Parisse, A. J. Tax reform for realty depreciation: for better or worse. Taxes, 54 September 1976 pp532-548.
3675 Rowe & Pitman. Property indices: do they make sense? London, Rowe & Pitman, 1982.
3676 Rowe & Pitman. Property shares - review of 1983 and prospects for 1984. London, Rowe & Pitman, 1984.
3677 Royal Institution of Chartered Surveyors. Finance in property: a memorandum of evidence to the Committee to Review the Functioning of Financial Institutions. London, Royal Institution of Chartered Surveyors, 1977.
3678 Royal Institution of Chartered Surveyors. The property boom, 1968-1973, and its collapse: a supplementary memorandum of evidence to the Committee to Review the Functioning of Financial Institutions. London, Royal Institution of Chartered Surveyors, 1978.
3679 Royal Institution of Chartered Surveyors. Property investment across the EEC: the RICS/Law Society's European Group 6th Annual joint meeting, Wednesday 8 December 1976. London, Royal Institution of Chartered Surveyors, 1976.
3680 Sack, Paul. Are attractive returns on unleveraged real estate worth taking a risk. Pensions and Investments, 5(4) 28 February 1977 pp23-24.
3681 Sanderson, I. J. V. Valuer's role in property portfolio management. Valuer(Australia), 27 April 1983 pp506-508, 539.
3682 Sandifar, L. L. The national directory of real estate financing sources. Englewood Cliffs, NJ, Prentice Hall, 1984.
3683 Schiller, R. and others. The property investment market. Accountant, supplement to 3 April 1980 pp19-21.
3684 Schmidt, C. F. Power in numbers. Real Estate Today, 9 July 1976 pp54-56.
3685 Schott, Francis. Real estate's stake in a stable dollar. Real Estate Review, 8(3) 1978 pp8-9.
3686 Segala, J. P. Redlining: an economic analysis. Federal Reserve Bank of Richmond: Economic Review, 66(6) 1980 pp3-13.
3687 Seldin, Maury. Land investment. Homewood, Ill., Dow Jones-Irwin, 1975.
3688 Seldin, Maury. Real estate investment for profit throgh appreciation. Reston, Va., Reston, 1980.
3689 Seldin, Maury. A time to buy, a time to sell. Real Estate Issues, 8(2) 1983 pp29-31.
3690 Seldin, Maury and Swesnik, Richard H. Real estate investment strategy. New York and Chichester, Wiley, 1979.
3691 Shapiro, Ivan. Case studies in creative real estate financing. Boston, Warren Gorham and Lamont, 1979. (Real Estate Review Portfolios 5A)

3692 Sheinfield, M. M. Walking through a real property arrangement. Real Estate Review, 6 Fall 1976 pp46-52.

3693 Shenkel, W. M. Real estate finance. Washington, American Institute of Banking, American Banks Association, 1977.

3694 Sherman, Paul. A reason for economic analysis. Estates Gazette, 264 (6106) 16 October 1982 p233.

3695 Simon, A. C. A new investor's guide to real estate. Hollywood, Ca., Future Shop, 1978. (1907 Whitley Ave, CA 90068)

3696 Simons, T. J. A. Property investment in the 80s. Accountant, 182 (5497) 19 June 1980 pp928-929.

3697 Simpkin, J. G. and Nielsen, G. C. Rise of project/construction management. Real Estate Review, 6 Winter 1977 pp47-53.

3698 Sirmans, C. F. and Jaffe, Austin J. The complete real estate investment handbook. Second edition. Englewood Cliffs, NJ, Prentice Hall, 1984. (First edition 1981)

3699 Sirmans, C. F. and Webb, J. R. Investment yield in the money, capital and real estate markets: a comparative analysis for 1951-1976. Real Estate Appraiser and Analyst, 44(6) 1978 pp40-46.

3700 Sirmans, C. F. and Webb, J. R. Real estate: the preferred choice of portfolio managers. Real Estate Review, 9(3) 1979 pp108-109.

3701 Sirmans, G. Stacey, Sirmans, C. F. and Smith, Stanley D. Cash equivalency valuation for creative financing methods. Appraisal Journal, 52(3) 1984 pp420-435.

3702 Sirota, D. Essentials of real estate finance. Second edition. Chicago, Real Estate Education Council, 1979. (First edition 1977)

3703 Sirota, D. Essentials of real estate investment. Second edition. Chicago, Real Estate Education Council, 1984.

3704 Sirota, D. Winning in real estate. Reston, Va., Reston, 1981.

3705 Smith, C. C. Complexities and perplexities in real estate financing. Buildings, 70 October 1976 pp48-52.

3706 Smith, D. The syndicator and the professional property manager. Journal of Property Management, 46(5) September/October 1982 p9+ .

3707 Smith, D. O. Geographical dispersion requirement for employer real property owned by a plan. Taxes, 55 May 1977 pp308-312.

3708 Smith, J. Analyzing investment alternatives. Real Estate Today, 9 July 1976 pp46-52.

3709 Smith, K. V. and Shulman, D. Performance of equity real estate investment trusts. Financial Analysts Journal, 32 September 1976 pp61-66.

3710 Snyder, E. A. Before you invest: questions and answers on real estate. Reston, Va., Reston, 1981.

3711 Sober, P. ED 18 and property investment companies. Accountant, 176 14 April 1977 pp417-419.

3712 Speedy, S. L. Financial appraisal. Wellington, New Zealand Institute of Valuers, 1982.

3713 Speedy, S. L. Property investment: inflation edition. Second edition. Wellington, Butt, 1980.

3714 Speedy, S. L. Recent problems in the hypothetical sub-divisional approach to value. New Zealand Valuer, 25(1) 1982 pp31-38.

3715 Speedy, S. L. Recent problems in the hypothetical sub-divisional approach to value. Valuer(Australia), 27 1983 pp725-732.

3716 Starchild, Adam. Using tax havens for U.S. real estate investment. Journal of Property Management, 43(1) January/February 1978 pp12-15.

3717 Stern, R. D. Investing in today's economy. Trusts and Estates, 121(5 1982 pp15-19.

3718 Stern, W. H. The new investor's guide to making money in real estate:

a strategist's handbook. New York, Grosset and Dunlap, 1976.
3719 Stevenson, H. H. Lessons from the mortgage trust experience. Real Estate Review, 6 Fall 1976 pp72-77.
3720 Stevenson, H. H. What went wrong with the REITs? Appraisal Journal, 45 April 1977 pp249-260.
3721 Stratton, Ian G. C. Building land and estates: their acquisition and development. London, Oyez Longman, 1983.
3722 Strohm, P. Hands-on management the key. Estates Gazette, 270(6184) 12 May 1984 p466.
3723 Swesnik, R. H. Acquiring and developing income-producing real estate. Reston, Va., Reston, 1979.
372 Sykes, S. The assessment of property investment risk. Journal of Valuation, 1(3) 1983 pp253-267.
3725 Taylor, T. R. Taxation for the investor in Australian real estate. International Property Investment Journal, 2(1) 1984 pp1-26.
3726 Temple, D. M. Real estate finance in California. Santa Monica, Ca., Goodyear Publishing, 1977.
3727 Temple, D. M. Real estate investment for the '80s: how to build financial security in the face of inflation. Chicago, Il., Contemporary Books, 1981.
3728 Tims, F. B. and Neider, L. J. Introduction to real estate investments. California, Calfornia Certified Public Accountants Foundation for Education and Research, 1975.
3729 Title insurance and real estate securities terminology. Sacramento, Ca., Real Estate Publishing Co., 1980.
3730 Tockarshewsky, J. B. Reducing the risks in construction lending. Real Estate Review, 7 Spring 1977 pp59-63.
3731 Travis, Richard M. Property investment strategy for the foreign investor. International Property Investment Journal, 1(4) 1983 pp673-722.
3732 Trippi, R. R. Estimating the relationship between price and time to sale for investment property. Management Science, 23 April 1977 pp838-842.
3733 Trott, John. The future for development: the financier's viewpoint. Estates Gazette, 236 20/27 December 1975 pp859, 861.
3734 Troubled trusts doomed to linger or to die: strong REITs considered soundinvestments.National Real Estate Investor, 18 October 1976 pp46-48+ .
3735 Turner, C. Syndicates for the small investor. Management Today, April 1977 pp143-144.
3736 Unger, M. A. How to invest in real estate. New York and London, McGraw Hill, 1976.
3737 Unger, M. A. and Melicher, R. W. Real estate finance. Cincinatti, South Western Publishing, 1978.
3738 Valachi, Donald J. Calculating true yields on wraparounds. Real Estate Review, 6 Winter 1977 pp92-99.
3739 Valachi, Donald J. Determining the value of a real estate investment. Real Estate Review, 7 Winter 1978 pp64-67.
3740 Valachi, Donald J. On interpreting the Internal Rate of Return on a real estate investment. New Zealand Valuer, 25(5) March 1983 pp278-284. (Reprinted from Real Estate Appraiser and Analyst, 47(1) 1981 pp35-42.)
3741 Valachi, Donald J. The three faces of IRR. Real Estate Review, Fall 1978 pp74-78.
3742 Walters, D. W. The intelligent investor's guide to real estate. New York and Chichester, Wiley, 1980.
3743 Ward, C. The evaluation of risk. Estates Gazette, 260(6056) 17 Oct-

ober 1981 pp253-256.
3744 Ward, C. W. R. Arbitrage and investment in commercial property. Journal of Business Finance and Accounting, 9(1) 1982 pp93-108.
3745 Waters, William. The ABCs of real estate investing. Supervisory Management, 26(11) 1981 pp40-41.
3746 Webb, James R. and Sirmans, C. F. Yields and risk measures for real estate, 1966-1977. Journal of Portfolio Management, 7(1) 1980 pp14-19.
3747 Webster, Bernard. Some implications of private sector investment in new industrial property for local authority planning. in Chiddick, David and Millington, Alan F. Land management: new directions. London, Spon, 1984. pp182-188.
3748 Weinberg, M. Property investment: an individual viewpoint. Estates Gazette, 238 5 June 1976 pp703-705, 707, 709.
3749 Weinstein, Marvin W. An 'at risk' rule in real estate. Real Estate Law Journal, 8(1) 1979 pp47-50.
3750 Wendt, Paul F. Estimating interest and recapture rates - miracle or mirage. Appraisal Journal, 46 July 1978 pp397-408.
3751 Wendt, Paul F. The future of investment in real estate. California Management Review, 25(4) 1983 p110-120.
3752 Wendt, Paul F. Perspectives on real estate investment. Berkeley, Ca., University of California, Institute of Business and Economic Research, 1982. (Report 82-45)
3753 Wendt, Paul F. and Cerf, Alan R. Real estate investment analysis and taxation. Second edition. New York, McGraw Hill, 1979.
3754 When is an investment not an investment? Property Letter, 315 November 1981 pp7-13.
3755 Whisler, W. D. Analyzing the effects of deviations from forecasts in real estate investment analysis. Appraisal Journal, 45 January 1977 pp35-48.
3756 White, John R. American real estate remains an attractive investment. Appraisal Journal, 49(4) 1981 pp485-493.
3757 White, John R. Nonfeasance with feasibility = failure: improving the quality of feasibility studies. Urban Land, 35(9) 1976 pp5-9.
3758 White, John R. Real estate appraisals: how they pay off for investors. Appraisal Journal, 1977 pp49-55.
3759 White, W. L. Price indexing for time adjustments. Appraisal Journal, 48 January 1980 pp15-23.
3760 Whitmore, G. Foreign investors need strategy before committment. National Real Estate Investor, 25(10) 1983 pp60-62.
3761 Wiedemer, J. P. Real estate finance. Second edition. Reston, Va., Reston, 1977. (First edition 1974)
3762 Wiedemer, J. P. Real estate investment. Second edition. Reston, Va., Reston, 1982. (First edition 1979)
3763 Wiley, Robert J. Real estate investment. New York, Ronald Press, 1977.
3764 Wiley, Robert J. Real estate investment analysis: an empirical study. Appraisal Journal, 44 October 1976 pp586-592.
3765 Wofford, Larry E. and Moses, Edward A. Relationship between capital markets and real estate investment yield: theory and application. Real Estate Appraiser and Analyst, 44 November 1978 pp51-61.
3766 Wofford, Larry E. and Preddy, R. Keith. Real estate investment perception: a multi-dimensional analysis. American Real Estate and Urban Economics Association Journal, 6(1) 1978 pp22-36.
3767 Wofford, Larry E. and others. Using capital market theory in real estate appraisal: evidence from securities markets. Real Estate Appraiser and Analyst, 48 1982 pp34-39.
3768 Woolever, Michael H. and Olsen, Bradley A. Managing pension fund

properties: the prohibited transaction rules of ERISA. Journal of Property Management, 48(3) May/June 1983 p6+ .

3769 Woy, J. B. Investment methods: a bibliographic guide. New York, Bowker, 1973.

3770 Wurtzebach, C. H. Institutional explanation of poor REIT performance. Appraisal Journal, 45 January 1977 pp103-109.

3771 Wurtzebach, C. H. and Kim, K. S. Investment analysis and decision making framework for real estate development. American Real Estate and Urban Economics Association Journal, 7 1979 pp410-426.

3772 Yannacone, V. J. 1973 revisited: investors facing new energy crisis. National Real Estate Investor, 21(5) 1979 pp36,176.

3773 Young, Michael S. Evaluating the risk of investment real estate. Real Estate Appraiser and Analyst, 43(5) 1977 pp39-45.

3774 Zalaznick, Charles. Real estate development and construction financing. New York, Practising Law Institute, 1978. (Real Estate Law and Practice Course Handbook Series 154)

3775 Zeikel, Arthur. Real estate equity investing. Journal of Accounting, Auditing and Finance, 3(4) 1980 pp375-382.

3776 Zell, Samuel. Emma's allure, or foreign capital seeks a new home. Real Estate Review, 6(4) 1977 pp31-36.

Company studies

Many brief notes describe the current progress of the many property companies, both investment and real estate agencies. Most relate to present developments only. They will be found in the pages of the weekly and monthly journals, worldwide. Examples might be those in Estates Gazette or Chartered Surveyor Weekly, National Real Estate Investor or Real Estate Review. They are too numerous to list all. Most longer studies are initiated by the company concerned and often published by them, used for publicity, or even held, unpublished, in the archives. Those below are a few representative examples.

3777 Baldock, D. A history of the London Auction Mart. Estates Gazette, 268(6158) 29 October 1983 pp458-460, 462, 464.

3778 Barber, Derek. Humberts into the eighties: a history of Humberts Chartered Surveyors 1842-1980. London, Humberts, 1980.

3779 Barty-King, Hugh. Scratch a surveyor ... the nearest anyone will ever come to telling the story of Drivers Jonas. London, Heinemann, 1975.

3780 Erdman, E. People and property. London, Batsford, 1982.

3781 Laing & Cruikshank. A & J Mucklow Group plc. London, Laing & Cruikshank, 1983,

3782 Laing & Cruikshank. Hammerson Property Investment and Development Corporation plc. London, Laing & Cruikshank, 1983,

3783 Laing & Cruikshank. Stock Conversion and Investment Trust. London, Laing & Cruikshank, 1982.

3784 MEPC's base for recovery. Accountant, 176 13 January 1977 pp48+.

3785 Panmure Gordon & Co. Reviews of various companies: for private circulation.

3786 Peagam, Norman. The Reichmanns never gamble. Euromoney, June 1984 pp37-45.

3787 Pickford, D. How Halsmere does it. Chartered Surveyor Weekly, 5(2) 13 October 1983 pp94-96.(Regular series reviewing company progress)

3788 Richard Ellis. An historical review. London, Richard Ellis, 1982.

3789 Scrimgeour, Kemp-Gee & Co. Detailed company reports on each of nearly fifty companies.

3790 St Quintin. _A history of St Quintin Chartered Surveyors 1831-1981_. London, St Quintin (Management Services) Ltd, 1981

3791 Valuation problems for Town & City. _Accountant_, 175 7 October 1976 p419.

3792 Wates, N. _The battle for Tolmers Square_. London, Routledge Kegan Paul, 1976.

3793 Wates, N. _Tolmers destroyed: a report on the activities of property speculators Stock Conversion and Investment Trust in Tolmers Square and their effect on a community_. London, Tolmers Village Association, 1974.

3794 Watson, John. _Savills: a family and a firm 1652-1977_. London, Hutchinson Benham, 1977.

Appendix A
Dictionaries and encyclopaedias

Abraham, S. V. Real estate dictionary and reference guide. Orange, Ca., Career Publishing, 1979.

Allen, R. D. and Wolfe, T. E. The Allen and Wolfe illustrated dictionary of real estate. New York and Chichester, Wiley, 1983.

Allen, R. D. and Wolfe, T. E. Real estate almanac. New York, Wiley, 1980.

American Institute of Real Estate Appraisers. Real estate appraisal terminology. Second edition. Chicago, American Institute of Real Estate Appraisers, 1980.

Arnold, A. L. and Kusnet, J. The Arnold encyclopaedia of real estate. New York, Warren Gorham and Lamont, 1978.

Bagby, J. R. and M. L. G. Real estate dictionary. Englewood Cliffs, NJ, Institute for Business Planning, 1981.

Baraoh, S. T. Encyclopaedia of real estate appraising forms and model reports. Englewood Cliffs, NJ, Prentice Hall, 1983.

Boyce, B. N. Real estate appraisal terminology. Cambridge, Ma., Ballinger for American Institute of Real Estate Appraisers, 1975.

Brown, H. E. and Page, D. J. The language of real estate in Michigan. Chicago, Real Estate Education Council, 1979.

Brownstone, D. M. and French, I. M. The Van Nostrand Reinhold real estate dictionary. New York, Van Nostrand Reinhold, 1981.

Chapman, D. H. Technical terms for property people. London, Estates Gazette, 1973.

Freshman, S. K. Real estate, finance and syndication glossary. Beverley Hills, Ca., Law and Capital Dynamics, 1979.

Friedman, Edith J. ed. Encyclopaedia of real estate appraising. Third edition. Englewood Cliffs, NJ, Prentice Hall, 1978.

Friedman, J. P., Harris, J. C. and Lindeman, Bruce. Dictionary of real estate terms. Woodbury, NY, Barron's Educational Series, 1984.

Glossary of property terms - I. Estates Gazette, 267(6145) 30 July 1983 pp428-429. (Beginning of a series running throughout 1984)

Gross, J. S. Illustrated encyclopaedic dictionary of real estate. Englewood Cliffs, NJ, Prentice Hall, 1978. (First edition 1969 as Illustrated encyclopaedic dictionary of real estate terms)

Harrison, H. S. and J. S. Illustrated dictionary of real estate and appraisal. Reston, Va., Reston, 1982.

Hemphill, T. and C. F. The essential dictionary of real estate terminology. Englewood Cliffs, NJ, Prentice Hall, 1982.

Johnsich, J. R. Modern real estate dictionary. no place, Canfield Press, 1975.

Lukers, R. C. The dictionary of real estate appraisal. Chicago, American Institute of Real Appraisers, 1984.

Lyons, P. J. with Bowyer, M. J. Real estate investor's desk encyclopaedia. Reston, Va., Reston, 1982.

McMahon, J. The McGraw-Hill real estate pocket guide: up-to-date terms and tables for the real estate professional. New York, McGraw Hill, 1979.

McLean, A. J. Real estate terms and definitions. Santa Monica, Ca., Delphi Information Sciences Corp, 1980.

Miles, M. J. Encyclopaedia of real estate formulas and tables. Englewood Cliffs, NJ, Prentice Hall, 1978.

O'Donnell, P. T. and Maleady, E. L. Dictionary of real estate terminology. Philadelphia, Saunders, 1975.

Real Estate and Stock Institute of Victoria. A glossary of terms and standard abbreviations used in real estate and valuation practice. Melbourne, Real Estate and Stock Institute, 1981(?).

Real estate appraisal terminology. Second edition. Chicago, Appraisal Institute, 1981.

Reilly, J. W. The language of real estate. Chicago, Real Estate Education Council, 1977.

Rieger, G. L. The language of real estate in Ohio. Chicago, Real Estate Education Council, 1978.

Talamo, J. The real estate dictionary. Second edition. Boston, Financial Publishing, 1979. (First edition, Anaheim, Box 5136, Cal 92804, The author, 1975)

Volpe, C. C. Running Press glossary of real estate language. Philadelphia, Running Press, 1977.

Appendix B
Journals

This list provides an indication of some of the titles covering property matters which are available in the various countries. Many titles from the text are listed as well as some which were not analysed, either because they were unavailable or because they were judged to be too newsy with insufff-icient articles of note. As part of the work involved in compiling this bibliography letters were sent to many of those not available in England requesting sample copies and indexes. Although the response was poor, where possible, information is included in the list below indicating the type of content. A blank indicates that this was not known and although known to relate to real estate a copy was not seen.

Address information should be located using the current edition of Ulrich's International Periodicals Directory, or any other periodicals directory. It is not given here as addresses date quickly. Many organisations and publishers also have local agents whose addresses are often listed making it unnecessary to contact them in their country of origin. It would not be possible to give them all accurately.

Australia

Developer, quarterly, Institute of Real Estate Development;
Melbourne Cityscope, 3 per annum, Cityscope Publications; newsy and property listing.
North Sydney Cityscope, 3 per annum, Cityscope Publications; newsy and property listing.
Real Estate Agents and Valuers Society. Land and Building, quarterly, Breda Publications;
Real Estate and Stock Journal, quarterly, Real Estate and Stock Institute of Victoria;
Real Estate Journal, monthly, Real Estate Institute of Queensland; news with short articles.
Real Estate Journal, monthly, Real Estate Institute of New South Wales; (tabloid).
Sydney Cityscope, 3 per annum, Cityscope Publications; news and property listing.
Valuer, semi-annual, Australian Institute of Valuers;
Victorian Real Estate Monitor, weekly, Hill Group Publicatons;

Appendix B: Journals

Canada

Appraisal Institute Digest, 5-6 per annum, Appraisal Institute of Canada;
Canadian Appraiser, formerly AIM(Appraisal Institute Magazine), quarterly, Appraisal Insitute of Canada; news with scholarly articles.
Canadian Real Estate, bi-monthly, Canadian Real Estate Association; tabloid, news.
Ontario Real Estate Law Guide, monthly, CCH Canadian Ltd.;
Real Estate News, weekly, Toronto Real Estate Board;
Real Property Reports, monthly, Carswell Legal publications; articles.
Realtor,monthly, Toronto Real Estate Board;

Great Britain

Chartered Surveyor Weekly, weekly, formerly Chartered Surveyor, monthly, Royal Institution of Chartered Surveyors; mix of news with short articles.
Conveyancer and Property Lawyer, bi-monthly, Sweet & Maxwell;scholarly
Country Landowner, monthly, Country Landowners Association; news with a few longer articles.
Estate Agent, quarterly, National Association of Estate Agents; news.
Estates Gazette, weekly, Estates Gazette Ltd.; both news and longer scholarly, articles.
Estates Times, weekly, Estates Times Ltd.; newspaper with occasional longer articles.
Journal of Valuation, quarterly, Henry Stewart publications;scholarly.
Land Development Studies, quarterly, E & F N Spon; scholarly.
Property Business,(formerly Estates Times Review), monthly supplement to Estates Times; longer news articles and surveys.
Property Journal, bi-monthly, British Property Federation; news.
Rent Review, quarterly, Henry Stewart Publications; scholarly.
Valuer, 10 per annum, Incorporated Society of Valuers and Auctioneers; news with short articles.

Ireland

Estate and Property News, monthly, Keltic Enterprises Ltd.; news.

New Zealand

New Zealand Valuer, quarterly, New Zealand Institute of Valuers; scholarly with news items.

United States

A O M A Newsletter, monthly, Apartment Owners and Managers Association of America;
Advisor, quarterly, Real Estate Commission, Department of Insurance, State of New Jersey;
American Real Estate and Urban Economics Association Journal, quarterly, American Real Estate and Urban Economics Association;scholarly
Appraisal Digest, quarterly, New York State Society of Real Estate Appraisers;
Appraisal Journal, quarterly, American Institute of Real Estate Appraisers, National Association of Realtors; scholarly.
Appraiser,monthly, American Institute of Real Estate Appraisers, National Association of Realtors; news bulletin.

<u>Assessment Digest</u>, bimonthly, International Association of Assessing Officers; articles on techniques with news.
<u>Business Atlanta</u>, monthly, Communication Channels Inc.; news, with short articles.
<u>Business Facilities</u>, (formerly A I P R (American Industrial Properties Report) 10 per annum, Bus Fac Publishing; news, short articles and area reviews.
<u>CAAS News</u>, quarterly, Computer Assisted Appraisal Section, International Association of Assessing Officers; short informative articles although primarily a newssheet.
<u>California Real Estate Magazine</u>, monthly, California Association of Rea ltors;
<u>Florida Realtor</u>, monthly, Florida Association of Realtors; news.
<u>Industrial Real Estate Market Survey</u>, semi-annual, Society of Industrial Realtors;
<u>International Property Investment Journal</u>, quarterly, Harwood Academic; scholarly.
<u>Investing in Real Estate</u>, monthly, Harcourt Brace Jovanovich Newsletter Bureau;
<u>Journal of Property Management</u>, bi-monthly, Institute of Real Estate Management, National Association of Realtors; scholarly.
<u>Journal of Real Estate Education</u>, quarterly, National Association of Realtors;
<u>Journal of Real Estate Taxation</u>, quarterly, Warren Gorham and Lamont Inc.; scholarly.
<u>Mortgage and Real Estate Executives Report</u>, fortnightly, Warren Gorham and Lamont Inc; news.
<u>National Real Estate Investor</u>, monthly, Communication Channels Inc.; news and articles.
<u>New England Real Estate Journal</u>, weekly, Roland G Hopkins; news.
<u>New-Jersey Realtor</u>, monthly, New Jersey Association of Realtors;
<u>News Bulletin</u>, monthly, International Association of Assessing Officers; news items relating to property tax.
<u>Operating Techniques and Products Bulletin</u>, monthly, Institute of Real Estate Management, National Association of Realtors;
<u>Personal Property Section News</u>, quarterly, International Association of Assessing Officers; news.
<u>Property Tax Journal</u>, quarterly, International Association of Assessing Officers; scholarly studies.
<u>Real Estate Appraiser and Analyst</u>, quarterly, Society of Real Estate Appraisers; news and longer articles.
<u>Real Estate Bulletin</u>, fortnightly, New York Chamber of Commerce and Industry;
<u>Real Estate Forum</u>, monthly, Real Estate Forum Inc.;
<u>Real Estate Intelligence Report</u>, monthly, Phillips Publishing Inc.; news.
<u>Real Estate Insider Newsletter</u>, weekly, Atcom Inc.; news
<u>Real Estate Investing Letter</u>, monthly, Harcourt Brace Jovanovich Newsletter Inc.; news.
<u>Real Estate Investment Ideas</u>, fortnightly, Institute for Business Planning Inc., Prentice-Hall Inc.;
<u>Real Estate Issues</u>, semi-annually, American Society of Real Estate Counselors of the National Association of Realtors; theoretical and practical studies in the whole real estate area.
<u>Real Estate Magazine</u>,(formerly <u>Chicagoland's Real Estate Advertiser</u>), fortnightly, Law Bulletin Publishing Company; (tabloid).
<u>Real Estate News</u>, quarterly, Real Estate Division, Department of Licensing, State of Washington; newsletter covering general news with one or two

articles.

Real Estate News(Chicago), weekly, Real Estate News Inc.;

Real Estate Record and Builder's Guide, weekly and quarterly, Real Estate News; Inc.;

Real Estate Review, quarterly, Warren Gorham and Lamont Inc.;scholarly

Real Estate Tax Planning News, quarterly, Taxplan Inc., by Ronald Brodie; newsletter summarising developments in Federal tax law.

Real Estate Today, 9 per annum, National Association of Realtors; many short topical articles.

Real Estate Weekly, weekly, Hagedorn Publishing Co.; New York area news.

Real Estate West, monthly, Grier & Co.; Denver, Colorado news.

Realtor, monthly, Washington (DC) Real Estate Council Inc.; short informative articles, with news.

Realtor News, weekly, National Association of Realtors; tabloid, news.

Realty, fortnightly, Leader Observer Inc.(New York); tabloid, news.

Realty and Building, weekly, Realty and Building Inc. (Chicago);

Realty Roundup, weekly, Real Estate Forum Inc. (New York);

Regardie's Magazine for Washington Business, bi-monthly, Real Estate Washington Inc.;

REIT Report, bi-monthly, National Association of Real Estate Investment Trusts;

Shopping Center World, monthly, Communication Channels Inc.; news with short articles.

Site seekers guide, monthly, Bus Fac Publishing Co. Inc.; directory of sites and contacts issued as a journal.

Southeast Real Estate News, weekly, Communication Channels Inc.; tabloid, news.

Southwest Real Estate News, monthly, Communication Channels Inc.; tabloid, news.

S R E A Briefs, fortnightly, Society of Real Estate Appraisers; news.

Strout World, monthly, Strout Realty Inc.; tabloid, news.

Tierra Grande, quarterly, Texas Real Estate Research Center, for real estate brokers.

Trend, quarterly, Texas Real Estate Research Center, Texas housing statistical data.

Valuation Magazine, semi-annual, American Society of Appraisers;

Washington Real Estate News, quarterly, Real Estate Division, Department of Licensing, State of Washington; News with one longer article.

Westchester Realtor, monthly, Westchester County Board of Realtors Inc. (New York);

Western Real Estate News, fortnightly, Business Extension Bureau (San Francisco);

Author index

Subject index

Place names and proper names not indexed in the author index are indexed here giving the state or country only for those places not in the United Kingdom and not already well known; e.g. for Aspen(Col) but not for Chicago or Barcelona. All terms relate to value, valuation and property, therefore these are not repeated continually. All terms should be understood in this context. Usual professional terminology is indexed throughout even where this means entering terms under adjectives rather than nouns.